SPURGEON
ON THE PSALMS

BOOK TWO

Psalm 26 through Psalm 50

SPURGEON
ON THE PSALMS

BOOK TWO

Psalm 26 through Psalm 50

CHARLES H. SPURGEON

Compiled and Edited by Beverlee J. Chadwick

BRIDGE
LOGOS

Alachua, Florida 32615

Bridge-Logos

Alachua, FL 32615 USA

Spurgeon on the Psalms: Book Two
Charles H. Spurgeon
Compiled and Edited by Beverlee J. Chadwick

Printed in the United States of America.

Library of Congress Catalog Card Number: 2015935709
International Standard Book Number 978-1-61036-140-8

Scripture quotations are from the *King James Version* of the Bible.

VP 04-07-15

TABLE OF CONTENTS

FOREWORD

CHARLES H. SPURGEON delighted in his study of the Psalms and prayed that his exposition of each verse would be of such benefit that it would cause the readers to search the Psalms further themselves. His commentary on every verse of the Psalms is extremely insightful and timelessly applicable to the life of every reader.

Spurgeon had thousands of sermons and many books published during his years of ministry. One of his greatest works—and considered by many to be "Spurgeon's magnum opus"—is his multi-volume exposition of the Psalms. His work on this book was composed, polished and penned over the span of half of his ministry years. Spurgeon's wife, Susannah, said that even if Charles Spurgeon had never written any other work, this would have been his permanent literary memorial.

Be prepared to read "Spurgeon on the Psalms" over and over again and experience the spiritual insight and enlightening truth of God's Word that will enhance your own spiritual walk with the Lord.

To the praise and glory of God.

Beverlee J. Chadwick, Senior Editor
Bridge-Logos, Inc.

Note: Charles H. Spurgeon's biography is printed in Spurgeon on the Psalms Book One of this six-book series from the Pure Gold Classics published by Bridge-Logos, Inc. Alachua, FL 32615.

PREFACE
VOLUME TWO

GREATLY ENCOURAGED by the generous reception awarded to my first volume, I have labored on with diligence, and am now able to present the reader with the second installment of my work. Whether life and health shall be given me to complete my task, remains with the gracious Preserver of men; but with His aid and allowance, my face is set towards that design, and I pray that my purpose may be achieved, if it be for the divine glory, and for the good of His Church.

In this volume, we have several of the more memorable and precious of Zion's songs. In commenting upon some of them, I have been overwhelmed with awe, and said with Jacob, *"How dreadful is this place! This is none other than the house of God"* [Genesis 28:17]. Especially was this the case with the fifty-first; I postponed expounding it week after week, feeling more and more my inability for the work. Often I sat down to it, and rose up again without having penned a line. It is a bush burning with fire yet not consumed, and out of it a voice seemed to cry to me, *"Draw not nigh hither: put off thy shoes from off thy feet."* [Exodus 3:5]. The Psalm is charged with an inspiration all divine, as if the Great Father were putting words into His child's mouth. Such a Psalm may be wept over, absorbed into the soul, and exhaled again in devotion; but commented on—ah but where is he who having attempted it can do other than blush at his defeat?

More and more is the conviction forced upon my heart that every man must traverse the territory of the Psalms himself if he would know what a goodly land they are. They flow with milk and honey, but not to strangers; they are

3

only fertile to lovers of their hills and vales. None but the Holy Spirit can give a man the key to the Psalms, and even He gives it rather to experience than to study. Happy is he who for himself knows the secret of the Psalms. I shall now proceed with another portion. The labor and research are exceedingly great, and my other occupations are very pressing, and therefore must crave the patience of the Christian public.
— C. H. Spurgeon, Clapham, November, 1870.

PSALM 26

PSALM 26:1–PSALM 26:12

Psalm 26:1 *Judge me, O Lord; for I have walked in mine integrity: I have trusted also in the Lord; therefore I shall not slide.*

EXPOSITION: Verse 1. *Judge me, O Jehovah.* A solemn appeal to the just tribunal of the heart searching God, warranted by the circumstances of the writer, so far as regarded the particular offences with which he was wrongly charged. Worried and worn out by the injustice of men, the innocent spirit flies from its false accusers to the throne of Eternal Right. He had better have a clear case who dares to carry his suit into the King's Bench of Heaven. Such an appeal as this is not to be rashly made on any occasion; and

as to the whole of our walk and conversation, it should never be made at all, unless we are justified in Christ Jesus: a far more fitting prayer for a sinful mortal is the petition, *Enter not into judgment with thy servant* [See Psalm 143:2].

For I have walked in mine integrity. [Psalm 26:1].

He held integrity as his principle, and walked in it as his practice. David had not used any traitorous or unrighteous means to gain the crown, or to keep it; he was conscious of having been guided by the noblest principles of honor in all his actions with regard to Saul and his family. What a comfort it is to have the approbation of one's own conscience! If there is peace within the soul, the blustering storms of slander which howl around us are of little consideration. When the little bird in my bosom sings a merry song, it is no matter to me if a thousand owls hoot at me from without. *I have trusted also in the Lord.* Faith is the root and sap of integrity. He who leans upon the Lord is sure to walk in righteousness.

David knew that God's covenant had given him the crown, and therefore he took no indirect or unlawful means to secure it; he would not slay his enemy in the cave, nor suffer his men at arms to smite him when he slept unguarded on the plain. Faith will work hard for the Lord, and in the Lord's way, but she refuses so much as to lift a finger to fulfill the devices of unrighteous cunning. Rebecca acted out a great falsehood in order to fulfill the Lord's decree in favor of Jacob—this was unbelief; but Abraham left the Lord to fulfill his own purposes, and took the knife to slay his son—this was faith. Faith trusts God to accomplish His own decrees. Why should I steal when God has promised to supply my need? Why should I avenge myself when I know that the Lord has adopted my cause? Confidence in God is a most effectual security against sin.

Therefore I shall not slide. Slippery as the way is, so that I walk like a man upon ice, yet faith keeps my heels from tripping, and will continue to do so. The doubtful ways of policy are sure sooner or later to give a fall to those who run therein, but the ways of honesty, though often rough, are always safe. We cannot trust in God if we walk crookedly;

but straight paths and simple faith bring the pilgrim happily to his journey's end.

Psalm 26:2 *Examine me, O Lord, and prove me; try my reins and my heart.*

EXPOSITION: Verse 2. There are three modes of trial here challenged, which are said in the original to refer to trial by touch, trial by smell, and trial by fire. The psalmist was so clear from the charge laid against him, that he submitted himself unconditionally to any form of examination, which the Lord might see fit to employ. *Examine me, O Lord.* Look me through and through; make a minute survey; put me to the question, cross-examine my evidence. *And prove me.* Put me again to trial; and see if I would follow such wicked designs as my enemies impute to me. *Try my reins and my heart.* Assay me as metals are assayed in the furnace, and do this to my most secret parts, where my affections hold their court; see, O God, whether or not I love murder, and treason, and deceit.

All this is a very bold appeal, and made by a man like David, who feared the Lord exceedingly, it manifests a most solemn and complete conviction of innocence. The expressions here used should teach us the thoroughness of the divine judgment, and the necessity of being in all things profoundly sincere, lest we be found wanting at the last. Our enemies are severe with us with the severity of spite, and this a brave man endures without fear; but God's severity is that of unswerving right. Who shall stand against such a trial? The sweet singer says: . . . *who can stand before His cold?* [See Psalm 147:17.] and we may well enquire, *who can stand before the heat of His justice?* [See Nahum 1:6.]

Psalm 26:3 *For thy lovingkindness is before mine eyes: and I have walked in thy truth.*

EXPOSITION: **Verse 3.** *For thy lovingkindness is before mine eyes.* An object of memory and a ground of hope. A sense of mercy received sets a fair prospect before the faithful mind in its gloomiest condition, for it yields visions of mercies yet to come, visions not visionary but real. Dwell, dear reader, upon that celestial word lovingkindness. It has a heavenly savor. Is it not an unmatchable word, unexcelled, unrivalled? The goodness of the Lord to us should be before our eyes as a motive actuating our conduct; we are not under the bondage of the law, but we are under the sweet constraints of grace, which are far more mighty, although far more gentle. Men sin with the law before their eyes, but divine love, when clearly seen, sanctifies the conversation. If we were not so forgetful of the way of mercy in which God walks toward us, we would be more careful to walk in the ways of obedience toward Him.

And I have walked in thy truth. The psalmist was preserved from sin by his assurance of the truthfulness of God's promise, which truth he endeavored to imitate as well as to believe. Observe from this verse that an experience of divine love will show itself in a practical following of divine truth; those who neglect either the doctrinal or practical parts of truth must not wonder if they lose the experimental enjoyment of it. Some talk of truth, it is better to walk in it. Some vow to do well in the future, but their resolutions come to nothing; only the regenerate man can say "I have walked in thy truth."

EXPOSITION:

Verses 4-5. So far from being himself an open offender against the laws of God, the psalmist had not even associated with the lovers of evil. He had kept aloof from the men of

PSALM 26

Belial. A man is known by his company, and if we have kept ourselves apart from the wicked, it will always be evidence in our favor should our character be impugned. He who was never in the parish is not likely to have stolen the corn. He who never went to sea is clearly not the man who scuttled the ship.

Psalm 26:4 *I have not sat with vain persons, neither will I go in with dissemblers.*

EXPOSITION: **Verse 4.** *I have not sat with vain persons.* True citizens have no dealings with traitors. David had no seat in the parliament of triflers. They were not his boon companions at feasts, nor his advisers in council, nor his associates in conversation. We must see, and speak, and trade, with men of the world, but we must on no account take our rest and solace in their empty society. Not only the profane, but the vain are to be shunned by us. All those who live for this life only are vain, chaffy,[1] frothy[2] men, quite unworthy of a Christian's friendship. Moreover as this vanity is often allied with falsehood, it is well to save ourselves altogether from this untoward generation, lest we should be led from bad to worse and from tolerating the vain should come to admire the wicked.

Neither will I go in with dissemblers. Since I know that hypocritical piety is double iniquity, I will cease all acquaintance with pretenders. If I must walk the same street, I will not enter the same door and spend my time in their society. The congregation of the hypocrites is not one with which we should cultivate communion; their ultimate rendezvous will be the lowest pit of hell, let us drop their acquaintance now! for we shall not desire it soon. They hang their beads

1. Worthless.
2. Of little substance.

9

around their necks and carry the devil in their hearts. This clause is in the future tense, to indicate that the writer felt no desire to begin an acquaintance with the characters whom up until then he had shunned. We must maintain the separated path with more and more circumspection as we see the great redemption day approaching. Those who would be transfigured with Jesus must not be disfigured by conformity to the world. The resolution of the psalmist suggests that even among professed followers of truth we must make distinctions, for as there are vain persons out of the Church, so there are dissemblers in it and both are to be shunned with scrupulous decision.

Psalm 26:5 *I have hated the congregation of evil doers; and will not sit with the wicked.*

EXPOSITION: **Verse 5.** *I have hated the congregation of evil doers.* A severe sentence, but not too severe. A man who does not hate evil terribly does not love good heartily. Men, as men, we must always love, for they are our neighbors, and therefore to be loved as ourselves; but evil doers, as such, are traitors to the Great King, and no loyal subject can love traitors. What God hates we must hate. The congregation or assembly of evil doers signifies violent men in alliance and conclave for the overthrow of the innocent; such synagogues of Satan are to be held in abhorrence. What a sad reflection it is that there should be a congregation of evil doers as well as a congregation of the upright, a church of Satan as well as a Church of God; a seed of the serpent as well as a seed of the woman; an old Babylon as well as a new Jerusalem: a great whore sitting upon many waters, to be judged in wrath, as well as a chaste bride of the Lamb to be crowned at His coming.

And will not sit with the wicked. Saints have a seat at

another table, and will never leave the King's dainties for the husks of the swine trough. Better to sit with the blind, and the halt, and the lame, at the table of mercy, than with the wicked in their feasts of ungodliness, yes, better to sit on Job's dunghill than on Pharaoh's throne. Let each reader be selective as to the company he keeps, for those we keep company with in this world, we are likely to keep company with in the next.

Psalm 26:6 *I will wash mine hands in innocency: so will I compass thine altar, O Lord:*

EXPOSITION: Verse 6. *I will wash mine hands in innocency.* He would publicly avow himself to be altogether clear of the accusations laid against him, and if any fault in other matters could be truthfully alleged against him, he would for the future abstain from it. The washing of the hands is a significant action to set forth our having no connection with a deed, as we still say, "I wash my hands of the whole business." As to perfect innocence, David does not here claim it, but he avows his innocence of the crimes whereof he was slanderously accused; there is, however, a sense in which we may be washed in absolute innocency, for the atoning blood makes us completely clean. We ought never to rest satisfied short of a full persuasion of our complete cleansing by Jesus' precious blood.

So will I compass thine altar O Lord. Priests unto God must take great care to be personally cleansed; the brazen laver was as needful as the golden altar; God's worship requires us to be holy in life. He who is unjust to man cannot be acceptably religious towards God. We must not bring our thank offerings with hands defiled with guilt. To love justice and purity is far more acceptable to God, than ten thousands of the fat of fed beasts. We see from this verse that holy minds delight in the worship of the Lord, and find their sweetest solace at His altar; and that it is their deepest concern never to enter upon any course of action which would unfit them for the most sacred communion with God. Our eye must be upon the altar which sanctifies both the giver and the gift, yet we must never draw from the atoning sacrifice an excuse for sin, but rather find in it a most convincing argument for holiness.

Psalm 26:7 *That I may publish with the voice of thanksgiving, and tell of all thy wondrous works.*

EXPOSITION: Verse 7. *That I may publish with the voice of thanksgiving.* David was so far instructed that he does not mention the typical offering, but discerns the spiritual offering which was intended thereby, not the groans of bullocks, but songs of gratitude the spiritual worshipper presents. To sound abroad the worthy praises of the God of all grace should be the everyday business of a pardoned sinner. Let men slander us as they will, let us not defraud the Lord of His praises; let dogs bark, but let us like the moon shine on. *And tell of all thy wondrous works.* God's people should not be tongue tied. The wonders of divine grace are enough to make the tongue of the dumb sing. God's works of love are wondrous if we consider the unworthiness of their objects, the costliness of their method, and the glory of their result. And as men find great pleasure in discoursing upon things remarkable and astonishing, so the saints rejoice to tell of the great things which the Lord has done for them.

Psalm 26:8 *Lord, I have loved the habitation of thy house, and the place where thine honour dwelleth.*

EXPOSITION: **Verse 8.** *Lord, I have loved the habitation of thy house.* Into the abodes of sin he would not enter, but the house of God he had long loved, and loved it still. We would be sad children if we did not love our Father's dwelling place. Though we own no sacred buildings, yet the Church of the living God is the house of God, and true Christians delight in her ordinances, services, and assemblies. O that all our days were Sabbaths!

And the place where thine honour dwelleth. In His Church where God is held in honor at all times, where He reveals himself in the glory of His grace, and is proclaimed by His people as the Lord of all. We come not together as the Lord's people to honor the preacher, but to give glory to God; such an occupation is most pleasant to the saints of the Most High. What are those gatherings where God is not honored, are they not an offence to His pure and holy eyes, and are they not a sad stumbling block to the people of God? It brings the scalding tear upon our cheek to hear sermons in which the honor of God is so far from being the preacher's object that one might almost imagine the preacher worshipped the dignity of manhood, and thought more of it than of the Infinite Majesty of God.

Psalm 26:9 *Gather not my soul with sinners, nor my life with bloody men:*

EXPOSITION: **Verse 9.** *Gather not my soul with sinners.* Lord, when, like fruit, I must be gathered, put me not in the same basket with the best of sinners, much less with the worst of them. The company of sinners is so distasteful to us here, that we cannot endure the thought of being bound up in the same bundle with them to all eternity. Our comfort is that the Great Husbandman discerns the tares from the wheat, and will find a separate place for distinct characters. In the former verses we see that the psalmist kept himself clear of profane persons, and this is to be understood as a reason why he should not be thrust into their company at the last. Let us think of the doom of the wicked, and the prayer of the text will forcibly rise to our lips; meanwhile, as we see the rule of judgment by which like is gathered to its like, we who have passed from death unto life have nothing to fear.

Nor my life with bloody men. Our soul sickens to hear them speak; their cruel dispatches, in which they treat the shooting of their fellow men as rare sport, are horrifying to us; Lord, let us not be shut up in the same prison with them; nay, the same paradise with such men would be a hell, if they remained as they are now.

Psalm 26:10 *In whose hands is mischief, and their right hand is full of bribes.*

EXPOSITION: **Verse 10.** *In whose hands is mischief.* They have both hands full of it, plotting it and carrying it out. *And their right hand,* with which they are most dexterous, *is full of bribes*; like thieves who would steal with impunity, they carry a bribe for the dogs of justice. He who gives bribes is every way as guilty as the man who takes them, and in the matter of our parliamentary elections the rich villain who gives the bribe is by far the worse. Bribery, in any form or shape, should be as detestable to a Christian as carrion to a dove, or garbage to a lamb. Let those whose dirty hands are fond of bribes remember that neither death nor the devil can be bribed to let them escape their well earned doom.

Psalm 26:11 *But as for me, I will walk in mine integrity: redeem me, and be merciful unto me.*

EXPOSITION: **Verse 11.** Here is the lover of godliness entering his personal protest against unrighteous gain. He is a Nonconformist, and is ready to stand alone in his Nonconformity. Like a live fish, he swims against the stream. Trusting in God, the psalmist resolves that the plain way of righteousness shall be his choice, and those who will, may prefer the tortuous paths of violence and deceit. Yet, he is by no means a boaster or a self righteous bragger of his own strength, for he cries for redemption and pleads for mercy. Our integrity is not absolute nor inherent, it is a work of grace in us, and is marred by human infirmity; we must, therefore, resort to the redeeming blood and to the throne of mercy, confessing that though we are saints among men, we must still bow as sinners before God.

Psalm 26:12 *My foot standeth in an even place: in the congregations will I bless the Lord.*

EXPOSITION: **Verse 12.** The song began in the minor, but it has now reached the major key. Saints often sing themselves into happiness. The even place upon which our foot stands is the sure, covenant faithfulness, eternal promise and immutable oath of the Lord of Hosts; there is no fear of falling from this solid basis, or of its being removed from under us. Established in Christ Jesus, by being vitally united to Him, we have nothing left to occupy our thoughts but the praises of our God. Let us not forsake the assembling of ourselves together, and when assembled, let us not be slow to contribute our portion of thanksgiving. Each saint is a witness to divine faithfulness, and should be ready with his testimony. As for the slanderers, let them howl outside the door while the children sing within.

Psalm 27

Psalm 27:1–Psalm 27:14

Psalm 27:1 *The Lord is my light and my salvation; whom shall I fear? the Lord is the strength of my life; of whom shall I be afraid?*

EXPOSITION: Verse 1. *The Lord is my light and my salvation.* Here is personal interest, "my light," "my salvation;" the soul is assured of it, and therefore, declaring it boldly. "My light;"—into the soul at the new birth divine light is poured as the precursor of salvation; where there is not enough light to see our own darkness and to long for the Lord Jesus, there is no evidence of salvation. Salvation finds us in the dark, but it does not leave us there; it gives light to those who sit in the valley of the shadow of death. After conversion our God is our joy, comfort, guide, teacher, and in every sense our light; He is light within, light around, light reflected from us, and light to be revealed to us. Note, it is not said merely that the Lord gives light, but that He "is" light; nor that He gives salvation, but that He is salvation; he, then, who by faith has laid hold upon God has all covenant blessings in his possession.

Every light is not the sun, but the sun is the father of all lights. This being made sure as a fact, the argument drawn from it is put in the form of a question, *Whom shall I fear?* A question which is its own answer. The powers of darkness are not to be feared, for the Lord, our light, destroys them; and the damnation of hell is not to be dreaded by us, for the Lord is our salvation. This is a very different challenge from that of boastful Goliath, for it is based upon a very different foundation; it rests not upon the conceited vigor of an arm of flesh, but upon the real power of the omnipotent *I AM*. *The Lord is the strength of my life.* Here is a third glowing epithet, to show that the writer's hope was fastened with a threefold cord which could not be broken. We may well accumulate terms of praise where the Lord lavishes deeds of grace. Our life derives all its strength from Him who is the author if it; and if He deigns to make us strong we cannot be weakened by all the machinations of the adversary. *Of whom shall I be afraid?* The bold question looks into the future as well as the present. "If God be for us, who can be against us?" [Romans 8:31], either now or in time to come?

Psalm 27:2 *When the wicked, even mine enemies and my foes, came upon me to eat up my flesh, they stumbled and fell.*

EXPOSITION: **Verse 2.** This verse records a past deliverance, and is an example of the way in which experience should be employed to reassure our faith in times of trial. Each word is instructive. *When the wicked.* It is a hopeful sign for us when the wicked hate us; if our foes were godly men it would be a sore sorrow, but as for the wicked their hatred is better than their love. *Even mine enemies and my foes.* There were many of them, they were of different sorts, but they were unanimous in mischief and hearty in hatred. *Came upon me*—advanced to the attack, leaping upon the victim like a lion upon its prey. *To eat up my flesh*, like cannibals they would make a full end of the man, tear him limb from limb, and make a feast for their malice.

The enemies of our souls are not deficient in ferocity; they yield no quarter, and ought to have none in return. See in what danger David was; in the grip and grasp of numerous, powerful, and cruel enemies, and yet observe his perfect safety and their utter discomfiture! *They stumbled and fell.* God's breath blew them off their legs. There were stones in the way which they never reckoned upon, and over these they made an ignominious tumble. This was literally true in the case of our Lord in Gethsemane, when those who came to take Him went backward and fell to the ground; and herein He was a prophetic representative of all wrestling believers who, rising from their knees shall, by the power of faith, throw their foes upon their faces.

Psalm 27:3 *Though an host should encamp against me, my heart shall not fear: though war should rise against me, in this will I be confident.*

EXPOSITION: **Verse 3.** *Though an host should encamp against me, my heart shall not fear.* Before the actual conflict, while as yet the battle is untried, the warrior's heart, being held in suspense, is very liable to become fluttered. The encamping host often inspires greater dread than the same host in actual affray. Young[3] tells us of some—"Who feel a thousand deaths in fearing one." Doubtless the shadow of anticipated trouble is, to timorous minds, a more prolific source of sorrow than the trouble itself, but faith puts a strengthening plaster to the back of courage, and throws out of the window the dregs of the cup of trembling. *Though war should rise against me, in this will I be confident.* When it actually comes to push of pike[4], faith's shield will ward off the blow; and if the first brush should be but the beginning

---

3. Quote by Edward Young in 1683.

4. A medieval and early modern warfare featuring two opposing columns of men colliding and pushing at the opposing column with long poles having very sharply pointed ends aimed to thrust into the opposing column.

of a war, yet faith's banners will wave in spite of the foe. Though battle could succeed battle, and one campaign could be followed by another, the believer will not be dismayed at the length of the conflict. Reader, this third verse is the comfortable and logical inference from the second, confidence is the child of experience. Have you been delivered out of great perils? then set up your flag, wait at your watch fire, and let the enemy do his worst.

Psalm 27:4 *One thing have I desired of the Lord, that will I seek after; that I may dwell in the house of the Lord all the days of my life, to behold the beauty of the Lord, and to enquire in his temple.*

EXPOSITION: Verse 4. *One thing.* Divided aims tend to distraction, weakness, disappointment. The man of one book is eminent; the man of one pursuit is successful. Let all our affections be bound up in one affection, and that affection set upon heavenly things. *Have I desired*—what we cannot at once attain, it is well to desire. God judges us very much by the desire of our hearts. He who rides a lame horse is not blamed by his master for want of speed, if he makes all the haste he can, and would make more if he could; God takes the will for the deed with His children.

Of the Lord. This is the right target for desires, this is the well into which to dip our buckets, this is the door to knock at, the bank to draw upon; desire of men, and lie upon the dunghill with Lazarus: desire of the Lord, and to be carried of angels into Abraham's bosom. Our desires of the Lord should be sanctified, humble, constant, submissive, fervent, and it is well if, as with the psalmist, they are all molten into one mass. Under David's painful circumstances we might have expected him to desire repose, safety, and a thousand other good things, but no, he has set his heart on the pearl, and leaves the rest.

That will I seek after. Holy desires must lead to resolute action. The old proverb says, "Wishers and the would-be are never good housekeepers," and "wishing never fills a sack." Desires are seed which must be sown in the good soil of activity, or they will yield no harvest. We shall find our desires to be like clouds without rain, unless followed up by practical endeavors. *That I may dwell in the house of the Lord all the days of my life.* For the sake of communion with the King, David longed to dwell always in the palace; so far from being wearied with the services of the Tabernacle, he longed to be constantly engaged in them, as his life-long pleasure. He desired above all things to be one of the household of God, a home born child, living at home with his Father. This is our dearest wish, only we extend it to those days of our immortal life which have not yet dawned. We pine for our Father's house above, the home of our souls; if we may but dwell there forever, we care but little for the goods or ills of this poor life. "Jerusalem the Golden"[5] is the one and only goal of our heart's longings.

To behold the beauty of the Lord. An exercise both for earthly and heavenly worshippers. We must not enter the assemblies of the saints in order to see and be seen, or merely to hear the minister; we must go to the gatherings of the righteous, intent upon the gracious object of learning more of the loving Father, more of the glorified Jesus, more of the mysterious Spirit, in order that we may the more lovingly admire, and the more reverently adore our glorious God. What a word that is, *the beauty of the Lord!* Think of it, dear reader! Better far—behold it by faith! What a sight will that be when every faithful follower of Jesus shall behold

---

5. A hymn written by Bernard of Morlaix in 1146 and translated to English by John M. Neal in 1858.

"the King in his beauty!" [See Isaiah 33:17.] Oh, for that infinitely blessed vision!

And to enquire in his temple. We should make our visits to the Lord's house enquirers' meetings. Not seeking sinners alone, but assured saints should be enquirers. We must enquire as to the will of God and how we may do it; as to our interest in the heavenly city, and how we may be more assured of it. We shall not need to make enquiries in Heaven, for there we shall know even as we are known; but meanwhile we should sit at Jesus' feet, and awaken all our faculties to learn of Him.

Psalm 27:5 *For in the time of trouble he shall hide me in his pavilion: in the secret of his tabernacle shall he hide me; he shall set me up upon a rock.*

EXPOSITION: **Verse 5.** This verse gives an excellent reason for the psalmist's desire after communion with God, namely, that he was thus secured in the hour of peril. *For in the time of trouble,* that needy time, that time when others forsake me, *he shall hide me in his pavilion:* he shall give me the best of shelter in the worst of danger. The royal pavilion was erected in the center of the army, and around it all the mighty men kept guard at all hours; thus in that divine sovereignty which almighty power is sworn to maintain, the believer peacefully is hidden, hidden not by himself furtively, but by the king, who hospitably entertains him. *In the secret of his tabernacle shall he hide me.* Sacrifice aids sovereignty in screening the elect from harm. No one of old dared to enter the most holy place on pain of death; and if the Lord has hidden his people there, what foe shall venture to molest them? *He shall set me up upon a rock.* Immutability, eternity, and infinite power here come to the aid of sovereignty and sacrifice. How blessed is the standing of the man whom God himself sets on high above his foes, upon an impregnable rock which never can be stormed! Well may we desire to dwell with the Lord who so effectually protects His people.

Psalm 27:6 *And now shall mine head be lifted up above mine enemies round about me: therefore will I offer in his tabernacle sacrifices of joy; I will sing, yea, I will sing praises unto the Lord.*

EXPOSITION: **Verse 6.** *And now shall mine head be lifted up above mine enemies round about me.* He is quite sure of it. Godly men of old prayed in faith, nothing wavering, and spoke of their answer to their prayers as a certainty. David was by faith so sure of a glorious victory over all those who beset him that he arranged in his own heart what he would do when his foes lay all prostrate before him; that arrangement was such as gratitude suggested.

Therefore will I offer in his tabernacle sacrifices of joy. That place, for which he longed in his conflict, should see his thankful joy in his triumphant return. He does not speak of jubilations to be offered in his palace, and feastings in his banqueting halls, but holy mirth he selects as most fitting for so divine a deliverance. *I will sing.* This is the most natural mode of expressing thankfulness. *Yea, I will sing praises unto the Lord.* The vow is confirmed by repetition, and explained by addition, which addition vows all the praise unto Jehovah. Let who will be silent, the believer when his prayer is heard, must and will make his praise to be heard also; and let who will sing unto the vanities of the world, the believer reserves his music for the Lord alone.

Psalm 27:7 *Hear, O Lord, when I cry with my voice: have mercy also upon me, and answer me.*

EXPOSITION: **Verse 7.** *Hear, O Lord, when I cry with my voice.* The pendulum of spirituality swings from prayer to praise. The voice which in the last verse was tuned to music is here turned to crying. As a good soldier, David knew how to handle his weapons, and found himself much at home with the weapon of "all prayer." Note his anxiety to be heard. Pharisees care not a fig for the Lord's hearing them, so long as they are heard of men, or charm their own pride with their sounding devotions; but with a genuine man, the Lord's ear is everything. The voice may be profitably used even in private prayer; for though it is unnecessary, it is often helpful, and aids in preventing distractions.

Have mercy also upon me. Mercy is the hope of sinners and the refuge of saints. All acceptable petitioners dwell much upon this attribute. *And answer me.* We may expect answers to prayer, and should not be easy without them any more than we should be if we had written a letter to a friend upon important business, and had received no reply.

Psalm 27:8 *When thou saidst, Seek ye my face; my heart said unto thee, Thy face, Lord, will I seek.*

EXPOSITION: **Verse 8.** In this verse we are taught that if we would have the Lord hear our voice, we must be careful to respond to His voice. The true heart should echo the will of God as the rocks among the Alps repeat in sweetest music the notes of the peasant's horn. Observe, that the command was in the plural, to all the saints, *Seek ye;* but the man of God turned it into the singular by a personal application, *Thy face, Lord, will I seek.* The voice of the Lord is very effectual where all other voices fail. *When thou saidst,* then my heart, my inmost nature was moved to an obedient reply. Note the promptness of the response—no sooner said than done; as soon as God said "seek," the heart said, "I will seek." Oh, for more of this holy readiness! I pray to God that we were more moldable to the divine hand, more sensitive of the touch of God's Spirit.

Psalm 27:9 *Hide not thy face far from me; put not thy servant away in anger: thou hast been my help; leave me not, neither forsake me, O God of my salvation.*

EXPOSITION: Verse 9. *Hide not thy face far from me.* The word "far" is not in the original, and is a very superfluous addition of the translators, since even the least hiding of the Lord's face is a great affliction to a believer. The command to seek the Lord's face would be a painful one if the Lord, by withdrawing himself, rendered it impossible for the seeker to meet with Him. A smile from the Lord is the greatest of comforts, His frown the worst of ills. *Put not thy servant away in anger.* Other servants had been put away when they proved unfaithful, as for instance, his predecessor Saul; and this made David, while conscious of many faults, most anxious that divine long suffering should continue him in favor. This is a most appropriate prayer for us under a similar sense of unworthiness.

Thou hast been my help. How truly can we join in this declaration; for many years, in circumstances of varied trial, we have been upheld by our God, and must and will confess our obligation. "Ingratitude," it is said, "is natural to fallen man," but to spiritual men it is unnatural and detestable. *Leave me not, neither forsake me.* A prayer for the future, and an inference from the past. If the Lord had meant to leave us, why did He begin with us? Past help is but a waste of effort if the soul now be deserted. The first petition, "leave me not," may refer to temporary desertions, and the second word to the final withdrawal of grace, both are to be prayed against; and concerning the second, we have immutable promises to urge. *O God of my salvation.* A sweet title worthy of much meditation.

Psalm 27:10 *When my father and my mother forsake me, then the Lord will take me up.*

EXPOSITION: Verse 10. *When my father and my mother forsake me.* These dear relations will be the last to desert me, but if the milk of human kindness should dry up even from their breasts, there is a Father who never forgets. Some of the greatest of the saints have been cast out by their families, and persecuted for righteousness' sake. *Then the Lord will take me up.* Will espouse my cause, will uplift me from my woes, will carry me in His arms, will elevate me above my enemies, and will at last receive me to His eternal dwelling place.

Psalm 27:11 *Teach me thy way, O Lord, and lead me in a plain path, because of mine enemies.*

EXPOSITION: Verse 11. *Teach me thy way, O Lord.* He does not pray to be indulged with his own way, but to be informed as to the path in which the righteous Jehovah would have him walk. This prayer evinces a humble sense of personal ignorance, great teachableness of spirit, and cheerful obedience of heart. *Lead me in a plain path.* Help is here sought as well as direction; we not only need a map of the way, but a guide to assist us in the journey. A path is here desired which shall be open, honest, straightforward, in opposition to the way of cunning, which is intricate, tortuous, dangerous. Good men seldom succeed in fine speculations and doubtful courses; plain simplicity is the best spirit for an heir of Heaven: let us leave shifty tricks and political expediencies to the citizens of the world—New Jerusalem has plain men for its citizens. Esau was a cunning hunter; Jacob was a plain man, dwelling in tents. *Because of mine enemies.* These will catch us if they can, but the way of manifest, simple honesty is safe from their rage. It is wonderful to observe how honest simplicity baffles and outwits the craftiness of wickedness. Truth is wisdom. "Honesty is the best policy."

Psalm 27:12 *Deliver me not over unto the will of mine enemies: for false witnesses are risen up against me, and such as breathe out cruelty.*

EXPOSITION: Verse 12. *Deliver me not over unto the will of mine enemies;* or I shall be like a victim cast to the lions, to be rent in pieces and utterly devoured. God be thanked that our foes cannot have their way with us, or Smithfield[6] would soon be on a blaze again.

For false witnesses are risen up against me. Slander is an old fashioned weapon out of the armory of hell, and is still in plentiful use; and no matter how holy a man may be, there will be some who will defame him. "Give a dog an ill name, and hang him;" but glory be to God, the Lord's people are not dogs, and their ill names do not injure them. *And such as breathe out cruelty.* It is their vital breath to hate the good; they cannot speak without cursing them; such was Paul before conversion. They who breathe out cruelty may well expect to be sent to breathe their native air in hell; let persecutors beware!

Psalms 27:13 *I had fainted, unless I had believed to see the goodness of the Lord in the land of the living.*

---

6. Burning of the Protestant Martyrs at Smithfield in England.

27

EXPOSITION: **Verse 13.** Faintness of heart is a common infirmity; even he who slew Goliath was subject to its attacks. Faith puts its bottle of cordial to the lip of the soul, and so prevents fainting. Hope is Heaven's balm for present sorrow. In this land of the dying, it is our blessedness to be looking and longing for our fair portion in the land of the living, whence the goodness of God has banished the wickedness of man, and where holy spirits charm with their society those persecuted saints who were vilified and despised among men. We must believe to see, not see to believe; we must wait the appointed time, and stay our soul's hunger with foretastes of the Lord's eternal goodness which shall soon be our feast and our song.

Psalm 27:14 *Wait on the Lord: be of good courage, and he shall strengthen thine heart: wait, I say, on the Lord.*

EXPOSITION: **Verse 14.** *Wait on the Lord.* Wait at His door with prayer; wait at His foot with humility; wait at His table with service; wait at His window with expectancy. Suitors often win nothing but the cold shoulder from earthly patrons after long and obsequious waiting; he speeds best whose patron is in the skies. *Be of good courage.* A soldier's motto. Be it mine. Courage we shall need, and for the exercise of it we have as much reason as necessity, if we are soldiers of King Jesus. *And he shall strengthen thine heart.* He can lay the plaster right upon the weak place. Let the heart be strengthened, and the whole machine of humanity is filled with power; a strong heart makes a strong arm. What strength is this which God himself gives to the heart? Read the "Book of Martyrs,[7]" and see its glorious deeds of prowess; go to

---

7. *Foxe's Book of Martyrs from the Pure Gold Classics line is available from Bridge-Logos, Inc.*

God rather, and get such power yourself. *Wait, I say, on the Lord.* David, in the words "I say," sets his own private seal to the word which, as an inspired man, he had been moved to write. It is his testimony as well as the command of God, and indeed he who writes these scanty notes has himself found it so sweet, so reviving, so profitable to draw near to God, that on his own account he also feels bound to write, "Wait, I SAY, on the Lord."

PSALM 28

PSALM 28:1–PSALM 28:9

Psalm 28:1 *Unto thee will I cry, O Lord my rock; be not silent to me: lest, if thou be silent to me, I become like them that go down into the pit.*

EXPOSITION: **Verse 1.** *Unto thee will I cry, O Lord, my rock.* A cry is the natural expression of sorrow, and is a suitable utterance when all other modes of appeal fail us; but the cry must be alone directed to the Lord, for to cry to man is to waste our entreaties upon the air. When we consider the readiness of the Lord to hear, and His ability to aid, we shall see good reason for directing all our appeals at once to the God of our salvation, and shall use language of firm resolve like that in the text, "I will cry." The immutable Jehovah is our rock, the immovable foundation of all our hopes and our refuge in time of trouble: we are fixed in our determination to flee to Him as our stronghold in every hour of danger. It will be in vain to call to the rocks in the Day of Judgment, but our rock attends to our cries.

Be not silent to me. Mere formalists may be content without answers to their prayers, but genuine suppliants cannot; they are not satisfied with the results of prayer itself in calming the mind and subduing the will—they must go further and obtain actual replies from Heaven, or they cannot rest; and those replies they long to receive at once, if possible; they dread even a little of God's silence. God's voice is often so terrible that it shakes the wilderness; but His silence is equally full of awe to an eager suppliant. When God seems to close His ear, we must not therefore close our mouths, but rather cry with more earnestness; for when our note grows shrill with eagerness and grief, He will not long deny us a hearing. What a dreadful case would we be in if the Lord should become forever silent to our prayers! This thought suggested itself to David, and he turned it into a plea, thus teaching us to argue and reason with God in our prayers.

Lest, if thou be silent to me, I become like them that go down into the pit. Deprived of the God who answers prayer, we should be in a more pitiable plight than the dead in the grave, and would soon sink to the same level as the lost in hell. We must have answers to prayer: ours is an urgent case of dire necessity; surely the Lord will speak peace to our agitated minds, for He never can find it I His heart to permit His own elect to perish.

Psalm 28:2 *Hear the voice of my supplications, when I cry unto thee, when I lift up my hands toward thy holy oracle.*

EXPOSITION: **Verse 2.** This is much to the same effect as the first verse, only that it refers to future as well as present pleadings. Hear me! Hear me! *Hear the voice of my supplications!* This is the burden of both verses. We cannot be put off with a refusal when we are in the spirit of prayer; we labor, use importunity, and agonize in supplications until a hearing is granted us. The word "supplications," in the plural, shows the number, continuance, and variety of a good man's prayers, while the expression "hear the voice," seems to hint that there is an inner meaning, or heart voice, about which spiritual men are far more concerned than for their outward and audible utterances. A silent prayer may have a louder voice than the cries of those priests who sought to awaken Baal with their shouts. *When I lift up my hands* *toward thy holy oracle:* which holy place was the type of our Lord Jesus; and if we would gain acceptance, we must turn ourselves evermore to the blood besprinkled mercy seat of His atonement. Uplifted hands have ever been a form of devout posture, and are intended to signify a reaching upward towards God, a readiness, an eagerness to receive the blessing sought after. We stretch out empty hands, for we are beggars; we lift them up, for we seek heavenly supplies; we lift them towards the mercy seat of Jesus, for there our expectation dwells. O that whenever we use devout gestures, we may possess contrite hearts, that speak well with God.

Psalm 28:3 *Draw me not away with the wicked, and with the workers of iniquity, which speak peace to their neighbours, but mischief is in their hearts.*

EXPOSITION: **Verse 3.** *Draw me not away with the wicked.* They shall be dragged off to hell like felons of old drawn on a hurdle to Tyburn,[8] like logs drawn to the fire, like fagots to the oven. David fears lest he should be bound up in their bundle, drawn to their doom; and the fear is an appropriate one for every godly man. The best of the wicked are dangerous company in time, and would make terrible companions for eternity; we must avoid them in their pleasures, if we would not be confounded with them in their miseries. *And with the workers of iniquity.* These are overtly sinful, and their judgment will be sure; Lord, do not make us to drink of their cup. Activity is found with the wicked even if it be lacking to the righteous. Oh! to be "workers" for the Lord.

Which speak peace to their neighbours, but mischief is in their hearts. They have learned the manners of the place

---

8. Place of the gallows.

to which they are going: the doom of liars is their portion forever, and lying is their conversation on the road. Soft words, oily with pretended love, are the deceitful meshes of the infernal net in which Satan catches the precious life; many of his children are learned in his abominable craft, and fish with their father's nets, almost as cunningly as he himself could do it. It is a sure sign of baseness when the tongue and the heart do not ring to the same note. Deceitful men are more to be dreaded than wild beasts: it would be better to be shut up in a pit with serpents than to be compelled to live with liars. He, who cries "peace" too loudly, means to sell it if he can get his price. "Good wine needs no bush:"[9] if he were so very peaceful he would not need to say so; he means mischief, make sure of that.

Psalm 28:4 *Give them according to their deeds, and according to the wickedness of their endeavours: give them after the work of their hands; render to them their desert.*

EXPOSITION: Verse 4. When we view the wicked simply as such, and not as our fellow men, our indignation against sin leads us entirely to coincide with the acts of divine justice which punish evil, and to wish that justice might use her power to restrain by her terrors the cruel and unjust. But still the desires of the present verse, as our version renders it, are not readily made consistent with the spirit of the Christian dispensation, which seeks rather the reformation than the punishment of sinners. If we view the words before us as prophetic, or as in the future tense, declaring a fact, we are probably nearer to the true meaning than that given in our version. Ungodly reader, what will be your lot when

---

9. From "As You Like It" by William Shakespeare.

the Lord deals with you according to your just deserts, and weighs out to you His wrath, not only in proportion to what you have actually done, but according to what you would have done if you could? Our endeavors are taken as facts; God takes the will for the deed, and punishes or rewards accordingly. Not in this life, but certainly in the next, God will repay His enemies to their faces, and give them the wages of their sins. Not according to their fawning words, but after the measure of their mischievous deeds, will the Lord mete out vengeance to them that know Him not.

Psalm 28:5 *Because they regard not the works of the Lord, nor the operation of his hands, he shall destroy them, and not build them up.*

EXPOSITION: **Verse 5.** *Because they regard not the works of the Lord, nor the operation of his hands.* God works in creation—nature teems with proofs of His wisdom and goodness, yet purblind[10] atheists refuse to see Him: He works in providence, ruling and overruling, and His hand is very manifest in human history, yet the infidel will not discern Him: He works in grace—remarkable conversions are still met with on all hands, yet the ungodly refuse to see the operations of the Lord. Where angels wonder, carnal men despise. God condescends to teach, and man refuses to learn. *He shall destroy them*: he will make them "behold, and wonder, and perish." If they will not see the hand of judgment upon others, they shall feel it upon themselves. Both soul and body shall be overwhelmed with utter destruction forever and ever. *And not build them up.* God's cure is positive and negative; His sword has two edges, and cuts right and left. Their heritage of evil shall prevent the ungodly receiving any

---

10. Lacking in insight or discernment.

good; the ephah[11] shall be too full of wrath to contain a grain of hope. They have become like old, rotten, decayed houses of timber, useless to the owner, and harboring all manner of evil, and, therefore, the Great Builder will demolish them utterly. Incorrigible offenders may expect speedy destruction: they, who will not mend, shall be thrown away as worthless. Let us be very attentive to all the lessons of God's Word and work, lest being found disobedient to the divine will, we be made to suffer the divine wrath.

Psalm 28:6 *Blessed be the Lord, because he hath heard the voice of my supplications.*

EXPOSITION: **Verse 6.** *Blessed be the Lord.* Saints are full of benedictions; they are a blessed people, and a blessing people; but they give their best blessings, the fat of their sacrifices, to their glorious Lord. Our psalm was prayer up to this point, and now it turns to praise. They who pray well, will soon praise well: prayer and praise are the two lips of the soul; two bells to ring out sweet and acceptable music in the ears of God; two angels to climb Jacob's ladder: two altars smoking with incense; two of Solomon's lilies dropping sweet smelling myrrh; they are two young roes that are twins, feeding upon the mountain of myrrh and the hill of frankincense. *Because he hath heard the voice of my supplications.* Real praise is established upon sufficient and constraining reasons; it is not irrational emotion, but rises, like a pure spring, from the deeps of experience.

Answered prayers should be acknowledged. Do we not often fail in this duty? Would it not greatly encourage others, and strengthen ourselves, if we faithfully recorded divine goodness, and made a point of extolling it with our tongue?

---

11. Hebrew dry measure equal to a bushel.

God's mercy is not such an inconsiderable thing that we may safely venture to receive it without so much as thanks. We should shun ingratitude, and live daily in the heavenly atmosphere of thankful love.

Psalm 28:7 *The Lord is my strength and my shield; my heart trusted in him, and I am helped: therefore my heart greatly rejoiceth; and with my song will I praise him.*

EXPOSITION: **Verse 7.** Here is David's declaration and confession of faith, coupled with a testimony from his experience. *The Lord is my strength.* The Lord employs His power on our behalf, and moreover, infuses strength into us in our weakness. The psalmist, by an act of appropriating faith, takes the omnipotence of Jehovah to be his own. Dependence upon the invisible God gives great independence of spirit, inspiring us with confidence more than human. *And my shield.* Thus David found both sword and shield in his God. The Lord preserves His people from unnumbered ills; and the Christian warrior, sheltered behind his God, is far more safe than the hero when covered with his shield of brass or triple steel.

My heart trusted in him, and I am helped. Heart work is sure work; heart trust is never disappointed. Faith must come before help, but help will never be long behindhand. Every day the believer may say, "I am helped," for the divine assistance is vouchsafed us every moment, or we should go back unto perdition; when more manifest help is needed, we have but to put faith into exercise, and it will be given us. *Therefore my heart greatly rejoiceth; and with my song will I praise him.* The heart is mentioned twice to show the truth of his faith and his joy. Observe the adverb "greatly," we need not be afraid of being too full of rejoicing at the remembrance of grace received. We serve a great God; let us greatly rejoice in Him. A song is the soul's fittest method of giving vent to its happiness, it were well if we were more like the singing lark, and less like the croaking raven. When the heart is glowing, the lips should not be silent. When God blesses us, we should bless Him with all our heart.

Psalm 28:8 *The Lord is their strength, and he is the saving strength of his anointed.*

EXPOSITION: Verse 8. *The Lord is their strength.* The heavenly experience of one believer is a pattern of the life of all. To all the militant church, without exception, Jehovah is the same as He was to His servant David, "the least of them shall be as David." They need the same aid and they shall have it, for they are loved with the same love, written in the same book of life, and one with the same anointed Head. *And he is the saving strength of his anointed.* Here behold King David as the type of our Lord Jesus, our covenant Head, our anointed Prince, through whom all blessings come to us. He has achieved full salvation for us, and we desire saving strength from Him, and as we share in the unction which is so largely shed upon Him, we expect to partake of His salvation. Glory be unto the God and Father of our Lord Jesus Christ, who has magnified the power of His grace in His only begotten Son, whom He has anointed to be a Prince and a Savior unto His people.

Psalm 28:9 *Save thy people, and bless thine inheritance: feed them also, and lift them up for ever.*

EXPOSITION: Verse 9. This is a prayer for the church militant, written in short words, but full of weighty meaning. We must pray for the whole Church and not for ourselves alone. *Save thy people.* Deliver them from their enemies, preserve them from their sins, comfort them under their troubles, rescue them from their temptations, and ward off from them every ill. There is a plea hidden in the expression, thy people: for it may be safely concluded that God's interest in the Church, as His own portion, will lead Him to guard it from destruction.

Bless thine inheritance. Grant positive blessings, peace, plenty, prosperity, happiness; make all your dearly purchased and precious heritage to be comforted by your Spirit. Revive, refresh, enlarge, and sanctify your Church. *Feed them also.* Be a shepherd to your flock; let their bodily and spiritual wants be plentifully supplied. By your Word, and ordinances, direct, rule, sustain, and satisfy those who are the sheep of your hand. *And lift them up for ever.* Carry them in your arms on Earth, and then lift them into your bosom in Heaven. Elevate their minds and thoughts, spiritualize their affections, and make them heavenly, Christlike, and full of God. O Lord, answer our petition, for Jesus' sake.

PSALM 29

PSALM 29:1–PSALM 29:11

Psalm 29:1 *Give unto the Lord, O ye mighty, give unto the Lord glory and strength.*

EXPOSITION: **Verse 1.** *Give,* i.e., ascribe. Neither men nor angels can confer anything upon Jehovah, but they should recognize His glory and might, and ascribe it to Him in their songs and in their hearts. Unto the Lord and unto Him alone, must honor be given. Natural causes, as men call them, are God in action, and we must not ascribe power to them, but to the infinite Invisible who is the true source of all. *O ye mighty.* You great ones of Earth and of Heaven, kings and angels, join in rendering worship to the blessed and only Potentate; you lords among men need thus to be reminded, for you often fail where humbler men are ardent; but fail no longer, bow your heads at once, and loyally do homage to the King of kings. How frequently do grandees[12] and potentates think it beneath them to fear the Lord; but, when they have been led to extol Jehovah, their piety has been the greatest jewel in their crowns.

Give unto the Lord glory and strength, both of which men are too apt to claim for themselves, although they are the exclusive prerogatives of the self-existent God. Let crowns and swords acknowledge their dependence upon God. Not to your arms, O kings, give ye the glory, nor look for strength to your hosts of warriors, for all your pomp is but as a fading flower, and your might is as a shadow which declines. When

---

12. Noblemen

shall the day arrive when kings and princes shall count it their delight to glorify their God? "All worship is to be to God only," [See Romans 27.] let this be emblazoned on every coat of arms.

Psalm 29:2 *Give unto the Lord the glory due unto his name; worship the Lord in the beauty of holiness.*

EXPOSITION: **Verse 2.** *Give unto the Lord the glory due unto his name.* A third time the admonition is given, for men are backward in glorifying God, and especially great men, who are often too swollen with their own glory to spare time to give God His rightful praise, although nothing more is asked of them than is most just and right. Surely men should not need so much pressing to give what is due, especially when the payment is so pleasant. Unbelief and distrust, complaining and murmuring, rob God of His honor; in this respect, even the saints fail to give due glory to their King. *Worship the Lord,* bow before Him with devout homage and sacred awe, and let your worship be such as He appoints.

Worship of old was encumbered with ceremony, and men gathered around one dedicated building, whose solemn pomp was emblematic of the beauty of holiness. But now our worship is spiritual, and the architecture of the house and the garments of the worshipers are matters of no importance; the spiritual beauty of inward purity and outward holiness being far more precious in the eyes of our thrice holy God. O for grace ever to worship with holy motives and in a holy manner, as becomes saints! The call to worship in these two verses chimes in with the loud pealing thunder, which is the church bell of the universe ringing kings and angels, and all the sons of Earth to their devotions.

Psalm 29:3 *The voice of the Lord is upon the waters: the God of glory thundereth: the Lord is upon many waters.*

EXPOSITION: Verse 3. *The voice of the Lord is upon the waters.* The thunder is not only poetically but instructively called "the voice of God," since it peals from on high; it surpasses all other sounds, it inspires awe, it is entirely independent of man, and has been used on some occasions as the grand accompaniment of God's speech to Adam's sons.

There is a peculiar terror in a tempest at sea, when deep calls unto deep, and the raging sea echoes to the angry sky. No sight more alarming than the flash of lightning around the mast of the ship; and no sound more calculated to inspire reverent awe than the roar of the storm. The children of Heaven have often enjoyed the tumult with humble joy peculiar to the saints, and even those who know not God have been forced into unwilling reverence while the storm has lasted.

The glory of God thundereth. Thunder is in truth no mere electric phenomenon, but is caused by the interposition of God himself. Even the old heathen spoke of Jupiter Tonans;[13] but our modern wise men will have us believe in laws and forces, and anything or nothing so they may be rid of God. Electricity of itself can do nothing, it must be called and sent upon its errand; and until the almighty Lord commissions it, its bolt of fire is inert and powerless. As well might a rock of granite or a bar of iron fly in the midst of Heaven, as the lightning go without being sent by the great First Cause.

The Lord is upon many waters. Still the Psalmist's ear hears no voice but that of Jehovah, resounding from the

---

13. An epithet for Jupiter meaning the "thunderer."

43

multitudinous and dark waters of the upper ocean of clouds, and echoing from the innumerable billows of the storm tossed sea below. The waters above and beneath the firmament are astonished at the eternal voice. When the Holy Spirit makes the divine promise to be heard above the many waters of our soul's trouble, then is God as glorious in the spiritual world as in the universe of matter. Above us and beneath us all is the peace of God when He gives us quiet.

Psalm 29:4 *The voice of the Lord is powerful; the voice of the Lord is full of majesty.*

EXPOSITION: **Verse 4.** *The voice of the Lord is powerful.* An irresistible power attends the lightning of which the thunder is the report. In an instant, when the Lord wills it, the force of electricity produces amazing results. A writer upon this subject, speaks of these results as including a light of the intensity of the sun in its strength, a heat capable of fusing the most compact metals, a force in a moment paralyzing the muscles of the most powerful animals; a power suspending the all pervading gravity of the Earth, and an energy capable of decomposing and recomposing the closest affinities of the most intimate combinations. The poet, James Thompson, speaks of "the unconquerable lightning," in the poem called *"Summer,"* for it is the chief of the ways of God in physical forces, and none can measure its power.

As the voice of God in nature is so powerful, so is it in grace; the reader will do well to draw a parallel, and he will find much in the gospel which may be illustrated by the thunder of the Lord in the tempest. His voice, whether in nature or revelation, shakes both Earth and Heaven; see that you refuse not Him that speaks. If His voice is thus mighty, what must His hand be! Beware lest you provoke a blow.

The voice of the Lord is powerful; the voice of the Lord is full of majesty. The King of kings speaks like a king. As when a lion roars, all the beasts of the forest are still, so is the Earth hushed and mute while Jehovah thunders marvelously. "It is listening fear and dumb amazement all."[14]

As for the written Word of God, its majesty is apparent both in its style, its matter, and its power over the human mind; blessed be God, it is the majesty of mercy wielding a silver scepter; of such majesty the word of our salvation is full to overflowing.

Psalm 29:5 *The voice of the Lord breaketh the cedars; yea, the Lord breaketh the cedars of Lebanon.*

EXPOSITION: **Verse 5.** *The voice of the Lord breaketh the cedars.*

> The Four Seasons
> "Black from the stroke above,
> the smouldering pine
> Stands a sad shattered trunk."[15]

Noble trees fall prostrate beneath the mysterious bolt, or stand in desolation as mementoes of its power. Lebanon itself is not secure, high as it stands, and ancient as are its venerable woods: *Yea, the Lord breaketh the cedars of Lebanon.* The greatest and most venerable of trees or men, may not reckon upon immunity when the Lord is abroad in His wrath. The Gospel of Jesus has a like dominion over the most inaccessible of mortals; and when the Lord sends the word, it breaks hearts far stouter than the cedars.

---

14. Portion of poem by James Thompson written in 1855.
15. Poem: *"The Four Seasons"* by James Thompson, *written in 1855.*

45

Psalm 29:6 *He maketh them also to skip like a calf; Lebanon and Sirion like a young unicorn.*

EXPOSITION: **Verse 6.** *He maketh them also to skip like a calf; Lebanon and Sirion like a young unicorn.* Not only the trees, but the mountains themselves move as though they frisked and leaped like young bulls or antelopes. As our own poets would mention hills and valleys known to them, so the Psalmist hears the crash and roar among the ranges of Libanus[16], and depicts the tumult in graphic terms. Thus sings one of our own countrymen as "The Four Seasons" poem continues:

> "Amid Carnavon's mountains rages loud
> The repercussive roar: with mighty crash
> Into the flashing deep, from the rude rocks
> Of Penmaen Mawr, heaped hideous to the sky,
> Tumble the smitten cliffs; and Snowdon's peak,
> Dissolving, instant yields his wintry load.
> Far seen, the heights of heathy Cheviot blaze,
> And Thule bellows through her utmost isles."

The glorious gospel of the blessed God has more than equal power over the rocky obduracy[17] and mountainous pride of man. The voice of our dying Lord rent the rocks and opened the graves: His living voice still works the like wonders. Glory be to His name, the hills of our sins leap into His grave, and are buried in the red sea of His blood, when the voice of His intercession is heard.

Psalm 29:7 *The voice of the Lord divideth the flames of fire.*

---

16. A mountain range in Lebanon.
17. Unyieldingness.

EXPOSITION: **Verse 7.** *The voice of the Lord divideth the flames of fire.* As when sparks fly from the anvil by blows of a ponderous hammer, so the lightning attends the thundering strokes of Jehovah. The *"Four Seasons* poem" continues:

> The tempest growls; but as it nearer comes,
> And rolls its awful burden on the wind,
> The lightnings flash a larger curve, and more
> The noise astounds: till overhead a sheet
> Of livid flame discloses wide; then shuts
> And opens wider; shuts and opens still
> "At first heard solemn over the verge of heaven,
> Expansive, wrapping ether in a blaze."

The thunder seems to divide one flash from another, interposing its deepening roar between the flash which precedes it and the next. That the flashes are truly flames of fire is witnessed by their frequently falling upon houses, churches, etc., and wrapping them in a blaze. How easily could the Lord destroy His rebellious creatures with His hot thunderbolts! How gracious is the hand which spares such great offenders, when to crush them would be so easy! Flames of fire attend the voice of God in the gospel, illuminating and melting the hearts of men: by those He consumes our lusts and kindles in us a holy flame of ever aspiring love and holiness. Pentecost is a suggestive commentary upon this verse.

Psalm 29:8 *The voice of the Lord shaketh the wilderness; the Lord shaketh the wilderness of Kadesh.*

EXPOSITION: **Verse 8.** As the storm travelled, it burst over the desert. *The voice of the Lord shaketh the wilderness; the Lord shaketh the wilderness of Kadesh.* God courts not the applause of men—His grandest deeds are wrought where man's inquisitive glance is all unknown. Where no sound of man was heard, the voice of God was terribly distinct. The vast and silent plains trembled with affright. Silence did homage to the Almighty voice. Low lying plains must hear the voice of God as well as lofty mountains; the poor as well as the mighty must acknowledge the glory of the Lord. Solitary and barren places are to be gladdened by the gospel's heavenly sound. What a shaking and overturning power there is in the Word of God! Even the conservative desert quivers into progress when God decrees it.

Psalm 29:9 *The voice of the Lord maketh the hinds to calve, and discovereth the forests: and in his temple doth every one speak of his glory.*

EXPOSITION: **Verse 9.** *The voice of the Lord maketh the hinds to calve,* those timid creatures, in deadly fear of the tempest, drop their burdens in an untimely manner. Perhaps a better reading is, "the oaks to tremble," especially as this agrees with the next sentence, *and discovereth the forests.* The dense shades of the forest are lit up with the lurid glare of the lightning, and even the darkest recesses are for a moment laid bare.

> "The gloomy woods
> Start at the flash, and from their deep recesses
> Wide flaming out, their trembling
> inmates shake."[18]

Our first parents sought a refuge among the trees, but the voice of the Lord soon found them out, and made their hearts to tremble. There is no concealment from the fire glance of the Almighty—one flash of His angry eye turns midnight into noon. The gospel has a like revealing power

---

18. From *"Critical Essays"* #377, *by John Scott.*

48

in dark hearts, in a moment it lights up every dark recess of the heart's ungodliness, and bids the soul tremble before the Lord.

In his temple doth everyone speak of his glory. Those who were worshiping in the temple were led to speak of the greatness of Jehovah as they heard the repeated thunder claps. The whole world is also a temple for God, and when He rides abroad upon the wings of the wind, all things are vocal in His praise. We too, the redeemed of the Lord, who are living temples for His Spirit, as we see the wonders of His power in creation, and feel them in grace, unite to magnify His name. No tongue may be dumb in God's temple when His glory is the theme. The original appears to have the force of "every one crieth Glory," as though all things were moved by a sense of God's majesty to shout in ecstasy, "Glory, glory." Here is a good precedent for our Methodist friends and for the Gogoniants[19] of the zealous Welsh.

Psalm 29:10 *The Lord sitteth upon the flood; yea, the Lord sitteth King for ever.*

EXPOSITION: **Verse 10.** *The Lord sitteth upon the flood.* Flood follows tempest, but Jehovah is ready for the emergency. No deluge can undermine the foundation of His throne. He is calm and unmoved, however much the deep may roar and be troubled: His government rules the most unstable and boisterous of created things. Far out on the wild waste of waters, Jehovah "plants his footsteps in the sea, and rides upon the storm."[20] *Yea, the Lord sitteth King for ever.* Jesus has the government upon His shoulders eternally: our interests in the stormiest times are safe in His hands. Satan

---

19. Glory

20. A portion from the hymn, "God Moves in Mysterious Ways," and written by William Cowper in 1773.

is not a king, but Jehovah Jesus is; therefore let us worship Him, and rejoice evermore.

Psalm 29:11 *The Lord will give strength unto his people; the Lord will bless his people with peace.*

EXPOSITION: Verse 11. Power was displayed in the hurricane whose course this psalm so grandly pictures; and now, in the cool calm after the storm, that power is promised to be the strength of the chosen. He, who sets wings the unerring bolt, will give to His redeemed the wings of eagles; He, who shakes the Earth with His voice, will terrify the enemies of His saints, and give His children peace. Why are we weak when we have divine strength to flee to? Why are we troubled when the Lord's own peace is ours? Jesus the mighty God is our peace—what a blessing is this today! What a blessing it will be to us in that day of the Lord which will be in darkness and not light to the ungodly! Dear reader, is not this a noble psalm to be sung in stormy weather? Can you sing amid the thunder? Will you be able to sing when the last thunders are let loose, and Jesus judges the quick and dead? If you are a believer, the last verse is your heritage, and surely that will set you singing.

PSALM 30
PSALM 30:1–PSALM 30:12

Psalm 30:1 *I will extol thee, O Lord; for thou hast lifted me up, and hast not made my foes to rejoice over me.*

EXPOSITION: *"I will extol thee.* I will have high and honorable conceptions of you, and give them utterance in my best music. Others may forget you, murmur at you, despise you, blaspheme you, but "I will extol thee," for I have been favored above all others. I will extol your name, your character, your attributes, your mercy to me, your great forbearance to my people; but, especially will I speak well of you; I will extol thee, O Jehovah; this shall be my cheerful and constant employ. *For you have lifted me up.* Here is an antithesis, "I will exalt you, for you have exalted me." I would render according to the benefits received.

The Psalmist's praise was reasonable. He had a reason to give for the praise that was in his heart. He had been drawn up like a prisoner from a dungeon, like Joseph out of the pit, and therefore he loved his deliverer. Grace has uplifted us from the pit of hell, from the ditch of sin, from the Slough of Despond, from the bed of sickness, from the bondage of doubts and fears: have we no song to offer for all this? How high has our Lord lifted us? Lifted us up into the children's place, to be adopted into the family; lifted us up into union with Christ, "to sit together with him in heavenly places." [See Ephesians 2:6.]

Lift high the name of our God, for He has lifted us up

above the stars. *And hast not made my foes to rejoice over me.* This was the judgment which David most feared out of the three evils; he said, let me fall into the hand of the Lord, and not into the hand of man. Terrible indeed would be our lot if we were delivered over to the will of our enemies. Blessed be the Lord, we have been preserved from so dire a fate. The devil and all our spiritual enemies have not been permitted to rejoice over us; for we have been saved from the fowler's snare. Our evil companions, who prophesied that we should go back to our old sins, are disappointed. Those who watched for our halting, and would love to say, "Aha! Aha! So would we have it!" have watched in vain until now. O happy they whom the Lord keeps so consistent in character that the lynx eyes of the world can see no real fault in them. Is this our case? Let us ascribe all the glory to Him who has sustained us in our integrity.

Psalm 30:2 *O Lord my God, I cried unto thee, and thou hast healed me.*

EXPOSITION: **Verse 2.** *O Lord my God, I cried unto thee, and thou hast healed me.* David sent up prayers for himself and for his people when visited with the pestilence. He went at once to headquarters, and not roundabout to fallible means. God is the best physician, even for our bodily infirmities. We do very wickedly and foolishly when we forget God. It was a sin in Asa that he trusted to physicians and not to God. If we must have a physician, let it be so, but still let us go to our God first of all; and, above all, remember that there can be no power to heal in medicine of itself; the healing energy must flow from the divine hand. If our watch is out of order, we take it to the watchmaker; if our body or soul is in an evil plight, let us resort to Him who created them, and has unfailing skill to put them in right condition.

As for our spiritual diseases, nothing can heal these evils but the touch of the Lord Christ: if we do but touch the hem of His garment, we shall be made whole, while if we embrace all other physicians in our arms, they can do us no service.

O Lord my God. Observe the covenant name which faith uses—my God. Thrice happy is he who can claim the Lord himself to be his portion. Note how David's faith ascends the scale; he sang O Lord in the first verse, but it is O Lord my God, in the second. Heavenly heart music is an ascending thing, like the pillars of smoke which rose from the altar of incense. I cried unto thee. I could hardly pray, but I cried; I poured out my soul as a little child pours out its desires. I cried to my God: I knew to whom to cry; I did not cry to my friends, or to any arm of flesh. Hence the sure and satisfactory result—*Thou hast healed me.* I know it. I am sure of it. I have the evidence of spiritual health within me now: glory be to your name! Every humble suppliant with God, who seeks release from the disease of sin, shall speed as well as the Psalmists did, but those who will not so much as seek a cure, need not wonder if their wounds putrefy and their soul dies.

Psalm 30:3 *O Lord, thou hast brought up my soul from the grave: thou hast kept me alive, that I should not go down to the pit.*

EXPOSITION: **Verse 3.** *O Lord, thou hast brought up my soul from the grave.* Note, it is not "I hope so;" but it is, "Thou hast; thou hast; thou hast"—three times over. David is quite sure, beyond a doubt, that God has done great things for him, whereof he is exceeding glad. He had descended to the brink of the sepulcher, and yet was restored to tell of the forbearance of God; nor was this all, he stated that nothing but grace had kept him from the lowest hell, and this made him doubly thankful. To be spared from the grave is much; to be delivered from the pit is more; hence there is growing cause for praise, since both deliverances are alone traceable to the glorious right hand of the Lord, who is the only preserver of life, and the only Redeemer of our souls from hell.

Psalm 30:4 *Sing unto the Lord, O ye saints of his, and give thanks at the remembrance of his holiness.*

EXPOSITION: Verse 4. *Sing unto the Lord, O ye saints of his.* Join my song; assist me to express my gratitude. He felt that he could not praise God enough himself, and therefore he would enlist the hearts of others. *Sing unto the Lord, O ye saints of his.* David would not fill his choir with reprobates, but with sanctified persons, who could sing from their hearts. He calls to you, you people of God, because you are saints: and if sinners are wickedly silent, let your holiness constrain you to sing. You are His saints—chosen, blood bought, called, and set apart for God; sanctified on purpose that you should offer the daily sacrifice of praise.

Abound in this heavenly duty. *Sing unto the Lord.* It is a pleasing exercise; it is a profitable engagement. Do not need to be stirred up so often to so pleasant a service. And give thanks. Let your songs be grateful songs, in which the Lord's mercies shall live again in joyful remembrance. The very remembrance of the past should tune our harps, even if present joys be lacking. *At the remembrance of His holiness.* Holiness is an attribute which inspires the deepest awe, and demands a reverent mind; but still gives thanks at the remembrance of it. "Holy, holy, holy!" is the song of seraphim and cherubim; let us join it—not dolefully, as though we trembled at the holiness of God, but cheerfully, as humbly rejoicing in it.

Psalm 30:5 *For his anger endureth but a moment; in his favour is life: weeping may endure for a night, but joy cometh in the morning.*

EXPOSITION: **Verse 5.** *For his anger endureth but a moment.* David here alludes to those dispensations of God's providence which are the chastisement ordered in His paternal government towards His erring children, such as the plague which fell upon Jerusalem for David's sins; these are but short judgments, and they are removed as soon as real penitence sues for pardon and presents the great and acceptable sacrifice. What a mercy is this, for if the Lord's wrath smoked for a long season, flesh would utterly fail before Him. God puts up His rod with great readiness as soon as its work is done; He is slow to anger and swift to end it. If His temporary and fatherly anger is so severe that it needs to be short, what must be the terror of eternal wrath exercised by the Judge towards His adversaries?

In his favour is life. As soon as the Lord looked favorably upon David, the city lived, and the king's heart lived too. We die like withered flowers when the Lord frowns, but His sweet smile revives us as the dews refresh the field. His favor not only sweetens and cheers life, but it is life itself, the very essence of life. Who would know life; let him seek the favor of the Lord. *Weeping may endure for a night*; but nights are not forever. Even in the dreary winter the day star lights his lamp. It seems fit that in our nights the dews of grief should fall. When the Bridegroom's absence makes it dark within, it is right that the widowed soul should pine for a renewed sight of the Well beloved.

But joy cometh in the morning. When the Sun of Righteousness comes, we wipe our eyes, and joy chases out intruding sorrow. Who would not be joyful that knows Jesus? The first beams of the morning bring us comfort when

Jesus is the day dawn, and all believers know it to be so. Mourning only lasts to morning: when the night is gone the gloom shall vanish. This is advanced reasoning for saintly singing, and forcible reason it is; short nights and merry days call for the psaltery and harp.

Psalm 30:6 *And in my prosperity I said, I shall never be moved.*

EXPOSITION: **Verse 6.** *In my prosperity.* When all his foes were quiet and his rebellious son dead and buried, then was the time of peril. Many a vessel founders in a calm. No temptation is as bad as tranquility. *I said, I shall never be moved. "* Ah! David, you said more than was wise to say, or even to think, for God has founded the world upon the floods, to show us what a poor, mutable, moveable, inconstant world it is. Unhappy is he who builds upon it! He builds himself a dungeon for his hopes. Instead of conceiving that we shall never be moved, we ought to remember that we shall very soon be removed altogether.

Nothing is abiding beneath the moon. Because I happen to be prosperous today, I must not fancy that I shall be in my high estate tomorrow. As in a wheel, the uppermost spokes descend to the bottom in due course, so it is with mortal conditions. There is a constant revolution: many who are in the dust today shall be highly elevated tomorrow; while those who are now aloft shall soon grind the Earth. Prosperity had evidently turned the psalmist's head, or he would not have been so self-confident. He stood by grace, and yet forgot himself, and so met with a fall. Reader, is there not much of the same proud stuff in all our hearts? Let us beware lest the fumes of intoxicating success get into our brains and make fools of us also.

Psalm 30:7 *Lord, by thy favour thou hast made my mountain to stand strong: thou didst hide thy face, and I was troubled.*

EXPOSITION: **Verse 7.** *Lord, by thy favour thou hast made my mountain to stand strong.* He ascribed his prosperity to the Lord's favor—so far good, it is well to own the hand of the Lord in all our stability and wealth. But observe that the good in a good man is not unmingled good, for this was alloyed with carnal security. His state he compares to a mountain, a molehill would have been nearer—we never think too little of ourselves. He boasted that his mountain stood strong, and yet he had before, in Psalm 29, spoken of Sirion and Lebanon as moving like young unicorns. Was David's state more firm than Lebanon? Ah, vain conceit, too common to us all!

How soon the bubble bursts when God's people get conceit into their heads, and fancy that they are to enjoy immutability beneath the stars, and constancy upon this whirling orb. How touchingly and teachingly God corrected His servant's mistake: *Thou didst hide thy face, and I was troubled.* There was no need to come to blows, a hidden face was enough. This proves, first, that David was a genuine saint, for no hiding of God's face on Earth would trouble a sinner; and, secondly, that the joy of the saint is dependent upon the presence of his Lord. No mountain, however firm, can yield us rest when our communion with God is broken, and His face is concealed. However, in such a case, it is well to be troubled. The next best thing to basking in the light of God's countenance is to be thoroughly unhappy when that bliss is denied us.

"Lord, let me weep for nought for sin!
And after none but thee!
And then I would—O that I might,
A constant weeper be!"[21]

Psalm 30:8 *I cried to thee, O Lord; and unto the Lord I made supplication.*

EXPOSITION: **Verse 8.** *I cried to thee, O Lord.* Prayer is the unfailing resource of God's people. If they are driven to their wit's end, they may still go to the mercy seat. When an earthquake makes our mountain tremble, the throne of grace still stands firm, and we may come to it. Let us never forget to pray, and let us never doubt the success of prayer. The hand which wounds can heal: let us turn to Him who smites us, and He will be entreated of us. Prayer is better solace than Cain's building a city, or Saul's seeking for music. Mirth and carnal amusements are a sorry prescription for a mind distracted and despairing: prayer will succeed where all else fails.

Psalm 30:9 *What profit is there in my blood, when I go down to the pit? Shall the dust praise thee? shall it declare thy truth?*

EXPOSITION: **Verse 9.** In this verse we learn the form and method of David's prayer. It was an argument with God, an urging of reasons, a pleading of his cause. It was not a statement of doctrinal opinions, nor a narration of experience, much less a sly hit at other people under pretence of praying to God, although all these things and worse have been substituted for holy supplication at certain

---

21. Hymn #122, titled "The Spiritual Mourner" from the Hymnbook, "A Collection of Hymns Adapted to Public Worship" by John Ash and Caleb Evans.

prayer meetings. He wrestled with the angel of the covenant with vehement pleadings, and therefore he prevailed. Head and heart, judgment and affections, memory and intellect were all at work to spread the case aright before the Lord of love. *What profit is there in my blood, when I go down to the pit?"* Wilt you not lose a songster from your choir and one who loves to magnify you? *"Shall the dust praise thee? shall it declare thy truth?"* Will there not be one witness the less to your faithfulness and veracity? Spare, then, your poor unworthy one for your own name sake!

Psalm 30:10 *Hear, O Lord, and have mercy upon me: Lord, be thou my helper.*

EXPOSITION: Verse 10. *"Hear, O Lord, and have mercy upon me."* A short and comprehensive petition, available at all seasons, let us use it full often. It is the publican's prayer; be it ours. If God hears prayer, it is a great act of mercy; our petitions do not merit a reply. *Lord, be thou my helper.* Another compact, expressive, ever fitting prayer. It is suitable to hundreds of the cases of the Lord's people; it is well becoming in the minister when he is going to preach, to the sufferer upon the bed of pain, to the toiler in the field of service, to the believer under temptation, to the man of God under adversity; when God helps, difficulties vanish. He is the help of His people, a very present help in trouble. The two brief petitions of this verse are commended as encouraging exclamations to believers full of business, denied to those longer seasons of devotion which are the rare privilege of those whose days are spent in retirement.

Psalm 30:11 *Thou hast turned for me my mourning into dancing: thou hast put off my sackcloth, and girded me with gladness;*

EXPOSITION: **Verse 11:** Observe the contrast, God takes away the mourning of His people; and what does He give them instead of it? Quiet and peace? Ah yes, and a great deal more than that. *Thou hast turned for me my mourning into dancing.* He makes their hearts to dance at the sound of His name. He takes off their sackcloth. That is good. What a delight to be rid of the habiliments of woe! But what then? He clothes us. And how? With some common dress? No, but with that royal vestment which is the array of glorified spirits in Heaven.

Thou hast girded me with gladness. This is better than to wear garments of silk or cloth of gold, bedight[22] with embroidery and bespangled[23] with gems. Many a poor man wears this heavenly apparel wrapped around his heart, though fustian[24] and corduroy are his only outward garb; and such a man needs not envy the emperor in all his pomp. Glory be to you, O God, if, by a sense of full forgiveness and present justification, you have enriched my spiritual nature, and filled me with all the fullness of God.

Psalm 30:12 *To the end that my glory may sing praise to thee, and not be silent. O Lord my God, I will give thanks unto thee for ever.*

EXPOSITION: **Verse 12.** *To the end*—namely, with this view and intent—*that my glory*—that is, my tongue or my soul—*may sing praise to thee, and not be silent.* It would be a shameful crime, if, after receiving God's mercies, we should forget to praise Him. God would not have our tongues lie idle while so many themes for gratitude are spread on every hand. He would have no dumb [unable to speak] children

---

22. Decorated.
23. Embellished.
24. A cotton or linen like fabric with a raised nap.

in the house. They are all to sing in Heaven, and therefore they should all sing on Earth. Let us sing with the hymnists:

> "I would begin the music here,
> And so my soul should rise:
> Oh for some heavenly notes to bear
> My passions to the skies."[25]

O Lord my God, I will give thanks unto thee for ever.

Hymn: *My Jesus I Love Thee*[26]
"I will praise him in life; I will praise him in death;
I will praise him as long as he lendeth me breath;
And say when the death dew lays cold on my brow,
If ever I loved thee, my Jesus, it is now."

---

25. Verse 6 of a hymn based on Revelation 6 written by John Charles Ryle in 1868.
26. Words by Wm. R. Featherston, 1864 and music by Adoniram J. Gordon, 1876

PSALM 31
PSALM 31:1–31:24

Psalm 31:1 *In thee, O Lord, do I put my trust; let me never be ashamed: deliver me in thy righteousness.*

EXPOSITION: Verse 1. *In thee, O Lord, do I put my trust.* Nowhere else do I fly for shelter; let the tempest howl as it may. The psalmist has one refuge, and that the best one. He casts out the great sheet anchor of his faith in the time of storm. Let other things be doubtful, yet the fact that he relies on Jehovah, David lays down most positively; and he begins with it, lest by stress of trial he should afterwards forget it. This avowal of faith is the fulcrum[27] by means of which he labors to uplift and remove his trouble; he dwells upon it as a comfort to himself and a plea with God. No mention is made of merit, but faith relies upon divine favor and faithfulness, and upon that alone.

Let me never be ashamed. How can the Lord permit the man to be ultimately put to shame who depends alone upon Him? This would not be dealing like a God of truth and grace. It would bring dishonor upon God himself if faith were not in the end rewarded. It will be an ill day indeed for religion when trust in God brings no consolation and no assistance. *Deliver me in thy righteousness.* You are not unjust to desert a trustful soul, or to break your promises; you will vindicate the righteousness of your mysterious providence, and give me joyful deliverance. Faith dares to look even to the sword of justice for protection: while God is righteous, faith will not

---

27. A swivel on which a lever turns.

be left to be proved futile and fanatical. How sweetly the declaration of faith in this first verse sounds, if we read it at the foot of the Cross, beholding the promise of the Father as yes and amen through the Son; viewing God with faith's eye as He stands revealed in Jesus crucified.

Psalm 31:2 *"Bow down thine ear to me; deliver me speedily: be thou my strong rock, for an house of defence to save me."*

EXPOSITION: **Verse 2.** *"Bow down thine ear to me."* Condescend to my low estate; listen to me attentively as one who would hear every word. Heaven with its transcendent glories of harmony might well engross the divine ear, but yet the Lord has an hourly regard to the weakest moanings of His poorest people. *Deliver me speedily.* We must not set times or seasons, yet in submission we may ask for swift as well as sure mercy. God's mercies are often enhanced in value by the timely haste which He uses in their bestowal; if they came late they might be too late—but He rides upon a cherub, and flies upon the wings of the wind when He intends the good of His beloved.

Be thou my strong rock. Be my Engedi,[28] my Adullam;[29] my immutable, immovable, impregnable, sublime, resort. *For an house of defense to save me,* wherein I may dwell in safety, not merely running to you for temporary shelter, but abiding in you for eternal salvation. How very simply does the good man pray and yet with what weight of meaning! He uses no ornamental flourishes; he is too deeply in earnest to be otherwise than plain: it would be well if all who engage in public prayer would observe the same rule.

---

28. A refuge and oasis on the western shore of the Dead Sea.
29. A cave outside the town of Adullam where David sought refuge from Saul.

Psalm 31:3 *For thou art my rock and my fortress; therefore for thy name's sake lead me, and guide me.*

EXPOSITION: Verse 3. *For thou art my rock and my fortress.* Here the tried soul avows yet again its full confidence in God. Faith's repetitions are not vain. The avowal of our reliance upon God in times of adversity is a principle method of glorifying Him. Active service is good, but the passive confidence of faith is not one jot less esteemed in the sight of God. The words before us appear to embrace and fasten upon the Lord with a fiducial[30] grip which is not to be relaxed. The two personal pronouns, like sure nails, lay hold upon the faithfulness of the Lord. O for grace to have our heart fixed in firm unstaggering belief in God! The figure of a rock and a fortress may be illustrated to us in these times by the vast fortress of Gibraltar, often besieged by our enemies, but never wrested from us: ancient strongholds, though far from impregnable by our modes of warfare, were equally important in those remoter ages—when in the mountain fastnesses, feeble bands felt themselves to be secure. Note the singular fact that David asked the Lord to be his rock in Psalm 31:2, because He was his rock; and learn from it that we may pray to enjoy in experience what we grasp by faith. Faith is the foundation of prayer.

Therefore for thy name's sake lead me, and guide me. The psalmist argues like a logician by his usage of for and therefore. Since I do sincerely trust you, he says, O my God, be my director. To lead and to guide are two things very like each other, but patient thought will detect different shades of meaning, especially as the last may mean provide for me. The double word indicates an urgent need—we require double direction, for we are fools, and the way is rough.

---

30. Trustworthy.

Lead me as a soldier, guide me as a traveler! Lead me as a babe, guide me as a man; lead me when you are with me, but guide me even if you are absent; lead me by your hand, guide me by your Word. The argument used is one which is taken from the armory of free grace: not for my own sake, but for thy name's sake guide me. Our appeal is not to any fancied virtue in our own names, but to the glorious goodness and graciousness which shines resplendent in the character of Israel's God. It is not possible that the Lord should suffer His own honor to be tarnished, but this would certainly be the case if those who trusted Him should perish. This was Moses' plea, *What wilt thou do unto thy great name?* [See Joshua 7:9.]

Psalm 31:4 *Pull me out of the net that they have laid privily for me: for thou art my strength.*

EXPOSITION: **Verse 4.** *Pull me out of the net that they have laid privily for me.* The enemies of David were cunning as well as mighty; if they could not conquer him by power, they would capture him by craft. Our own spiritual foes are of the same order—they are of the serpent's brood, and seek to ensnare us by their guile. The prayer before us supposes the possibility of the believer being caught like a bird; and, indeed, we are so foolish that this often happens. So deftly does the fowler do his work that simple ones are soon surrounded by it. The text asks that even out of the meshes of the net the captive one may be delivered; and this is a proper petition, and one which can be granted; from between the jaws of the lion and out of the belly of hell can eternal love rescue the saint. It may need a sharp pull to save a soul from the net of temptation, and a mighty pull to extricate a man from the snares of malicious cunning, but the Lord is equal to every emergency, and the most skillfully placed nets of the hunter shall never be able to hold His chosen ones. Woe unto those who are so clever at net laying: they who tempt others shall be destroyed themselves. Villains who lay traps in secret shall be punished in public.

For thou art my strength. What an inexpressible sweetness is to be found in these few words! How joyfully may we enter upon labors, and how cheerfully may we endure sufferings when we can lay hold upon celestial power. Divine power will rend asunder all the toils of the foe, confound their politics and frustrate their knavish tricks; he is a happy man who has such matchless might engaged upon his side. Our own strength would be of little service when embarrassed in the nets of base cunning, but the Lord's strength is ever available; we have but to invoke it and we shall find it near at hand. If by faith we are depending alone upon the strength of the strong God of Israel, we may use our holy reliance as a plea in supplication.

Psalm 31:5 *Into thine hand I commit my spirit: thou hast redeemed me, O Lord God of truth.*

EXPOSITION: **Verse 5.** *Into thine hand I commit my spirit.* These living words of David were our Lord's dying words, and have been frequently used by holy men in their hour of departure. Be assured that they are good, choice, wise, and solemn words; we may use them now and in the last tremendous hour. Observe the object of the good man's solicitude in life and death is not his body or his estate, but his spirit; this is his jewel, his secret treasure; if this be safe, all is well. See what he does with his pearl! He commits it to the hand of his God; it came from Him, it is His own, He has aforetime sustained it, He is able to keep it, and it is most fitting that He should receive it.

All things are safe in Jehovah's hands; what we entrust

to the Lord will be secure, both now and in that day of days towards which we are hastening. Without reservation the good man yields himself to his heavenly Father's hand; it is enough for him to be there; it is peaceful living and glorious dying to repose in the care of Heaven. At all times we should commit and continue to commit our all to Jesus' sacred care, then, though life may hang on a thread, and adversities may multiply as the sands of the sea, our soul shall dwell at ease, and delight itself in quiet resting places. *Thou hast redeemed me, O Lord God of truth.* Redemption is a solid base for confidence. David has not known Calvary as we have done, but temporal redemption cheered him; and shall not eternal redemption yet more sweetly console us? Past deliverances are strong pleas for present assistance. What the Lord has done He will do again, for He changes not. He is a God of veracity, faithful to His promises, and gracious to His saints; He will not turn away from His people.

Psalm 31:6 *I have hated them that regard lying vanities: but I trust in the Lord.*

EXPOSITION: **Verse 6.** *I have hated them that regard lying vanities.* Those who will not lean upon the true arm of strength are sure to make to themselves vain confidences. Man must have a god, and if he will not adore the only living and true God, he makes a fool of himself, and pays superstitious regard to a lie, and waits with anxious hope upon a base delusion. Those who did this were none of David's friends; he had a constant dislike of them: the verb includes the present as well as the past tense. He hated them for hating God; he would not endure the presence of idolaters; his heart was set against them for their stupidity and wickedness. He had no patience with their superstitious observances, and calls their idols vanities of emptiness, nothings of nonentity. Small courtesy is more than Romanists and Puseyists[31] deserve for their fooleries. Men who make gods of their riches, their persons, their wits, or anything else, are to be shunned by those whose faith rests upon God in Christ Jesus; and so far from being envied, they are to be pitied as depending upon utter vanities.

But I trust in the Lord. This might be very unfashionable, but the psalmist dared to be singular. Bad example should not make us less decided for the truth, but rather in the midst of general defection we should grow more bold. This adherence to his trust in Jehovah is the great plea employed all along: the troubled one flies into the arms of his God, and ventures everything upon the divine faithfulness.

Psalm 31:7 *I will be glad and rejoice in thy mercy: for thou hast considered my trouble; thou hast known my soul in adversities;*

EXPOSITION: **Verse 7.** *I will be glad and rejoice in thy mercy.* For mercy past he is grateful, and for mercy future, which he believingly anticipates, he is joyful. In our most importunate intercessions, we must find breathing time to bless the Lord: praise is never a hindrance to prayer, but rather a lively refreshment therein. It is delightful at intervals to hear the notes of the high sounding cymbals when the dolorous sackbut[32] rules the hour. Those two words, glad

---

31. Edward Bouverie Pusey, 1800-1882, English churchman, Professor of Hebrew at Oxford and a leader in the Oxford Movement. Puseyism The principles and teachings characteristic of a High-church party in the Church of England, originating in Oxford University in the early part of the nineteenth century: so called from one of the leaders in the Oxford Movement, Dr. E. B. Pusey, professor of Hebrew in the university. Also called Tractarianism or Ritualism.
32. A medieval instrument that resembles a trombone.

and rejoice, are an instructive reduplication, we need not stint ourselves in our holy triumph; this wine we may drink in bowls without fear of excess. *For thou hast considered my trouble.* Thou hast seen it, weighed it, directed it, fixed a bound to it, and in all ways made it a matter of tender consideration. A man's consideration means the full exercise of his mind; what must God's consideration be?

Thou hast known my soul in adversities. God owns His saints when others are ashamed to acknowledge them; He never refuses to know His friends. He thinks not the worse of them for their rags and tatters. He does not misjudge them and cast them off when their faces are lean with sickness, or their hearts heavy with despondency. Moreover, the Lord Jesus knows us in our pangs in a peculiar sense, by having a deep sympathy towards us in them all; when no others can enter into our griefs, from want of understanding them experimentally, Jesus dives into the lowest depths with us, comprehending the direst of our woes, because He has felt the same. Jesus is a physician who knows every case; nothing is new to Him. When we are so bewildered as not to know our own state, He knows us altogether. He has known us and will know us: O for grace to know more of Him! "Man, know yourself," is a good philosophic precept, but Man, *you are known by God,* is a superlative consolation. Adversities in the plural—*Many are the afflictions of the righteous.* [See Psalm 34:19.]

Psalm 31:8 *And hast not shut me up into the hand of the enemy: thou hast set my feet in a large room.*

EXPOSITION: **Verse 8.** *And hast not shut me up into the hand of the enemy.* To be shut up in one's hand is to be delivered over absolutely to his power; now, the believer is not in the hand of death or the devil, much less is he in the power of man. The enemy may get a temporary advantage over us, but we are like men in prison with the door open; God will not let us be shut up, He always provides a way of escape.

Thou hast set my feet in a large room. Blessed be God for liberty: civil liberty is valuable, religious liberty is precious, spiritual liberty is priceless. In all troubles we may praise God if these are left. Many saints have had their greatest enlargements of soul when their affairs have been in the greatest straits. Their souls have been in a large room when their bodies have been lying in "Bonner's coal hole"[33], or in some other narrow dungeon. Grace has been equal to every emergency; and more than this, it has made the emergency an opportunity for displaying itself.

Psalm 31:9 *Have mercy upon me, O Lord, for I am in trouble: mine eye is consumed with grief, yea, my soul and my belly.*

EXPOSITION: **Verse 9.** *Have mercy upon me, O Lord, for I am in trouble.* Now, the man of God comes to a particular and minute description of his sorrowful case. He unbosoms[34] his heart, lays bare his wounds, and expresses his inward desolation. This first sentence pithily comprehends all that follows; it is the text for his lamenting discourse. Misery moves mercy—no more reasoning is needed. *Have mercy* is the prayer; the argument is as prevalent as it is plain and personal; *I am in trouble. Mine eye is consumed with grief.* Dim and sunken eyes are plain indicators of failing health. Tears draw their salt from our strength, and floods of them are very apt to consume the source from which they

---

33. An underground dungeon named after the Catholic Bishop of London.
34. Unburdens his heart felt trouble to God.

71

spring. God would have us tell Him the symptoms of our disease, not for His information, but to show our sense of need. *Yea, my soul and my belly* (or body). Soul and body are so intimately united, that one cannot decline without the other feeling it. We, in these days, are not strangers to the double sinking which David describes; we have been faint with physical suffering, and distracted with mental distress: when two such seas meet, it is well for us that the Pilot at the helm is at home in the midst of the water floods, and makes storms to become the triumph of His art.

Psalm 31:10 *For my life is spent with grief, and my years with sighing: my strength faileth because of mine iniquity, and my bones are consumed.*

EXPOSITION: Verse 10. *For my life is spent with grief, and my years with sighing.* It had become his daily occupation to mourn; he spent all his days in the dungeon of distress. The sap and essence of his existence was being consumed, as a candle is wasted while it burns. His adversities were shortening his days, and digging for him an early grave. Grief is a sad market to spend all our wealth of life in, but a far more profitable trade may be driven there than in Vanity Fair; it is better to go to the house of mourning than the house of feasting. Black is good wear. The salt of tears is a healthy medicine. Better spend our years in sighing than in sinning. The two members of the sentence before us convey the same idea; but there are no idle words in Scripture, the reduplication is the fitting expression of fervency and importunity.

My strength faileth because of mine iniquity. David sees to the bottom of his sorrow, and detects sin lurking there. It is profitable trouble which leads us to trouble ourselves about our iniquity. Was this the psalmist's foulest crime which now gnawed at his heart, and devoured his strength?

Very probably it was so. Sinful morsels, though sweet in the mouth, turn out to be poison in the bowels: if we wantonly give a portion of our strength to sin, it will by and by take the remainder from us. We lose physical, mental, moral, and spiritual vigor by iniquity. *And my bones are consumed.* Weakness penetrated the innermost parts of his system, the firmest parts of his frame felt the general decrepitude. A man is in a piteous plight when he comes to this.

Psalm 31:11 *I was a reproach among all mine enemies, but especially among my neighbours, and a fear to mine acquaintance: they that did see me without fled from me.*

EXPOSITION: **Verse 11.** *I was a reproach among all mine enemies.* They were pleased to have something to throw at me; my mournful estate was music to them, because they maliciously interpreted it to be a judgment from Heaven upon me. Reproach is little thought of by those who are not called to endure it, but he who passes under its lash knows how deep it wounds. The best of men may have the bitterest foes, and be subject to the cruelest taunts. *But especially among my neighbours.* Those who are nearest can stab the sharpest. We feel most the slights of those who should have shown us sympathy. Perhaps David's friends feared to be identified with his declining fortunes, and therefore turned against him in order to win the mercy if not the favor of his opponents. Self-interest rules the most of men: ties the most sacred are soon snapped by its influence, and actions of the utmost meanness are perpetrated without scruple.

And a fear to mine acquaintance. The more intimate before, the more distant did they become. Our Lord was denied by Peter, betrayed by Judas, and forsaken by all in the hour of His utmost need. All the herd turns against a wounded deer. The milk of human kindness curdles when a despised believer is the victim of slanderous accusations.

They that did see me without fled from me. Afraid to be seen in the company of a man so thoroughly despised those who once courted his society hastened from him as though he had been infected with the plague. How villainous a thing is slander which can thus make an eminent saint, once the admiration of his people, to become the general butt, the universal aversion of mankind! To what extremities of dishonor may innocence be reduced!

Psalm 31:12 *I am forgotten as a dead man out of mind: I am like a broken vessel.*

EXPOSITION: **Verse 12.** *I am forgotten as a dead man out of mind.* All David's youthful prowess was now gone from remembrance; he had been the savior of his country, but his services were buried in oblivion. Men soon forget the deepest obligations; popularity is evanescent[35] to the last degree: he who is in every one's mouth today may be forgotten by all tomorrow. A man had better be dead than be smothered in slander. Of the dead we say nothing but good, but in the psalmist's case they said nothing but evil. We must not look for the reward of philanthropy this side of Heaven, for men pay their best servants but sorry wages, and turn them out of doors when no more is to be got out of them. *I am like a broken vessel,* a thing useless, done for, worthless, cast aside, forgotten. Sad condition for a king! Let us see herein the portrait of the King of kings in His humiliation, when He made himself of no reputation, and took upon Him the form of a servant.

---

35. Temporary.

Psalm 31:13 *For I have heard the slander of many: fear was on every side: while they took counsel together against me, they devised to take away my life.*

EXPOSITION: Verse 13. *For I have heard the slander of many.* One slanderous viper is death to all comfort—what must be the venom of a whole brood? What the ear does not hear the heart does not rue; but in David's case the accusing voices were loud enough to break in upon his quiet—foul mouths had grown so bold, that they poured forth their falsehoods in the presence of their victim. Shimei was but one of a class, and his cry of "Go up, thou bloody man," was but the common speech of thousands of the sons of Belial. All Beelzebub's pack of hounds may be in full cry against a man, and yet he may be the Lord's anointed. *Fear was on every side.* He was encircled with fearful suggestions, threatenings, remembrances, and forebodings; no quarter was clear from incessant attack.

While they took counsel together against me, they devised to take away my life. The ungodly act in concert in their onslaughts upon the excellent of the Earth: it is to be wondered at that sinners should often be better agreed than saints, and generally set about their wicked work with much more care and foresight than the righteous exhibit in holy enterprises. Observe the cruelty of a good man's foes! They will be content with nothing less than his blood—for this they plot and scheme. Better to fall into the power of a lion than under the will of malicious persecutors, for the beast may spare its prey if it be fed to the full, but malice is unrelenting and cruel as a wolf. Of all fiends the most cruel is envy. How sorely was the psalmist bestead[36] when the poisoned arrows of a thousand bows were all aimed at

---

36. Put in peril.

his life! Yet in all this his faith did not fail him, nor did his God forsake him. Here is encouragement for us.

Psalm 31:14 *But I trusted in thee, O Lord: I said, Thou art my God.*

EXPOSITION: **Verse 14.** *But I trusted in thee, O Lord.* Notwithstanding all afflicting circumstances, David's faith maintained its hold, and was not turned aside from its object. What a blessed saving clause is this! So long as our faith, which is our shield, is safe, the battle may go hard, but its ultimate result is no matter of question; if that could be torn from us, we would be as surely slain as were Saul and Jonathan upon the high places of the field. *I said, Thou art my God.* He proclaimed aloud his determined allegiance to Jehovah. He was no fair weather believer, he could hold to his faith in a sharp frost, and wrap it about him as a garment fitted to keep out all the ills of time. He who can say what David did need not envy Cicero his eloquence: *Thou art my God,* has more sweetness in it than any other utterance which human speech can frame. Note that this adhesive faith is here mentioned as an argument with God to honor His own promise by sending a speedy deliverance.

Psalm 31:15 *My times are in thy hand: deliver me from the hand of mine enemies, and from them that persecute me.*

EXPOSITION: **Verse 15.** *"My times are in thy hand.* The sovereign arbiter of destiny holds in His own power all the issues of our life; we are not waifs and strays upon the ocean of fate, but are steered by infinite wisdom towards our desired haven. Providence is a soft pillow for anxious heads, an anodyne[37] for care, and a grave for despair. *Deliver me from the hand of mine enemies, and from them that persecute me.* It is lawful to desire escape from persecution if it be the Lord's will; and when this may not be granted us in the form which we desire, sustaining grace will give us deliverance in another form, by enabling us to laugh to scorn all the fury of the foe.

Psalm 31:16 *Make thy face to shine upon thy servant: save me for thy mercies' sake.*

EXPOSITION: Verse 16. *Make thy face to shine upon thy servant.* Give me the sunshine of Heaven in my soul, and I will defy the tempests of Earth. Permit me to enjoy a sense of your favor, O Lord, and a consciousness that you are pleased with my manner of life, and all men may frown and slander as they will. It is always enough for a servant if he pleases his master; others may be dissatisfied, but he is not their servant, they do not pay him his wages, and their opinions have no weight with him. *Save me for thy mercies' sake.* The good man knows no plea but mercy; whoever might urge legal pleas David never dreamed of it.

Psalm 31:17 *Let me not be ashamed, O Lord; for I have called upon thee: let the wicked be ashamed, and let them be silent in the grave.*

EXPOSITION: Verse 17. *Let me not be ashamed, O Lord; for I have called upon thee.* Put not my prayers to the blush! Do not fill profane mouths with jeers at my confidence in my God. *Let the wicked be ashamed, and let them be silent in the grave.* Cause them to their amazement to see my wrongs righted and their own pride horribly

---

37. Medicine.

confounded. A milder spirit rules our prayers under the gentle reign of the Prince of Peace, and, therefore, we can only use such words as these in their prophetic sense, knowing as we do full well, that shame and the silence of death are the best portion that ungodly sinners can expect. That which they desired for despised believers shall come upon themselves by a decree of retributive justice, at which they cannot cavil—"As he loved mischief, so let it come upon him."

Psalm 31:18 *Let the lying lips be put to silence; which speak grievous things proudly and contemptuously against the righteous.*

EXPOSITION: **Verse 18.** *Let the lying lips be put to silence.* A right good and Christian prayer; who but a bad man would give liars more license than need be? May God silence them either by leading them to repentance, by putting them to thorough shame, or by placing them in positions where what they may say will stand for nothing. *Which speak grievous things proudly and contemptuously against the righteous.* The sin of slanderers lies partly in the matter of their speech; they speak grievous things; things cutting deep into the feelings of good men, and wounding them sorely in that tender place—their reputations. The sin is further enhanced by the manner of their speech; they speak proudly and contemptuously; they talk as if they themselves were the cream of society, and the righteous the mere scum of vulgarity. Proud thoughts of self are generally attended by debasing estimates of others.

The more room we take up ourselves, the less we can afford our neighbors. What wickedness it is that unworthy characters should always be the loudest in railing at good men! They have no power to appreciate moral worth of which they are utterly destitute, and yet they have the effrontery to mount the judgment seat, and judge the men compared with who they are as so much chaff. Holy indignation may well prompt us to desire anything which may rid the world of such unbearable impertinence and detestable arrogance.

Psalm 31:19 *Oh how great is thy goodness, which thou hast laid up for them that fear thee; which thou hast wrought for them that trust in thee before the sons of men!*

EXPOSITION: Verse 19. *Oh how great is thy goodness.* Is it not singular to find such a joyful sentence in connection with so much sorrow? Truly the life of faith is a miracle. When faith led David to his God, she set him singing at once. He does not tell us how great was God's goodness was, for he could not; there are no measures which can set forth the immeasurable goodness of Jehovah, who is goodness itself. Holy amazement uses interjections where adjectives utterly fail. Notes of exclamation suit us when words of explanation are of no avail. If we cannot measure we can marvel; and though we may not calculate with accuracy, we can adore with fervency.

Which thou hast laid up for them that fear thee. The psalmist in contemplation divides goodness into two parts, that which is in store and that which is wrought out. The Lord has laid up in reserve for His people supplies beyond all count. In the treasury of the covenant, in the field of redemption, in the caskets of the promises, in the granaries of providence, the Lord has provided for all the needs which can possibly occur to His chosen. We ought often to consider the laid up goodness of God which has not yet been distributed to the chosen, but is already provided for them: if we are much in such contemplations, we shall be led to feel devout gratitude, such as glowed in the heart of David.

Which thou hast wrought for them that trust in thee before the sons of men! Heavenly mercy is not all hidden in the storehouse; in a thousand ways it has already revealed itself on behalf of those who are bold to avow their confidence in God; before their fellow men this goodness of the Lord has been displayed, that a faithless generation might stand rebuked. Overwhelming are the proofs of the Lord's favor to believers, history teems with amazing instances, and our own lives are full of prodigies of grace. We serve a good Master. Faith receives a large reward even now, but looks for her full inheritance in the future. Who would not desire to take his lot with the servants of a Master whose boundless love fills all holy minds with astonishment?

Psalm 31:20 *Thou shalt hide them in the secret of thy presence from the pride of man: thou shalt keep them secretly in a pavilion from the strife of tongues.*

EXPOSITION: Verse 20. *Thou shalt hide them in the secret of thy presence from the pride of man.* Pride is a barbed weapon: the proud man's contumely[38] is iron which enters into the soul; but those who trust in God, are safely housed in the Holy of holies, the innermost court, into which no man may dare intrude; here in the secret dwelling place of God the mind of the saint rests in peace, which the foot of pride cannot disturb. Dwellers at the foot of the Cross of Christ grow callous to the sneers of the haughty. The wounds of Jesus distil a balsam which heals all the scars which the jagged weapons of contempt can inflict upon us; in fact, when armed with the same mind which was in Christ Jesus, the heart is invulnerable to all the darts of pride.

---

38. Disrespect or insult.

Thou shalt keep them secretly in a pavilion from the strife of tongues. Tongues are more to be dreaded than beasts of prey—and when they strive, it is as though a whole pack of wolves were let loose; but the believer is secure even in this peril, for the royal pavilion of the King of kings shall afford him quiet shelter and serene security. The secret tabernacle of sacrifice and the royal pavilion of sovereignty afford a double security to the Lord's people in their worst distresses. Observe the immediate action of God, *Thou shalt hide, Thou shalt keep,* the Lord himself is personally present for the rescue of His afflicted.

Psalm 31:21 *Blessed be the Lord: for he hath shewed me his marvellous kindness in a strong city.*

EXPOSITION: Verse 21. *Blessed be the Lord.* When the Lord blesses us we cannot do less than bless Him in return. *For he hath shewed me his marvellous kindness in a strong city.* Was this in Mahanaim, where the Lord gave him victory over the hosts of Absalom? Or did he refer to Rabbath of Ammon, where he gained signal triumphs? Or, best of all, was Jerusalem the strong city where he most experienced the astonishing kindness of his God? Gratitude is never short of subjects; her Ebenezers[39] stand so close together as to wall up her path to Heaven on both sides. Whether in cities or in hamlets our blessed Lord has revealed himself to us, we shall never forget the hallowed spots: the lonely mount of Hermon, or the village of Emmaus, or the rock of Patmos, or the wilderness of Horeb, are all alike renowned when God manifests himself to us in robes of love.

---

39. Stones of Help.

Psalm 31:22 *For I said in my haste, I am cut off from before thine eyes: nevertheless thou heardest the voice of my supplications when I cried unto thee.*

EXPOSITION: Verse 22. Confession of faults is always proper; and when we reflect upon the goodness of God, we ought to be reminded of our own errors and offences. *For I said in my haste.* We generally speak amiss when we are in a hurry. Hasty words are but for a moment on the tongue, but they often lie for years on the conscience. *I am cut off from before thine eyes.* This was an unworthy speech; but unbelief will have a corner in the heart of the firmest believer, and out of that corner it will vent many spiteful things against the Lord if the course of providence is not quite as smooth as nature might desire. No saint ever was, or ever could be, cut off from before the eyes of God, and yet no doubt many have thought so, and more than one has said so. May such dark suspicions be banished from our minds forever. *Nevertheless thou heardest the voice of my supplications when I cried unto thee.* What a mercy that if we believe not, yet God abides faithful, hearing prayer even when we are laboring under doubts which dishonor His name. If we consider the hindrances in the way of our prayers, and the poor way in which we present them, it is a wonder of wonders that they ever prevail with Heaven.

Psalm 31:23: *O love the Lord, all ye his saints: for the Lord preserveth the faithful and plentifully rewardeth the proud doer.*

EXPOSITION: Verse 23. *O love the Lord, all ye his saints.* A most affecting exhortation, showing clearly the deep love of the writer to his God: there is the more beauty in the expression, because it reveals love toward a smiting God, love which many waters could not quench. To bless Him who gives is easy, but to cling to Him who takes away is a work of grace. All the saints are benefited by the sanctified miseries of one, if they are led by earnest exhortations to love their Lord the better. If saints do not love the Lord, who will? Love is the universal debt of all the saved family: who would wish to be exonerated from its payment? Reasons for love are given, for believing love is not blind. *For the Lord preserveth the faithful.* They have to bide their time, but the recompense comes at last, and meanwhile all the cruel malice of their enemies cannot destroy them. *And plentifully rewardeth the proud doer.* This also is cause for gratitude: pride is so detestable in its acts that He, who shall mete out to it its righteous due, deserves the love of all holy minds.

Psalm 31:24 *Be of good courage, and he shall strengthen your heart, all ye that hope in the Lord.*

EXPOSITION: **Verse 24.** *Be of good courage.* Keep up your spirit; let no craven thoughts blanch your cheek. Fear weakens, courage strengthens. Victory waits upon the banners of the brave. *And he shall strengthen your heart.* Power from on high shall be given in the most effectual manner by administering force to the fountain of vitality. So far from leaving us, the Lord will draw very near to us in our adversity, and put His own power into us. *All ye that hope in the Lord.* Every one of you, lift up your heads and sing for joy of heart. God is faithful, and does not fail even His little children who do but hope, wherefore then should we be afraid?

PSALM 32

PSALM 32:1–32:11

Psalm 32:1 *Blessed is he whose transgression is forgiven, whose sin is covered.*

EXPOSITION: Verse 1. *Blessed.* Like the Sermon on the Mount, this Psalm begins with beatitudes. This is the second Psalm of benediction. The first Psalm describes the result of holy blessedness, the thirty-second details the cause of it. The first pictures the tree in full growth; this depicts it in its first planting and watering. He, who in the first Psalm is a reader of God's book, is here a suppliant at God's throne accepted and heard. *Blessed is he whose transgression is forgiven.* He is now blessed and ever shall be. Though he may be ever so poor, or sick, or sorrowful, he is blessed in very deed. Pardoning mercy is of all things in the world most to be prized, for it is the only and sure way to happiness. To hear from God's own Spirit the words, "absolvo te"[40] is joy unspeakable.

Blessedness is not in this case ascribed to the man who has been a diligent law keeper, for then it would never come to us, but rather to a lawbreaker, who by grace most rich and free has been forgiven. Self-righteous Pharisees have no portion in this blessedness. Over the returning prodigal, the word of welcome is here pronounced, and the music and dancing begin. A full, instantaneous, irreversible pardon of transgression turns the poor sinner's hell into Heaven, and makes the heir of wrath a partaker in blessing. The word

---

40. I absolve you.

rendered forgiven is in the original taken off or taken away, as a burden is lifted or a barrier removed.

What a lift is here! It cost our Savior a sweat of blood to bear our load, yes, it cost Him His life to bear it quite away. Samson carried the gates of Gaza, but what was that to the weight which Jesus bore on our behalf? *Whose sin is covered.* Covered by God, as the ark was covered by the mercy seat, as Noah was covered from the flood, as the Egyptians were covered by the depths of the sea. What a cover must that be which hides away forever from the sight of the all seeing God all the filthiness of the flesh and of the spirit! He, who has once seen sin in its horrible deformity, will appreciate the happiness of seeing it no more forever. Christ's atonement is the propitiation, the covering, the making an end of sin; where this is seen and trusted in, the soul knows itself to be now accepted in the Beloved, and therefore enjoys a conscious blessedness which is the antepast[41] of Heaven. It is clear from the text that a man may know that he is pardoned: where would be the blessedness of an unknown forgiveness? Clearly it is a matter of knowledge, for it is the ground of comfort.

Psalm 32:2 *Blessed is the man unto whom the Lord imputeth not iniquity, and in whose spirit there is no guile.*

EXPOSITION: Verse 2. *Blessed is the man unto whom the Lord imputeth not iniquity.* The word blessed is in the plural, oh, the blessedness's the double joys, the bundles of happiness, and the mountains of delight! Note the three words so often used to denote our disobedience: transgression, sin, and iniquity, are the three headed dog at the gates of hell, but

---

41. Foretaste.

our glorious Lord has silenced his barking for ever against His own believing ones. The trinity of sin is overcome by the Trinity of Heaven. Non imputation[42] is of the very essence of pardon: the believer sins, but his sin is not reckoned, not accounted to him. Certain divines froth at the mouth with rage against imputed righteousness, but for us, we see our sin not imputed, and to us may there be as Paul states it, "Righteousness imputed without works." [See Romans 4:11.] He is blessed indeed who has a substitute to stand for him to whose account all his debts may be set down. *And in whose spirit there is no guile.* He, who is pardoned, has in every case been taught to deal honestly with himself, his sin, and his God. Forgiveness is no sham, and the peace which it brings is not caused by playing tricks with conscience.

Self-deception and hypocrisy bring no blessedness, they may drug the soul into hell with pleasant dreams, but into the Heaven of true peace they cannot conduct their victim. Free from guilt, free from guile. Those who are justified from fault are sanctified from falsehood. A liar is not a forgiven soul. Treachery, double dealing, chicanery, dissimulation, are lineaments of the devil's children, but he who is washed from sin is truthful, honest, simple, and childlike. There can be no blessedness to tricksters with their plans, and tricks, and shuffling, and pretending: they are too much afraid of discovery to be at ease; their house is built on the volcano's brink, and eternal destruction must be their portion. Observe the three words to describe sin, and the three words to represent pardon, weigh them well, and note their meaning.

Psalm 32:3 *When I kept silence, my bones waxed old through my roaring all the day long.*

42. Not to ascribe sin to.

EXPOSITION: **Verse 3.** *When I kept silence.* When through neglect I failed to confess, or through despair dared not do so, *my bones,* those solid pillars of my frame, the stronger portions of my bodily constitution, *waxed old,* began to decay with weakness, for my grief was so intense as to sap my health and destroy my vital energy. What a killing thing is sin! It is a pestilent disease! A fire in the bones! While we smother our sin it rages within, and like a gathering wound swells horribly and torments terribly. *Through my roaring all the day long.* He was silent as to confession, but not as to sorrow. Horror at his great guilt drove David to incessant laments, until his voice was no longer like the articulate speech of man, but so full of sighing and groaning, that it resembled to hoarse roaring of a wounded beast. None knows the pangs of conviction but those who have endured them. The rack, the wheel, the flaming fagot are ease compared with the Tophet which a guilty conscience kindles within the breast: better to suffer all the diseases which flesh is heir to, than lie under the crushing sense of the wrath of almighty God. The Spanish inquisition with all its tortures was nothing to the inquest which conscience holds within the heart.

Psalm 32:4 *For day and night thy hand was heavy upon me: my moisture is turned into the drought of summer. Selah.*

EXPOSITION: **Verse 4.** *For day and night thy hand was heavy upon me.* God's finger can crush us—what must His hand be, and that pressing heavily and continuously! Under terrors of conscience, men have little rest by night, for the grim thoughts of the day dog them to their chambers and haunt their dreams, or else they lie awake in a cold sweat of dread. God's hand is very helpful when it uplifts, but it is awful when it presses down: better a world on the shoulder, like Atlas, than God's hand on the heart, like David.

My moisture is turned into the drought of summer. The sap of his soul was dried, and the body through sympathy appeared to be bereft of its needful fluids. The oil was almost gone from the lamp of life, and the flame flickered as though it would soon expire. Unconfessed transgression, like a fierce poison, dried up the fountain of the man's strength and made him like a tree blasted by the lightning, or a plant withered by the scorching heat of a tropical sun. Pity the poor soul when it has learned its sin but forgets its Savior, it goes hard with it indeed. *Selah.* It was time to change the tune, for the notes are very low in the scale, and with such hard usage, the strings of the harp are out of order: the next verse will surely be set to another key, or will rehearse a more joyful subject.

Psalm 32:5 *I acknowledge my sin unto thee, and mine iniquity have I not hid. I said, I will confess my transgressions unto the Lord; and thou forgavest the iniquity of my sin. Selah.*

EXPOSITION: **Verse 5.** *I acknowledged my sin unto thee.* After long lingering, the broken heart thought of what it ought to have done at the first, and laid bare its bosom before the Lord. The lancet must be let into the gathering ulcer before relief can be afforded. The least we can do, if we would be pardoned, is to acknowledge our fault; if we are too proud for this we doubly deserve punishment. *And mine iniquity have I not hid.* We must confess the guilt as well as the fact of sin. It is useless to conceal it, for it is well known to God; it is beneficial to us to own it, for a full confession softens and humbles the heart. We must as far as possible unveil the secrets of the soul, dig up the hidden

89

treasure of Achan,[43] and by weight and measure bring out our sins. I said. This was his fixed resolution.

I will confess my transgressions unto the Lord. Not to my fellow men or to the high priest, but unto Jehovah; even in those days of symbol the faithful looked to God alone for deliverance from sin's intolerable load, much more now, when types and shadows have vanished at the appearance of the dawn. When the soul determines to lay low and plead guilty, absolution is near at hand; hence we read, *And thou forgavest the iniquity of my sin.* Not only was the sin itself pardoned, but the iniquity of it; the virus of its guilt was put away and that at once, as soon as the acknowledgment was made. God's pardons are deep and thorough: the knife of mercy cuts at the roots of the ill weed of sin. *Selah.* Another pause is needed, for the matter is not such as may be hurried over.

> Pause, my soul, adore and wonder,
> Ask, O why such love to me?
> Grace has put me in the number
> Of the Saviour's family.
> Hallelujah!
> Thanks, eternal thanks, to thee.

Psalm 32:6 *For this shall every one that is godly pray unto thee in a time when thou mayest be found: surely in the floods of great waters they shall not come nigh unto him.*

EXPOSITION: **Verse 6.** *For this shall every one that is godly pray unto thee in a time when thou mayest be found.* If the psalmist means that on account of God's mercy others would become hopeful, his witness is true. Remarkable answers to prayer very much quicken the prayerfulness of other godly persons. Where one man finds a golden nugget others feel inclined to dig. The benefit of our experience to others should reconcile us to it. No doubt the case of David has led thousands to seek the Lord with hopeful courage who, without such an instance to cheer them, might have died in despair. Perhaps the psalmist meant for this favor or the like all godly souls would seek, and here, again, we can confirm his testimony, for all will draw near to God in the same manner as he did when godliness rules their heart. The mercy seat is the way to Heaven for all who shall ever come there.

There is, however, a set time for prayer, beyond which it will be unavailing; between the time of sin and the day of punishment mercy rules the hour, and God may be found, but when once the sentence has gone forth pleading will be useless, for the Lord will not be found by the condemned soul. O dear reader, slight not the accepted time, waste not the day of salvation. The godly pray while the Lord has promised to answer, the ungodly postpone their petitions until the Master of the house has risen up and shut to the door, and then their knocking is too late. What a blessing to be led to seek the Lord before the great devouring floods leap forth from their lairs, for then when they do appear we shall be safe.

Surely in the floods of great waters they shall not come nigh unto him. The floods shall come, and the waves shall rage, and toss themselves like Atlantic billows; whirlpools and waterspouts shall be on every hand, but the praying man shall be at a safe distance, most surely secured from every ill. David was probably most familiar with those great land floods which fill up, with rushing torrents, the beds of rivers which at other times are almost dry: these overflowing waters often did great damage, and, as in the case of the Kishon,[44] were sufficient to sweep away whole armies. From sudden and overwhelming disasters thus set forth in metaphor the true suppliant will certainly be held secure. He who is saved from sin has no need to fear anything else.

Psalm 32:7 *Thou art my hiding place; thou shalt preserve me from trouble; thou shalt compass me about with songs of deliverance. Selah.*

EXPOSITION: **Verse 7.** *Thou art my hiding place.* Terse, short sentences make up this verse, but they contain a world of meaning. Personal claims upon our God are the joy of spiritual life. To lay our hand upon the Lord with the clasp of a personal "my" is delight at its full. Observe that the same man, who in the fourth verse was oppressed by the presence of God, here finds a shelter in Him. See what honest confession and full forgiveness will do! The gospel of substitution makes Him to be our refuge who otherwise would have been our judge. *Thou shalt preserve me from trouble.* Trouble shall do me no real harm when the Lord is with me, rather it shall bring me much benefit, like the file which clears away the rust, but does not destroy the metal. Observe the three tenses, we have noticed the sorrowful past, the last sentence was a joyful present, this is a cheerful future.

Thou shalt compass me about with songs of deliverance. What a golden sentence! The man is encircled in song, surrounded by dancing mercies, all of them proclaiming the triumphs of grace. There is no breach in the circle, it completely rings him round; on all sides he hears music. Before him hope sounds the cymbals, and behind him gratitude beats the timbrel. Right and left, above and beneath, the

---

44. See Judges 5:21.

air resounds with joy, and all this for the very man who, a few weeks ago, was roaring all the day long. How great a change! What wonders grace has done and still can do! *Selah.* There was a need of a pause, for love so amazing needs to be pondered, and joy so great demands quiet contemplation, since language fails to express it.

Psalm 32:8 *I will instruct thee and teach thee in the way which thou shalt go: I will guide thee with mine eye.*

EXPOSITION: **Verse 8.** *I will instruct thee and teach thee in the way which thou shalt go.* Here the Lord is the speaker, and gives the psalmist an answer to his prayer. Our Savior is our instructor. The Lord himself deigns to teach His children to walk in the way of integrity, His holy Word and the monitions of the Holy Spirit are the directors of the believer's daily conversation. We are not pardoned that we may henceforth live after our own lusts, but that we may be educated in holiness and trained for perfection. A heavenly training is one of the covenant blessings which adoption seals to us: "All thy children shall be taught by the Lord."[45] Practical teaching is the very best of instruction, and they are thrice happy who, although they never sat at the feet of Gamaliel[46], and are ignorant of Aristotle,[47] and the ethics of the schools, have nevertheless learned to follow the Lamb whithersoever He goes. *I will guide thee with mine eye.* As servants take their cue from the master's eye, and a nod or a wink is all that they require, so should we obey the slightest hints of our Master, not needing thunderbolts to startle our incorrigible sluggishness, but being controlled by

---

45. See Isaiah 54:13.
46. See Acts 5:34.
47. A Greek philosopher and scientist.

whispers and love touches. The Lord is the great overseer, whose eye in providence overlooks everything. It is well for us to be the sheep of His pasture, following the guidance of His wisdom.

Psalm 32:9 *Be ye not as the horse, or as the mule, which have no understanding: whose mouth must be held in with bit and bridle, lest they come near unto thee.*

EXPOSITION: **Verse 9.** *Be ye not as the horse, or as the mule, which have no understanding.* Understanding separates man from a brute—let us not act as if we were devoid of it. Men should take counsel and advice, and be ready to run where wisdom points them the way. We need to be cautioned against stupidity of heart, for we are very apt to fall into it. We who ought to be as the angels, readily become as the beasts. *Whose mouth must be held in with bit and bridle, lest they come near unto thee.* It is much to be deplored that we so often need to be severely chastened before we will obey. We ought to be as a feather in the wind, wafted readily in the breath of the Holy Spirit, however, we lay like motionless logs, and stir not with Heaven itself in view.

Those cutting bits of affliction show how hard mouthed we are, those bridles of infirmity manifest our headstrong and willful manners. We would not be treated like mules if there was not so much of their stubbornness in us. If we will be fractious, we must expect to be kept in with a tight rein. Oh, for grace to obey the Lord willingly, lest like the willful servant, we are beaten with many stripes. John Calvin renders the last words, "Lest they kick against thee," a version more probable and more natural, but the passage is confessedly obscure—not however, in its general sense.

Psalm 32:10 *Many sorrows shall be to the wicked: but he that trusteth in the Lord, mercy shall compass him about.*

EXPOSITION: Verse 10. *Many sorrows shall be to the wicked.* Like refractory[48] horses and mules, they have many cuts and bruises. Here and hereafter the portion of the wicked is undesirable. Their joys are evanescent;[49] their sorrows are multiplying and ripening. He who sows sin will reap sorrow in heavy sheaves. Sorrows of conscience, of disappointment, and of terror, are the sinner's sure heritage in time, and then forever sorrows of remorse and despair. Let those who boast of present sinful joys, remember they shall be sorrows of the future and take warning. *But he that trusteth in the Lord, mercy shall compass him about.* Faith is here placed as the opposite of wickedness, since it is the source of virtue. Faith in God is the great smoother of life's cares and the answer to him who possesses it, and he dwells in an atmosphere of grace, surrounded with the bodyguard of mercies. May it be given to us of the Lord at all times to believe in the mercy of God, even when we cannot see traces of its working, for to the believer, mercy is as all surrounding as omniscience, and every thought and act of God is perfumed with it. The wicked have a hive of wasps around them, many sorrows; but we have a swarm of bees storing honey for us.

Psalm 32:11 *Be glad in the Lord, and rejoice, ye righteous: and shout for joy, all ye that are upright in heart.*

EXPOSITION: Verse 11. *Be glad.* Happiness is not only our privilege, but our duty. Truly we serve a generous God,

---

48. Stubborn.
49. Temporary.

since He makes it a part of our obedience to be joyful. How sinful are our rebellious murmurings! How natural does it seem that a man blest with forgiveness should be glad! We read of one who died at the foot of the scaffold because of the joy received at the receipt of his monarch's pardon; and shall we receive the free pardon of the King of kings, and yet pine in inexcusable sorrow? *In the Lord.* Here is the directory by which gladness is preserved from levity. We are not to be glad in sin, or to find comfort in corn, and wine, and oil, but in our God is to be the garden of our soul's delight. That there is a God and such a God, and that He is ours, ours forever, our Father and our reconciled Lord, is matter enough for a never ending psalm of rapturous joy.

And rejoice, ye righteous redouble your rejoicing, peal upon peal. Since God has clothed His choristers in the white garments of holiness, let them not restrain their joyful voices, but sing aloud and shout as those who find great spoil. *And shout for joy, all ye that are upright in heart.* Our happiness should be demonstrative; chill penury of love often represses the noble flame of joy, and men whisper their praises decorously where a hearty outburst of song would be far more natural. It is to be feared that the Church of the present day, through a craving for excessive propriety, is growing too artificial; so that enquirers' cries and believers' shouts would be silenced if they were heard in our assemblies. This may be better than boisterous fanaticism, but there is as much danger in the one direction as the other.

For our part, we are touched to the heart by a little sacred excess, and when godly men in their joy over leap the narrow bounds of decorum, we do not, like Michal, Saul's daughter, eye them with a sneering heart. [See 2 Samuel 6:16-23.] Note how the pardoned are represented as upright, righteous, and without guile; a man may have many faults and yet be saved, but a false heart is everywhere the damning mark. A man of twisting, shifty ways, of a crooked, crafty nature, is not saved, and in all probability never will be; for the ground which brings forth a harvest when grace is sown in it, may be weedy and waste, but our Lord tells us it is honest and good ground. Our observation has been that men of double tongues and tricky ways are the least likely of all men to be saved: certainly where grace comes it restores man's mind to its perpendicular, and delivers him from being doubled up with vice, twisted with craft, or bent with dishonesty. Reader, what a delightful Psalm! Have you, in perusing it, been able to claim a lot in the goodly land? If so, publish to others the way of salvation.

PSALM 33
PSALM 33:1–PSALM 33:22

Psalm 33:1 *Rejoice in the Lord, O ye righteous: for praise is comely for the upright.*

EXPOSITION: **Verse 1.** *Rejoice in the Lord.* Joy is the soul of praise. To delight ourselves in God is most truly to extol Him; even if we let no notes of song proceed from our lips. That God is, and that He is such a God, and our God, ours forever and ever, should wake within us an unceasing and overflowing joy. To rejoice in temporal comforts is dangerous, to rejoice in self is foolish, to rejoice in sin is fatal, but to rejoice in God is heavenly. He who would have a double Heaven must begin below to rejoice like those above. *O ye righteous.* This is peculiarly your duty, your obligations are greater, and your spiritual nature more adapted to the work, be first then in the glad service. Even the righteous are not always glad, and need to be stirred up to enjoy their privilege.

For praise is comely for the upright. God has an eye to things which are becoming. When saints wear their choral robes, they look fair in the Lord's sight. A harp suits a blood washed hand. No jewel more ornamental to a holy face than sacred praise. Praise is not comely from unpardoned professional singers; it is like a jewel of gold in a swine's snout. Crooked hearts make crooked music, but the upright are the Lord's delight. Praise is the dress of saints in Heaven, it is right that they should put it on below.

Psalm 33:2 *Praise the Lord with harp: sing unto him with the psaltery and an instrument of ten strings.*

EXPOSITION: **Verse 2.** *Praise the Lord with harp.* Men need all the help they can get to stir them up to praise. This is the lesson to be gathered from the use of musical instruments under the old dispensation. Israel was at school, and used childish things to help her to learn; but in these days, when Jesus gives us spiritual manhood, we can make melody without strings and pipes. We who do not believe these things to be expedient in worship, lest they should mar its simplicity, do not affirm them to be unlawful, and if any George Herbert or Martin Luther can worship God better by the aid of well tuned instruments, who shall gainsay [dispute] their right? We do not need them; they would hinder rather than help our praise, but if others are otherwise minded, are they not living in gospel liberty?

Sing unto him. This is the sweetest and best of music. No instrument like the human voice. As a help to singing the instrument is alone to be tolerated, for keys and strings do not praise the Lord. *With the psaltery and an instrument of ten strings.* The Lord must have a full octave, for all notes are His, and all music belongs to Him. Where several pieces of music are mentioned, we are taught to praise God with all the powers which we possess.

Psalm 33:3 *Sing unto him a new song; play skilfully with a loud noise.*

EXPOSITION: **Verse 3.** *Sing unto him a new song.* All songs of praise should be unto Him. Singing for singing's sake is worth nothing; we must carry our tribute to the King, and not cast it to the winds. Do most worshippers do this? Our faculties should be exercised when we are magnifying the Lord, so as not to run in an old groove without thought; we ought to make every hymn of praise a new song. To keep up the freshness of worship is a great thing, and in private it is indispensable. Let us not present old worn out praise, but put life, and soul, and heart, into every song, since we have new mercies every day, and see new beauties in the work and word of our Lord. *Play skilfully.* It is wretched to hear God praised in a slovenly manner. He deserves the best that we have. Every Christian should endeavor to sing according to the rules of the art, so that he may keep time and tune with the congregation. The sweetest tunes and the sweetest voices, with the sweetest words, are all too little for the Lord our God; let us not offer Him limping rhymes, set to harsh tunes, and growled out by discordant voices. *With a loud noise.* Heartiness should be conspicuous in divine worship. Well bred whispers are disreputable here. It is not that the Lord cannot hear us, but that it is natural for great exultation to express itself in the loudest manner. Men shout at the sight of their kings: shall we offer no loud hosannas to the Son of David?

Psalm 33:4 *For the word of the Lord is right; and all his works are done in truth.*

EXPOSITION: Verse 4. *For the word of the Lord is right.* His ordinances both natural, moral, and spiritual, are right, and especially His incarnate Word, who is the Lord our Righteousness. Whatever God has ordained must be good, and just, and excellent. There are no anomalies in God's universe, except what sin has made; His Word of command made all things good. When we look at His Word of promise, and remember its faithfulness, what excellent reasons we have for joy and thankfulness!

And all his works are done in truth. His work is the

outflow of His Word, and it is true to it. He neither does nor says anything wrong; in deed and speech He agrees with himself and the purest truth. There is no lie in God's Word, and no sham in His works; in Creation, providence, and revelation, unalloyed truth abounds. To act truth as well as to utter it is divine. Let not children of God ever yield their principles in practice any more than in heart. What a God we serve! The more we know of Him, the more our better natures approve His surpassing excellence; even His afflicting works are according to His truthful Word.

> "Why should I complain of want or distress,
> Afflictions or pain? he told me no less;
> The heirs of salvation, I know from his word,
> Through much tribulation must follow their Lord."[50]

God writes with a pen that never blots, speaks with a tongue that never slips, acts with a hand which never fails. Bless His name.

Psalm 33:5 *He loveth righteousness and judgment: the earth is full of the goodness of the Lord.*

EXPOSITION: **Verse 5.** *He loveth righteousness and judgment.* The theory and practice of right He intensely loves. He not only approves the true and the just, but His inmost soul delights therein. The character of God is a sea, every drop of which should become a wellhead of praise for His people. The righteousness of Jesus is peculiarly dear to the Father, and for its sake He takes pleasure in those to whom it is imputed. Sin, on the other hand, is infinitely abhorrent to the Lord, and woe unto those who die in it; if He sees no

---

50. Hymn #37 in the *Olney Hymnal.* "Begone Unbelief." The words were written by John Newton and the music was composted by W. Oliver in 1779.

righteousness in them, He will deal righteously with them, and judgment stern and final will be the result. *The earth is full of the goodness of the Lord.* Come hither, astronomers, geologists, naturalists, botanists, chemists, miners, all of you who study the works of God, for all your truthful stories confirm this declaration. From the midge[51] in the sunbeam to leviathan in the ocean all creatures possess the bounty of the Creator. Even the pathless desert blazes with some undiscovered mercy, and the caverns of ocean conceal the treasures of love. Earth might have been as full of terror as of grace, but instead it is full of and overflows with kindness. He who cannot see it, and yet lives in it as the fish lives in the water, deserves to die. If Earth is full of mercy, what must Heaven be where goodness concentrates its beams?

Psalm 33:6 *By the word of the Lord were the heavens made; and all the host of them by the breath of his mouth.*

EXPOSITION: Verse 6. *By the word of the Lord were the heavens made.* The angelic heavens, the sidereal [the constellations and fixed stars] heavens, and the firmament or terrestrial heavens, were all made to start into existence by a word; what if we say by the Word, "For without him was not anything made that is made." It is interesting to note the mention of the Spirit in the next clause, *and all the host of them by the breath of his mouth; the* breath is the same as is elsewhere rendered Spirit. Thus the three persons of the Godhead unite in creating all things. How easy for the Lord to make the most ponderous orbs, and the most glorious angels! A word, a breath could do it. It is as easy

---

51. Gnat

for God to create the universe as for a man to breathe, far easier, for man breathes not independently, but borrows the breath in his nostrils from his Maker. It may be gathered from this verse that the constitution of all things is from the Infinite Wisdom, for His Word may mean His appointment and determination. A wise and merciful Word has arranged, and a living Spirit sustains all the creation of Jehovah.

Psalm 33:7 *He gathereth the waters of the sea together as an heap: he layeth up the depth in storehouses.*

EXPOSITION: Verse 7. *He gathereth the waters of the sea together as an heap.* The waters were once scattered like corn strewn upon a threshing floor: they are now collected in one spot as a heap. Who else could have gathered them into one channel but their great Lord, at whose bidding the waters fled away? The miracle of the Red Sea is repeated in nature day by day, for the sea which now invades the shore under the impulse of sun and moon, would soon devour the land if bounds were not maintained by the divine decree. *He layeth up the depth in storehouses.* The depths of the main are God's great cellars and storerooms for the tempestuous element. Vast reservoirs of water are secreted in the bowels of the Earth, from which issue our springs and wells of water. What a merciful provision for a pressing need? May not the text also refer to the clouds, and the storehouse of hail, and snow, and rain, those treasures of merciful wealth for the fields of Earth? These aqueous masses are not piled away as in lumber rooms, but in storehouses for future beneficial use. Abundant tenderness is seen in the foresight of our heavenly Joseph, whose granaries are already filled against Earth's time of need. These stores might have been, as once they were, the ammunition of vengeance, they are now a part of the commissariat[52] of mercy.

Psalm 33:8 *Let all the earth fear the Lord: let all the inhabitants of the world stand in awe of him.*

EXPOSITION: **Verse 8.** *Let all the earth fear the Lord.* Not only Jews, but Gentiles. The psalmist was not a man blinded by national prejudice; he did not desire to restrict the worship of Jehovah to the seed of Abraham. He looks for homage even to far off nations. If they are not well enough instructed to be able to praise, at least let them fear. There is an inferior kind of worship in the trembling which involuntarily admits the boundless power of the thundering God. A defiant blasphemer is out of place in a world covered with tokens of the divine power and Godhead: the whole earth cannot afford a spot congenial for the erection of a synagogue of Atheism, nor a man in whom it is becoming to profane the name of God. *Let all the inhabitants of the world stand in awe of him.* Let them forsake their idols, and reverently regard the only living God. What is here placed as a wish may also be read as a prophecy: the adoration of God will yet be universal.

Psalm 33:9 *For he spake, and it was done; he commanded, and it stood fast.*

EXPOSITION: **Verse 9.** *For he spake, and it was done.* Creation was the fruit of a word. Jehovah said, "Light be," and light was. The Lord's acts are sublime in their ease and instantaneousness. "What a word is this?" This was the wondering enquiry of old, and it may be ours to this day. *He commanded, and it stood fast.* Out of nothing creation

---

52. Supply

stood forth, and was confirmed in existence. The same power which first uplifted, now makes the universe to abide; although we may not observe it, there is as great a display of sublime power in confirming as in creating. Happy is the man who has learned to lean his all upon the sure Word of Him who built the skies!

Psalm 33:10 *The Lord bringeth the counsel of the heathen to nought: he maketh the devices of the people of none effect.*

EXPOSITION: **Verse 10.** *The Lord bringeth the counsel of the heathen to nought.* While His own will is done, He takes care to anticipate the willfulness of His enemies. Before they come to action He vanquishes them in the council chamber; and when, well armed with craft, they march to the assault, He frustrates their knaveries, [treacheries] and makes their promising plots to end in nothing. Not only the folly of the heathen, but their wisdom too, shall yield to the power of the Cross of Jesus: what a comfort is this to those who have to labor where false belief, and philosophy, falsely so called, are set in opposition to the truth as it is in Jesus. *He maketh the devices of the people of none effect.* Their persecutions, slanders, falsehoods, are like puff balls flung against a granite wall—they produce no result at all; for the Lord overrules the evil, and brings good out of it. The cause of God is never in danger: infernal craft is outwitted by infinite wisdom, and satanic malice held in check by boundless power.

Psalm 33:11 *The counsel of the Lord standeth for ever, the thoughts of his heart to all generations.*

EXPOSITION: **Verse 11.** *The counsel of the Lord standeth for ever.* He changes not His purpose, His decree is not frustrated, and his designs are accomplished. God has chosen predestination according to the counsel of His will, and none of the devices of His foes can thwart His decree for a moment. Men's purposes are blown to and fro like the thread of the gossamer or the down of the thistle, but the eternal purposes are firmer than the Earth. *The thoughts of his heart to all generations.* Men come and go, sons follow their sires to the grave, but the undisturbed mind of God moves on in unbroken serenity, producing ordained results with unerring certainty. No man can expect his will or plan to be carried out from age to age; the wisdom of one period is the folly of another, but the Lord's wisdom is always wise, and His designs run on from century to century. His power to fulfill His purposes is by no means diminished by the lapse of years. He who was absolute over Pharaoh in Egypt is not one whit the less today the King of kings and Lord of lords; still do His chariot wheels roll onward in imperial grandeur, none being for a moment able to resist His eternal will.

Psalm 33:12 *Blessed is the nation whose God is the Lord; and the people whom he hath chosen for his own inheritance.*

EXPOSITION: **Verse 12.** *Blessed is the nation whose God is the Lord.* Israel was happy in the worship of the only true God. It was the blessedness of the chosen nation to have received a revelation from Jehovah. While others groveled before their idols, the chosen people were elevated by a spiritual religion which introduced them to the invisible God, and led them to trust in Him. All who confide in the Lord are blessed in the largest and deepest sense, and none can reverse the blessing. *And the people whom he hath chosen for his own inheritance.* Election is at the bottom of it all. The divine choice rules the day; none take Jehovah to be their God until He takes them to be His people. What an ennobling choice this is! We are selected to no mean estate, and for no ignoble[53] purpose: we are made the peculiar domain and delight of the Lord our God. Being so blessed, let us rejoice in our portion, and show the world by our lives that we serve a glorious Master.

Psalm 33:13 *The Lord looketh from heaven; he beholdeth all the sons of men.*

EXPOSITION: **Verse 13.** *The Lord looketh from heaven.* The Lord is represented as dwelling above and looking down below; seeing all things, but peculiarly observing and caring for those who trust in Him. It is one of our choicest privileges to be always under our Father's eye, to be never out of sight of our best Friend. *He beholdeth all the sons of men.* All Adam's sons are as well watched as was Adam himself, their lone progenitor [ancestor] in the Garden of Eden. Ranging from the frozen pole to the scorching equator, dwelling in hills and valleys, in huts and palaces, alike doth the divine eye regard all the members of the family of man.

Psalm 33:14 *From the place of his habitation he looketh upon all the inhabitants of the earth.*

EXPOSITION: **Verse 14.** *From the place of his habitation he looketh upon all the inhabitants of the earth.* Here the sentiment is repeated: it is worth repeating, and it needs repeating, for man is most prone to forget it. As great men sit at their windows and watch the crowd below, so doth the Lord; He gazes intently upon His responsible creatures, and forgets nothing of what He sees.

---

53. Untitled

Psalm 33:15 *He fashioneth their hearts alike; he considereth all their works.*

EXPOSITION: Verse 15. *He fashioneth their hearts alike.* By which is meant that all hearts are equally fashioned by the Lord, kings' hearts as well as the hearts of beggars. The text does not mean that all hearts are created originally alike by God; such a statement would scarcely be true, since there is the utmost variety in the constitutions and dispositions of men. All men equally owe the possession of life to the Creator, and have therefore no reason to boast themselves. What reason has the vessel to glorify itself in the presence of the potter? *He considereth all their works.* Not in vain does God see men's acts: He ponders and judges them. He reads the secret design in the outward behavior, and resolves the apparent good into its real elements. This consideration foretokens a judgment when the results of the divine thoughts will be meted out in measures of happiness or woe. Consider your ways, O man, for God considers them!

Psalm 33:16 *There is no king saved by the multitude of an host: a mighty man is not delivered by much strength.*

EXPOSITION: Verse 16. *There is no king saved by the multitude of an host.* Mortal power is a fiction, and those who trust in it are dupes. Rows of closely compacted ranks of armed men have failed to maintain an empire, or even to save their monarch's life when a decree from the court of Heaven has gone forth for the empire's overthrow. The all seeing God preserves the poorest of His people when they are alone and friendless, but ten thousand armed men cannot ensure safety to him whom God leaves to destruction.

A mighty man is not delivered by much strength. So far

from guarding others, the valiant veteran is not able to deliver himself. When his time comes to die, neither the force of his arms nor the speed of his legs can save him. The weakest believer dwells safely under the shadow of Jehovah's throne, while the mightiest sinner is in peril every hour. Why do we talk so much of our armies and our heroes? The Lord alone has strength, and let Him alone have praise.

Psalm 33:17 *An horse is a vain thing for safety: neither shall he deliver any by his great strength.*

EXPOSITION: **Verse 17.** *An horse is a vain thing for safety.* Military strength among the Orientals lay much in horses and scythed chariots, but the psalmist calls them a lie, a deceitful confidence. Surely the knight upon his gallant steed may be safe, either by valor or by flight? Not so, his horse shall bear him into danger or crush him with its fall. *Neither shall he deliver any by his great strength.* Thus the strongest defenses are less than nothing when most needed. God only is to be trusted and adored. Sennacherib with all his cavalry is not a match for one angel of the Lord, Pharaoh's horses and chariots found it vain to pursue the Lord's anointed, and so shall all the leaguered might of Earth and hell find themselves utterly defeated when they rise against the Lord and His chosen.

Psalm 33:18 *Behold, the eye of the Lord is upon them that fear him, upon them that hope in his mercy;*

EXPOSITION: **Verse 18.** *Behold.* For this is a greater wonder than hosts and horses, a surer confidence than chariots or shields. *The eye of the Lord is upon them that fear him.* That eye of peculiar care is their glory and defense. None can take them at unawares, for the celestial watcher foresees the designs of their enemies, and provides against them. They who fear God need not fear anything else; let them fix their eye of faith on Him, and His eye of love will always rest upon them. *Upon them that hope in his mercy.* This one would think to be a small evidence of grace, and yet it is a valid one. Humble hope shall have its share as well as courageous faith. Say, my soul, is not this an encouragement to you? Do you not hope in the mercy of God in Christ Jesus? Then the Father's eye is as much upon you as upon the elder born of the family. These gentle words, like soft bread, are meant for babes in grace, who need infant's food.

Psalm 33:19 *To deliver their soul from death, and to keep them alive in famine.*

EXPOSITION: **Verse 19.** *To deliver their soul from death.* The Lord's hand goes with His eye; He sovereignly preserves those whom He graciously observes. Rescues and restorations hedge around the lives of the saints; death cannot touch them until the King signs His warrant and gives him leave, and even then his touch is not so much mortal as *immortal; he does not so much kill us as kill our mortality. And to* keep them alive in famine. Gaunt famine knows its master. God has meal and oil for His Elijahs somewhere. *Verily thou shalt be fed* [See Psalm 37:3.] is a divine provision for the man of faith. The Preserver of men will not suffer the soul of the righteous to famish. Power in human hands is outmatched by famine, but God is good at a pinch, and proves His bounty under the most straitened circumstances. Believer, wait upon your God in timely patience. His eye is upon you, and His hand will not long delay.

Psalm 33:20 *Our soul waiteth for the Lord: he is our help and our shield.*

EXPOSITION: **Verse 20.** *Our soul waiteth for the Lord.* Here the godly avow their reliance upon Him whom the Psalm extols. To wait is a great lesson. To be quiet in expectation, patient in hope, single in confidence, is one of the bright attainments of a Christian. Our soul, our life, must hang upon God; we are not to trust Him with a few gewgaws [trinkets], but with all we have and are. *He is our help and our shield.* Our help in labor, our shield in danger. The Lord answers all things to His people. He is their all in all. Note the three "ours" in the text. These holdfast words are precious. Personal possession makes the Christian man; all else is mere talk.

Psalm 33:21 *For our heart shall rejoice in him, because we have trusted in his holy name.*

EXPOSITION: **Verse 21.** *For our hearts shall rejoice in him.* The duty commended and commanded in the first verse is here presented to the Lord. We, who trust, cannot but be of a glad heart; our inmost nature must triumph in our faithful God. *Because we have trusted in his holy name.* The root of faith in due time bears the flower of rejoicing. Doubts breed sorrow, confidence creates joy.

Psalm 33:22 *Let thy mercy, O Lord, be upon us, according as we hope in thee.*

EXPOSITION: **Verse 22.** Here is a large and comprehensive prayer to close with. It is an appeal for mercy, which even joyful believers need; and it is sought for in a proportion which the Lord has sanctioned. According to your faith be it unto you, is the Master's word, and He will not fall short of the scale which He has himself selected. Yet, Master, do more than this when hope is faint, and bless us far above what we ask or even think.

PSALM 34
PSALM 34:1–PSALM 34:22

Psalm 34:1 *I will bless the Lord at all times: his praise shall continually be in my mouth.*

EXPOSITION: **Verse 1.** *I will bless the Lord at all times.* He is resolved and fixed, I will; he is personally and for himself determined, let others do as they may; he is intelligent in head and inflamed in heart—he knows to whom the praise is due, and what is due, and for what and when. To Jehovah, and not to second causes is our gratitude to be rendered. The Lord has by right a monopoly in His creatures' praise. Even when a mercy may remind us of our sin with regard to it, as in this case David's deliverance from the Philistine monarch was sure to do, we are not to rob God of His need of honor because our conscience justly awards a censure to our share in the transaction. Though the hook was rusty, yet God sent the fish, and we thank Him for it. At all times, in every situation, under every circumstance, before, in and after trials, in bright days of glee, and dark nights of fear. He would never be done praising, because he would never be satisfied that he had done enough; always feeling that he fell short of the Lord's deserving. Happy is he whose fingers are wedded to his harp. He who praises God for mercies shall never want a mercy for which to praise. To bless the Lord is never unseasonable.

His praise shall continually be in my mouth, not in my heart merely, but in my mouth too. Our thankfulness is not to be a dumb thing; it should be one of the daughters of music. Our tongue is our glory, and it ought to reveal the glory of God. What a blessed mouthful is God's praise! How sweet, how purifying, how perfuming! If men's mouths were always thus filled, there would be no repining against God, or slander of neighbors. If we continually rolled this dainty morsel under our tongue, the bitterness of daily affliction would be swallowed up in joy. God deserves blessing with the heart, and extolling with the mouth—good thoughts in the prayer closet, and good words in the world.

Psalm 34:2 *My soul shall make her boast in the Lord: the humble shall hear thereof, and be glad.*

EXPOSITION: **Verse 2.** *My soul shall make her boast in the Lord.* Boasting is a very natural propensity, and if it were used as in this case, the more it was indulged the better. The exultation of this verse is no mere tongue bragging, "the soul" is in it, the boasting is meant and felt before it is expressed. What scope there is for holy boasting in Jehovah! His person, attributes, covenant, promises, works, and a thousand things besides, are all incomparable, unparalleled, matchless; we may cry them up as we please, but we shall never be convicted of vain and empty speech in so doing. Truly he who writes these words of comment has nothing of his own to boast of, but much to lament over and yet none shall stop him of his boast in God so long as he lives.

The humble shall hear thereof, and be glad. They are usually grieved to hear boastings; they turn aside from vaunting [gloating or puffed up] and lofty speeches, but boasting in the Lord is quite another matter; by this the most lowly are consoled and encouraged. The confident expressions of tried believers are a rich solace to their brethren of less experience. We ought to talk of the Lord's goodness on purpose that others may be confirmed in their trust in a faithful God.

Psalm 34:3 *O magnify the Lord with me, and let us exalt his name together.*

EXPOSITION: Verse 3. *O magnify the Lord with me.* Is this request addressed to the humble? If so it is most fitting. Who can make God great but those who feel themselves to be little? He bids them help him to make the Lord's fame greater among the sons of men. Jehovah is infinite, and therefore cannot really be made greater, but His name grows in manifested glory as He is made known to His creatures, and thus He is said to be magnified. It is well when the soul feels its own inability adequately to glorify the Lord, and therefore stirs up others to the gracious work; this is good both for the man himself and for his companions. No praise can excel that which lays us prostrate under a sense of our own nothingness, while divine grace like some topless Alp rises before our eyes and sinks us lower and lower in holy awe. *Let us exalt his name together.* Social, congregated worship is the outgrowth of one of the natural instincts of the new life. In Heaven it is enjoyed to the full, and Earth is like Heaven where it abounds.

Psalm 34:4 *I sought the Lord, and he heard me, and delivered me from all my fears.*

EXPOSITION: Verse 4. *I sought the Lord, and he heard me.* It must have been in a very confused manner that David prayed, and there must have been much of self-sufficiency in his prayer, or he would not have resorted to methods of such dubious morality as pretending to be mad and behaving as a lunatic; yet his poor limping prayer had an acceptance and brought him succor: the more reason for then celebrating the abounding mercy of the Lord. We may seek God even when we have sinned. If sin could blockade the mercy seat it would be all over with us, but the mercy is that there are gifts even for the rebellious, and an advocate for men who sin.

And delivered me from all my fears. God makes a perfect work of it. He clears away both our fears and their causes, all of them without exception. Glory be to His name, prayer sweeps the field, slays all the enemies and even buries their bones. Note the egoism of this verse and of those preceding it; we need not blush to speak of ourselves when in so doing we honestly aim at glorifying God, and not at exalting ourselves. Some are foolishly squeamish upon this point, but they should remember that when modesty robs God it is most immodest.

Psalm 34:5 *They looked unto him, and were lightened: and their faces were not ashamed.*

EXPOSITION: **Verse 5.** *They looked unto him, and were lightened.* The psalmist avows that his case was not at all peculiar, it was matched in the lives of all the faithful; they too, each one of them on looking to their Lord were brightened up, their faces began to shine, their spirits were uplifted. What a means of blessing one look at the Lord may be! There is life, light, liberty, love, everything in fact, in a look at the crucified One. Never did a sore heart look in vain to the good Physician; never a dying soul turned its darkening eye to the brazen serpent to find its virtue gone. *And their faces were not ashamed.* Their faces were covered with joy but not with blushes. He who trusts in God has no need to be ashamed of his confidence, time and eternity will both justify his reliance.

Psalm 34:6 *This poor man cried, and the Lord heard him, and saved him out of all his troubles.*

EXPOSITION: **Verse 6.** *This poor man cried.* Here he returns to his own case. He was poor indeed and so utterly friendless that his life was in great jeopardy; but he cried in his heart to the protector of his people and found relief. His prayer was a cry, for brevity and bitterness, for earnestness and simplicity, for artlessness and grief; it was a poor man's cry, but it was none the less powerful with Heaven, *for the Lord heard him* and to be heard of God is to be delivered; and so it is added that the *Lord saved him out of all his troubles.* At once and altogether David was cleanly rid of all his woes. The Lord sweeps our griefs away as men destroy a hive of hornets, or as the winds clear away the mists. Prayer can clear us of troubles as easily as the Lord made riddance of the frogs and flies of Egypt when Moses entreated him. This verse is the psalmist's own personal testimony: he being dead yet speaks. Let the afflicted reader take heart and be of good courage.

Psalm 34:7 *The angel of the Lord encampeth round about them that fear him, and delivereth them.*

EXPOSITION: **Verse 7.** *The angel of the Lord.* The covenant angel, the Lord Jesus, at the head of all the bands of Heaven, surrounds with His army the dwellings of the saints. Like hosts entrenched so are the ministering spirits encamped around the Lord's chosen, to serve and succor,[54] to defend and console them. *Encampeth round about them that fear him.* On every side the watch is kept by warriors of sleepless eyes, and the Captain of the Host is one whose prowess none can resist. *And delivereth them.* We little know

54. Help

119

how many providential deliverances we owe to those unseen hands which are charged to bear us up lest we dash our foot against a stone.

Psalm 34:8 *O taste and see that the Lord is good: blessed is the man that trusteth in him.*

EXPOSITION: **Verse 8.** *O taste and see.* Make a trial, an inward, experimental trial of the goodness of God. You cannot see except by tasting for yourself; but if you taste you shall see, for this, like Jonathan's honey, enlightens the eyes. *That the Lord is good.* You can only know this really and personally by experience. There is the banquet with its oxen and fatlings; its fat things full of marrow, and wine on the lees [skins and other particles that gather during the aging process that removed during the refining process] well refined; but their sweetness will be all unknown to you unless you make the blessings of grace your own, by a living, inward, vital participation in them. *Blessed is the man that trusteth in him.* Faith is the soul's taste; they who test the Lord by their confidence always find Him good, and they become themselves blessed. The second clause of the verse is the argument in support of the exhortation contained in the first sentence.

Psalm 34:9 *O fear the Lord, ye his saints: for there is no want to them that fear him.*

EXPOSITION: **Verse 9.** *O fear the Lord, ye his saints.* Pay to Him humble childlike reverence, walk in His laws, have respect to His will, tremble to offend Him, hasten to serve Him. Fear not the wrath of men, neither be tempted to sin through the virulence of their threats; fear God and fear nothing else. *For there is no want to them that fear him.*

Jehovah will not allow His faithful servants to starve. He may not give luxuries, but the promise binds Him to supply necessaries, and He will not run back from His Word. Many whims and wishes may remain unfulfilled, but real wants the Lord will supply. The fear of the Lord or true piety is not only the duty of those who avow themselves to be saints, that is, persons set apart and consecrated for holy duties, but it is also their path of safety and comfort. Godliness has the promise of the life which now is. If we were to die like dogs, and there were no hereafter, yet it would be well for our own happiness' sake to fear the Lord. Men seek a patron and hope to prosper; he prospers surely who has the Lord of Hosts to be his friend and defender.

Psalm 34:10 *The young lions do lack, and suffer hunger: but they that seek the Lord shall not want any good thing.*

EXPOSITION: Verse 10. *The young lions do lack, and suffer hunger.* They are fierce, cunning, strong, in all the vigor of youth, and yet they sometimes howl in their ravenous hunger, and even so crafty, designing, and oppressing men, with all their sagacity and unscrupulousness, often come to want; yet simple minded believers, who dare not act as the greedy lions of Earth, are fed with food convenient for them. To trust God is better policy than the craftiest politicians can teach or practice. *But they that seek the Lord shall not want any good thing.* No really good thing shall be denied to those whose first and main end in life is to seek the Lord. Men may call them fools, but the Lord will prove them wise. They shall win where the world's wiseacres lose their all, and God shall have the glory of it.

Psalm 34:11 *Come, ye children, hearken unto me: I will teach you the fear of the Lord.*

EXPOSITION: **Verse 11.** *Come, ye children.* Though a warrior and a king, the psalmist was not ashamed to teach children. Teachers of youth belong to the true peerage; their work is honorable, and their reward shall be glorious. Perhaps the boys and girls of Gath had made sport of David in his seeming madness, and if so, he here aims by teaching the rising race to undo the mischief which he had done aforetime. Children are the most hopeful persons to teach—wise men who wish to propagate their principles take care to win the ear of the young.

Hearken unto me: I will teach you the fear of the Lord. So far as they can be taught by word of mouth, or learned by the hearing of the ear, we are to communicate the faith and fear of God, instilling upon the rising generation the principles and practices of piety. This verse may be the address of every Sabbath school teacher to his class, and of every parent to his children. It is not without instruction in the art of teaching. We should be winning and attractive to the youngsters, bidding them "come," and not repelling them with harsh terms. We must get them away, apart from toys and sports, and try to occupy their minds with better pursuits; for we cannot teach them well while their minds are full of other things. We must drive at the main point always, and keep the fear of the Lord ever uppermost in our teachings, and in so doing we may discreetly cast our own personality into the scale by narrating our own experiences and convictions.

Psalm 34:12 *What man is he that desireth life, and loveth many days, that he may see good?*

EXPOSITION: **Verse 12.** Life spent in happiness is the desire of all, and he who can give the young a receipt for leading a happy life deserves to be popular among them. Mere existence is not life; the art of living, truly, really, and joyfully living, it is not given to all men to know. To teach men how to live and how to die is the aim of all useful religious instruction. The rewards of virtue are the baits with which the young are to be drawn to morality. While we teach piety to God we should also dwell much upon morality towards man.

Psalm 34:13 *Keep thy tongue from evil, and thy lips from speaking guile.*

EXPOSITION: **Verse 13.** *Keep thy tongue from evil.* Guard with careful diligence that dangerous member, the tongue, lest it utter evil, for that evil will recoil upon you and mar the enjoyment of your life. Men cannot spit forth poison without feeling some of the venom burning their own flesh. *And thy lips from speaking guile.* Deceit must be very earnestly avoided by the man who desires happiness. A crafty schemer lives like a spy in the enemy's camp, in constant fear of exposure and execution. Clean and honest conversation, by keeping the conscience at ease, promotes happiness, but lying and wicked talk stuffs our pillow with thorns, and makes life a constant whirl of fear and shame. David had tried the tortuous policy, but he here denounces it, and begs others if they want to live long and well to avoid with care the doubtful devices of guile.

Psalm 34:14 *Depart from evil, and do good; seek peace, and pursue it.*

EXPOSITION: **Verse 14.** *Depart from evil.* Go away from it. Not merely take your hands off, but yourself off. Live not near the pest house. Avoid the lion's lair, leave the viper's nest. Set a distance between yourself and temptation. *And do good.* Be practical, active, energetic, persevering in good. Positive virtue promotes negative virtue; he who does good is sure to avoid evil. *Seek peace.* Not merely prefer it, but with zeal and care endeavor to promote it. Peace with God, with your own heart, with your fellow man, and search after this as the merchantman after a precious pearl.

Nothing can more effectually promote our own happiness than peace; strife awakens passions which eat into the heart with corroding power. Anger is murder to one's own self, as well as to its objects. *And pursue it.* Hunt after it, chase it with eager desire. It may soon be lost, indeed, nothing is harder to retain, but do your best, and if enmity should arise let it be no fault of yours. Follow after peace when it shuns you; be resolved not to be of a contentious spirit. The peace which you thus promote will be returned into your own bosom, and be a perennial spring of comfort to you.

Psalm 34:15 *The eyes of the Lord are upon the righteous, and his ears are open unto their cry.*

EXPOSITION: **Verse 15.** *The eyes of the Lord are upon the righteous.* He observes them with approval and tender consideration; they are so dear to Him that He cannot take His eyes off them; He watches each one of them as carefully and intently as if there were only that one creature in the universe. *His ears are open unto their cry.* His eyes and ears are thus both turned by the Lord towards His saints; His whole mind is occupied about them: if slighted by all others they are not neglected by Him. Their cry He hears at once, even as a mother is sure to hear her sick babe; the cry may be broken, plaintive, unhappy, feeble, unbelieving, yet the Father's quick ear catches each note of lament or appeal, and He is not slow to answer His children's voice.

Psalm 34:16 *The face of the Lord is against them that do evil, to cut off the remembrance of them from the earth.*

EXPOSITION: **Verse 16.** *The face of the Lord is against them that do evil.* God is not indifferent to the deeds of sinners, but He sets His face against them, as we say, being determined that they shall have no countenance and support, but shall be thwarted and defeated. He is determinately resolved that the ungodly shall not prosper; He sets himself with all His might to overthrow them. *To cut off the remembrance of them from the earth.* He will stamp out their fires; their honor shall be turned into shame, their names forgotten or accursed. Utter destruction shall be the lot of all the ungodly.

Psalm 34:17 *The righteous cry, and the Lord heareth, and delivereth them out of all their troubles.*

EXPOSITION: **Verse 17.** *The righteous cry.* Like Israel in Egypt, they cry out under the heavy yoke of oppression, both of sin, temptation, care, and grief. *And the Lord heareth*; He is like the night watchman, who no sooner hears the alarm bell than He flies to relieve those who need Him. *And delivereth them out of all their troubles.* No net of trouble can so hold us that the Lord cannot free us. Our afflictions may be numerous and complicated, but prayer can set us free from them all, for the Lord will show himself strong on our behalf.

Psalm 34:18 *The Lord is nigh unto them that are of a broken heart; and saveth such as be of a contrite spirit.*

EXPOSITION: **Verse 18.** *The Lord is nigh unto them that are of a broken heart.* Near in friendship to accept and console. Broken hearts think God far away, when He is really most near them; their eyes are so held in sorrow that they see not their best friend. Indeed, He is with them, and in them, but they know it not. They run hither and thither, seeking peace in their own works, or in experiences, or in proposals and resolutions, whereas the Lord is near them, and the simple act of faith will reveal Him. *And saveth such as be of a contrite spirit.* What a blessed token for good is a repentant, mourning heart! Just when the sinner condemns himself, the Lord graciously absolves him. If we chasten our own spirits the Lord will spare us. He never breaks with the rod of judgment those who are already sore with the rod of conviction. Salvation is linked with contrition.

Psalm 34:19 *Many are the afflictions of the righteous: but the Lord delivereth him out of them all.*

EXPOSITION: **Verse 19.** *Many are the afflictions of the righteous.* Thus are they made like Jesus their covenant Head. Scripture does not flatter us like the story books with the idea that goodness will secure us from trouble; on the contrary, we are again and again warned to expect tribulation while we are in this body. Our afflictions come from all points of the compass, and are as many and as tormenting as the mosquitoes of the tropics. It is the earthly portion of the elect to find thorns and briars growing in their pathway, to lie down among them, finding their rest broken and disturbed by sorrow. BUT, blessed but, how it takes the sting out of the previous sentence!

But the Lord delivereth him out of them all. Through troops of ills Jehovah shall lead His redeemed unscathed and triumphant. There is an end to the believer's affliction and a joyful end too. None of his trials can hurt so much as a hair of his head; neither can the furnace hold him for a moment after the Lord bids him come forth from it. Hard would be the lot of the righteous if this promise, like a bundle of camphor, were not bound up in it, but this sweetens all. The same Lord who sends the afflictions will also recall them when His design is accomplished, but He will never allow the fiercest of them to rend and devour His beloved.

Psalm 34:20 *He keepeth all his bones: not one of them is broken.*

EXPOSITION: **Verse 20.** *He keepeth all his bones: not one of them is broken.* David had come off with kicks and cuffs, but no broken bones. No substantial injury occurs to the saints. Eternity will heal all their wounds. Their real self is safe; they may have flesh wounds, but no part of the essential fabric of their being shall be broken. This verse may refer to frequent providential protections granted to the saints; but as good men have had broken limbs as well as others, it cannot absolutely be applied to bodily preservations; but must, it seems to me, be spiritually applied to great injuries of soul, which are forever prevented by divine love. Not a bone of the mystical body of Christ shall be broken, even as His corporeal frame was preserved intact. Divine love watches over every believer as it did over Jesus; no fatal injury shall happen to us, we shall neither be halt or maimed in the Kingdom of God, but shall be presented after life's trials are over without spot or wrinkle or any such thing,

SPURGEON ON THE PSALMS

being preserved in Christ Jesus, and kept by the power of God through faith unto salvation.

Psalm 34:21 *Evil shall slay the wicked: and they that hate the righteous shall be desolate.*

EXPOSITION: **Verse 21.** *Evil shall slay the wicked.* Their adversaries shall be killing; they are not medicine, but poison. Ungodly men only need rope enough and they will hang themselves; their own iniquities shall be their punishment. Hell itself is but evil fully developed, torturing those in whom it dwells. Oh happy are they who have fled to Jesus to find refuge from their former sins, such, and such only will escape. *And they that hate the righteous shall be desolate.* They hated the best of company, and they shall have none; they shall be forsaken, despoiled, wretched, despairing. God makes the viper poison itself. What desolation of heart the damned feel, and how richly have they deserved it!

Psalm 34:22 *The Lord redeemeth the soul of his servants: and none of them that trust in him shall be desolate.*

EXPOSITION: **Verse 22.** *The Lord redeemeth the soul of his servants*—with price and with power, with blood and with water. All providential helps are a part of the redemption by power, hence the Lord is said still to redeem. All thus ransomed belong to Him who bought them—this is the law of justice and the verdict of gratitude. Joyfully will we serve Him who so graciously purchases us with His blood, and delivers us by His power. *And none of them that trust in him shall be desolate.* Faith is the mark of the ransomed, and wherever it is seen, though in the least and meanest of the saints, it ensures eternal salvation. Believer, you shall never be deserted, forsaken, given up to ruin. God, even your God, is your guardian and friend, and bliss is yours.

PSALM 35

PSALM 35:1–PSALM 35:28

Psalm 35:1 *Plead my cause, O Lord, with them that strive with me: fight against them that fight against me.*

EXPOSITION: **Verse 1.** *Plead my cause, O Lord, with them that strive with me.* Plead against those who plead against me; strive with my strivers; contend with my contenders. If they urge their suit in the law court, Lord, meet them there, and beat them at their own weapons. Every saint of God shall have this privilege: the accuser of the brethren shall be met by the Advocate of the saints. *Fight against them that fight against me.* If my advisers try force as well as fraud, be a match for them; oppose your strength to their strength. Jesus does this for all His beloved—for them He is both intercessor and champion; whatever aid they need they shall receive from Him, and in whatever manner they are assaulted they shall be effectually defended. Let us not fail to leave our case into the Lord's hand. Vain is the help of man, but ever effectual is the interposition of Heaven. What is here asked for as a boon may be regarded as a promise to all the saints; in judgment they shall have a divine advocate, in warfare a divine protection.

Psalm 35:2 *Take hold of shield and buckler, and stand up for mine help.*

EXPOSITION: **Verse 2.** *Take hold of shield and buckler, and stand up for mine help.* In vivid metaphor the Lord is pictured as coming forth armed for battle, and interposing himself between His servant and His enemies. The greater and lesser protections of providence may be here intended by the two defensive weapons, and by the Lord's standing up is meant His active and zealous preservation of His servant in the perilous hour. This poetic imagery shows how the psalmist realized the existence and power of God; and thought of Him as a real and actual personage, truly working for His afflicted.

Psalm 35:3 *Draw out also the spear, and stop the way against them that persecute me: say unto my soul, I am thy salvation.*

EXPOSITION: Verse 3. *Draw out also the spear, and stop the way against them that persecute me.* Before the enemy comes to close quarters the Lord can push them off as with a long spear. To stave off trouble is no mean act of loving-kindness. As when some valiant warrior with his lance blocks up a defile [a narrow pass], and keeps back a host until his weaker brethren have made good their escape, so does the Lord often hold the believer's foes at bay until the good man had taken breath, or clean fled from his foes. He often gives the foes of Zion some other work to do and so gives rest to His Church. What a glorious idea is this of Jehovah blocking the way of persecutors, holding them at the pike's end [a spearhead attached to a long pole or pikestaff], and giving time for the hunted saint to elude the pursuit! *Say unto my soul, I am thy salvation.* Besides holding off the enemy, the Lord can also calm the mind of His servant by express assurance from His own mouth that he is, and shall be, safe under the Almighty wing. An inward persuasion of security in God is of all things the most precious in the furnace of persecution. One word from the Lord quiets all our fears.

Psalm 35:4 *Let them be confounded and put to shame that seek after my soul: let them be turned back and brought to confusion that devise my hurt.*

EXPOSITION: **Verse 4.** *Let them be confounded and put to shame that seek after my soul.* There is nothing malicious here, the slandered man simply craves for justice, and the petition is natural and justifiable. Guided by God's good spirit the psalmist foretells the everlasting confusion of all the haters of the righteous. Shameful disappointment shall be the portion of the enemies of the gospel, nor would the most tender hearted Christian have it otherwise: viewing sinners as men, we love them and seek their good, but regarding them as enemies of God, we cannot think of them with anything but detestation, and a loyal desire for the confusion of their devices. No loyal subject can wish well to rebels. Squeamish sentimentality may object to the strong language here used, but in their hearts all good men wish confusion to mischief makers.

Psalm 35:5 *Let them be as chaff before the wind: and let the angel of the Lord chase them.*

EXPOSITION: **Verse 5.** *Let them be as chaff before the wind.* They were swift enough to attack, let them be as swift to flee. Let their own fears and the alarms of their consciences unman them so that the least breeze of trouble shall carry them hither and thither. Ungodly men are worthless in character, and light in their behavior, being destitute of solidity and fixedness; it is but just that those that make themselves chaff should be treated as such. When this imprecation is fulfilled in graceless men, they will find it an awful thing to be forever without rest, without peace of mind, or stay of soul, hurried from fear to fear, and from misery to misery.

And let the angel of the Lord chase them. Fallen angels shall haunt them, good angels shall afflict them. To be pursued by avenging spirits will be the lot of those who delight in persecution. Observe the whole scene as the psalmist sketches it: the furious foe is first held at bay, then turned back, then driven to headlong flight, and chased by fiery messengers from whom there is no escape. His pathway becomes dark and dangerous, and his destruction overwhelming.

Psalm 35:6 *Let their way be dark and slippery: and let the angel of the Lord persecute them.*

EXPOSITION: **Verse 6.** *Let their way be dark and slippery.* What terrors are gathered here! No light, no foothold, and a fierce avenger at their heels! What a doom is appointed for the enemies of God! They may rage and rave today, but how altered will be their plight before long! *And let the angel of the Lord persecute them.* He will follow them hot foot, as we say, never turning aside, but like a trusty pursuivant [messenger] serving the writ of vengeance upon them, and arresting them in the name of unflinching justice. Woe, woe, woe, unto those who touch the people of God; their destruction is both swift and sure.

Psalm 35:7 *For without cause have they hid for me their net in a pit, which without cause they have digged for my soul.*

EXPOSITION: **Verse 7.** In this verse the psalmist brings forward the gravamen [grievance or complaint] of his charge against the servants of the devil. *For without cause*—without my having injured, assailed, or provoked them; out of their own spontaneous malice *have they hid for me their net in a pit,* even as men hunt for their game with cunning and deception. Innocent persons have often been ruined by traps set for them, into which they have fallen as guilelessly as beasts which stumble into concealed pits, and are taken as in a net. It is no little thing to be able to feel that the enmity which assails us is undeserved—not caused by any willful offence on our part. Twice does David assert in one verse that his adversaries plotted against him without cause. Net making and pit digging require time and labor, and both of these the wicked will expend cheerfully if they may but overthrow the people of God. Fair warfare belongs to honorable men, but the assailants of God's Church prefer mean, ungenerous schemes, and so prove their nature and their origin. We must all of us be on our guard, for gins[55] and pitfalls are still the favorite weapons of the powers of evil.

Psalm 35:8 *Let destruction come upon him at unawares; and let his net that he hath hid catch himself: into that very destruction let him fall.*

EXPOSITION: Verse 8. *Let destruction come upon him at unawares.* This tremendous imprecation is frequently fulfilled. God's judgments are often sudden and signal. Death enters the persecutor's house without pausing to knock at the door. The thunderbolt of judgment leaps from its hiding place, and in one crash the wicked are broken forever. *And let his net that he hath hid catch himself: into that very destruction let him fall.* There is a lex talionis[56] with God which often works most wonderfully. Men set traps and catch their own fingers. They throw up stones, and they fall upon their own heads. How often Satan outwits himself, and burns his fingers with his own coals! This will doubtless be one of

---

55. A snare or trap.
56. The Law of the Talion: an eye for an eye or a tooth for a tooth.

the aggravations of hell, that men will torment themselves with what were once the fond devices of their rebellious minds. They curse and are cursed; they kick the pricks and tear themselves; they pour forth floods of fire, and it burns within and without.

Psalm 35:9 *And my soul shall be joyful in the* LORD: *it shall rejoice in his salvation.*

EXPOSITION: **Verse 9.** *And my soul shall be joyful in the Lord.* Thus rescued, David ascribes all the honor to the Judge of the right; to his own valorous arm he offers no sacrifice of boasting. He turns away from his adversaries to his God, and finds a deep unbroken joy in Jehovah, and in that joy his spirit revels. *It shall rejoice in his salvation.* We do not triumph in the destruction of others, but in the salvation given to us of God. Prayer heard should always suggest praise. It would be well if we were more demonstrative in our holy rejoicing. We rob God by suppressing grateful emotions.

Psalm 35:10 *All my bones shall say, Lord, who is like unto thee, which deliverest the poor from him that is too strong for him, yea, the poor and the needy from him that spoileth him?*

EXPOSITION: **Verse 10.** As the tongue was not enough to bless God with, David makes every limb vocal. *All my bones shall say, Lord, who is like unto thee?* His whole anatomy he would make resonant with gratitude. Those bones which were to have been broken by my enemies shall now praise God; every one of them shall bring its tribute, ascribing unrivalled excellence to Jehovah the Savior of His people. Even if worn to skin and bone, yet my very skeleton shall magnify the Lord, *which deliverest the poor from him that is too strong for him, yea, the poor and the needy from him that spoileth him.* God is the champion, the true knight errant of all oppressed ones. Where there is so much condescension, justice, kindness, power, and compassion, the loftiest songs should be rendered. Come, dear reader, have you not been delivered from sin, Satan, and death, and will you not bless the Redeemer? You were poor and weak, but in due time Christ sought you, and set you free. O magnify the Lord today, and speak well of His name.

Psalm 35:11 *False witnesses did rise up; they laid to my charge things that I knew not.*

EXPOSITION: Verse 11. *False witnesses did rise up.* This is the old device of the ungodly, and we must not wonder if it be used against us as against our Master. To please Saul, there were always men to be found mean enough to impeach David. *They laid to my charge things that I knew not.* He had not even a thought of sedition; he was loyal even to excess; yet they accused him of conspiring against the Lord's anointed. He was not only innocent, but ignorant of the fault alleged. It is well when our hands are so clean that no trace of dirt is upon them.

Psalm 35:12 *They rewarded me evil for good to the spoiling of my soul.*

EXPOSITION: Verse 12. *They rewarded me evil for good.* This is devilish; but men have learned the lesson well of the old Destroyer, and practice it most perfectly. *To the spoiling of my soul.* They robbed him of comfort, and even would have taken his life had it not been for special rescues from the hand of God. The wicked would strip the righteous naked to their very soul: they know no pity. There are only such limits to human malice as God himself may see fit to place.

Psalm 35:13 *But as for me, when they were sick, my clothing was sackcloth: I humbled my soul with fasting; and my prayer returned into mine own bosom.*

EXPOSITION: **Verse 13.** *But as for me, when they were sick, my clothing was sackcloth.* David had been a man of sympathy; he had mourned when Saul was in ill health, putting on the weeds[57] of sorrow for him as though he were a near and dear friend. His heart went into mourning for his sick master. *I humbled my soul with fasting.* He prayed for his enemy, and made the sick man's case his own, pleading and confessing as if his own personal sin had brought on the evil. This showed a noble spirit in David, and greatly aggravated the baseness of those who now so cruelly persecuted him. *And my prayer returned into mine own bosom.* Prayer is never lost: if it blesses not those for whom intercession is made, it shall bless the intercessors. Clouds do not always descend in showers upon the same spot from which the vapors ascended, but they come down somewhere; and even so do supplications in some place or other yield their showers of mercy. If our dove finds no rest for the sole of her foot among our enemies, it shall fly into our bosoms and bring an olive branch of peace in its mouth. How sharp is the contrast all through this Psalm between the righteous and his enemies! We must be earnest to keep the line of demarcation broad and clear.

57. A black garment or arm band signifying a period of grieving.

Psalm 35:14 *I behaved myself as though he had been my friend or brother: I bowed down heavily, as one that mourneth for his mother.*

EXPOSITION: Verse 14. *I behaved myself as though he has been my friend or brother*: I waited upon him assiduously, comforted him affectionately, and sympathized with him deeply. This may refer to those days when David played on the harp, and chased away the evil spirit from Saul. *I bowed down heavily, as one that mourneth for his mother.* He bowed his head as mourners do. The strongest natural grief was such as he felt when they were in trouble. The mother usually wins the deepest love, and her loss is most keenly felt: such was David's grief. How few professors in these days have such bowels of compassion; and yet under the gospel there should be far more tender love than under the law. Had we more hearty love to manhood, and care for its innumerable ills, we might be far more useful; certainly we should be infinitely more Christ like. "He prayeth best that lovest best."[58]

Psalm 35:15 *But in mine adversity they rejoiced, and gathered themselves together: yea, the abjects gathered themselves together against me, and I knew it not; they did tear me, and ceased not:*

EXPOSITION: Verse 15. *But in mine adversity they rejoiced.* In my halting they were delighted. My lameness was sport to them. Danger was near, and they sang songs over my expected defeat. How glad are the wicked to see a good man limp! "Now," say they, "he will meet with his downfall." *And gathered themselves together,* like kites and vultures around

---

58. Quote from *"The Rime of the Ancient Mariner"* by *Samuel Taylor Coleridge.*

a dying sheep. They found a common joy in my ruin, and a recreation in my sorrow, and therefore met together to keep the feast. They laid their heads together to devise, and their tongues to deceive. *Yea, the abjects*[59] *gathered themselves together against me."* Those who deserved horsewhipping, fellows the soles of whose feet needed the bastinado[60], came together to plot, and held secret meetings to plan my harm.

Like curs around a sick lion, the mean wretches taunted and insulted one whose name had been their terror. The very cripples hobbled out to join the malicious crew. How unanimous are the powers of evil; how heartily do men serve the devil; and none decline his service because they are not endowed with great abilities! *I knew it not.* It was all done behind my back. What a fluster the world may be in, and the cause of it all may not even know that he has given offence. *They did tear me, and ceased not.* It is such dainty work to tear to pieces a good man's character, that when slanderers have their hand in they are loath to leave off. A pack of dogs tearing their prey is nothing compared with a set of malicious gossips mauling the reputation of a worthy man. The reason lovers of the gospel are not at this time rent and torn as in the old days of Mary, Queen of Scots is to be attributed to the providence of God rather than to the gentleness of men.

Psalm 35:16 *With hypocritical mockers in feasts, they gnashed upon me with their teeth.*

EXPOSITION: **Verse 16.** *With hypocritical mockers in feasts, they gnashed upon me with their teeth.* Like professional

---

59. Mean and contemptible revilers.
60. A form of torture in which the soles of the feet are beaten with a whip.

buffoons who grin around the banquet to make sport, so they made a business of jeering at the good man; not, however, out of mirth, but from violent, insatiable hatred. Like cake scoffers, or men who will jeer for a bit of bread, these hireling miscreants [wrongdoers] persecuted David in order to get a bellyful for themselves from Saul's table: having moreover an inward grudge against the son of Jesse because he was a better man than themselves. Very forcibly might our Lord have used the words of these verses! Let us not forget to see the Despised and Rejected of men here painted to the life. Calvary and the ribald crew around the Cross seem brought before our eyes.

Psalm 35:17 *Lord, how long wilt thou look on? rescue my soul from their destructions, my darling from the lions.*

EXPOSITION: **Verse 17.** *Lord, how long wilt thou look on?* Why be a mere spectator? Why so neglectful of your servant? Are you indifferent? Do you not care that we perish? We may thus reason with the Lord. He permits us this familiarity. There is a time for our salvation, but to our impatience it often seems to be very slow in coming; yet wisdom has ordained the hour, and nothing shall delay it. *Rescue my soul from their destructions.* From their many devices; their multiplied assaults, be pleased to set me free. *My darling,* my lovely, only, precious soul, do rescue *from the lions.* His enemies were fierce, cunning, and strong as young lions; God only could deliver him from their jaws, to God he therefore addresses himself.

Psalm 35:18 *I will give thee thanks in the great congregation: I will praise thee among much people.*

EXPOSITION: Verse 18. *I will give thee thanks in the great congregation.* Notable deliverances must be recorded, and their fame emblazoned. All the saints should be informed of the Lord's goodness. The theme is worthy of the largest assembly, the experience of a believer is a subject fit for an assembled universe to hear of. Most men publish their griefs; good men should proclaim their mercies. *I will praise thee among much people.*

Among friends and foes will I glorify the God of my salvation. Praise—personal praise, public praise, perpetual praise—should be the daily revenue of the King of Heaven. Thus, for the second time, David's prayer ends in praise, as indeed all prayers should.

Psalm 35:19 *Let not them that are mine enemies wrongfully rejoice over me: neither let them wink with the eye that hate me without a cause.*

EXPOSITION: Verse 19. He earnestly prays that as they have no cause for their enmity, they may have no cause for triumph either in his folly, sin, or overthrow. Neither let them wink with the eye that hates me without a cause. The winking of the eye was the low bred sign of congratulation at the ruin of their victim, and it may also have been one of their scornful gestures as they gazed upon him whom they despised. To cause hatred is the mark of the wicked, to suffer it causelessly is the lot of the righteous. God is the natural Protector of all who are wronged, and He is the enemy of all oppressors.

Psalm 35:20 *For they speak not peace: but they devise deceitful matters against them that are quiet in the land.*

EXPOSITION: **Verse 20.** *For they speak not peace.* They love it not; how can they speak it? They are such troublers themselves that they cannot judge others to be peaceable. Out of the mouth comes what is in the heart. Riotous men charge others with sedition. *But they devise deceitful matters against them that are quiet in the land.* David would rather have been an orderly citizen, but they labored to make him a rebel. He could do nothing right, all his dealings were misrepresented. This is an old trick of the enemy to brand good men with S.S.[61] on their cheeks, though they have ever been a harmless race, like sheep among wolves. When mischief is meant, mischief is soon made. Unscrupulous partisans could even charge Jesus with seeking to overturn Caesar, much more will they thus accuse his household. At this very hour, those who stand up for the crown rights of King Jesus are called enemies of the Church, favorers of Popery, friends of Atheists, levelers,[62] Red Republicans[63], and it is hard to say what else. Billingsgate[64] and Babylon are in league.

Psalm 35:21 *Yea, they opened their mouth wide against me, and said, Aha, aha, our eye hath seen it.*

EXPOSITION: **Verse 21.** *Yea, they opened their mouth wide against me.* As if they would swallow him. Uttering great lies which needed wide mouths. They set no bounds to their infamous charges, but poured out wholesale abuse, trusting that if all did not stick, some of it would. *And said, Aha, aha, our eye hath seen it.* Glad to find out a fault or a

---

61. Sower of Sedition
62. A radical who advocates the abolition of social distinctions.
63. A political party in France at the time of the revolution of 1858.
64. Billingsgate: a coarse and abusive language.

misfortune or to swear they had seen evil where there was none. Malice has but one eye; it is blind to all virtue in its enemy. Eyes can generally see what hearts wish. A man with a speck in his eye sees a spot in the sun. How like a man is to a donkey when he brays over another's misfortunes. How like to a devil when he laughs a hyena laugh over a good man's blunder. Malice is folly, and when it holds a festival its tones and gestures far exceed all the freaks and mummeries of the Lord of Misrule.[65]

Psalm 35:22 *This thou hast seen, O Lord: keep not silence: O Lord, be not far from me.*

EXPOSITION: **Verse 22.** *This thou hast seen, O Lord.* Here is comfort. Our heavenly Father knows all our sorrow. Omniscience is the saint's candle which never goes out. A father will not long endure to see his child abused. Shall not God avenge his own elect? *Keep not silence.* Rebuke your enemies and mine, O Lord. A word will do it. Clear my character, comfort my heart. *O Lord, be not far from me.* Walk the furnace with me. Stand in the pillory[66] at my side. The sweet presence of God is the divine cordial of the persecuted; His painful absence would be their deepest misery.

Psalm 35:23 *Stir up thyself, and awake to my judgment, even unto my cause, my God and my Lord.*

EXPOSITION: **Verse 23.** *Stir up thyself.* Be ready. Prove that you are not an indifferent witness to all this infamy.

---

65. A peasant or sub-deacon appointed to be in charge of drunken revelries and wild partying.

66. A block of wood on a post with holes for the neck and the wrists, offenders were locked into it to be scorned by passersby.

Awake to my judgment. Take the scepter and summon the great assize[67] vindicate justice, avenge oppression. Do not tarry as men do who sleep. *Even unto my cause, my God and my Lord.* He claims a nearness to his God, he holds Him with both hands; he leaves his case with the righteous Judge. He begs that the suit may be brought on, heard, tried, and verdict given. It is good for a man when his conscience is so clear that he dares to make such an appeal.

Psalm 35:24 *Judge me, O Lord my God, according to thy righteousness; and let them not rejoice over me.*

EXPOSITION: Verse 24. The appeal is here repeated; the plaintiff feels that the joy of his accusers will be short lived as soon as impartial justice rules. The oppressors' wrong, the proud man's contumely, the fool's grimace—all will cease when the righteous Lord sits down upon the judgment seat.

Psalm 35:25 *Let them not say in their hearts, Ah, so would we have it: let them not say, We have swallowed him up.*

EXPOSITION: Verse 25. *Let them not say in their hearts, Ah, so would we have it: let them not say, We have swallowed him up.* Disappoint them of their prey when their mouths are ready to swallow it. Saints are too dear a morsel for the powers of evil; God will not give His sheep over to the wolfish jaws of persecutors. Just when they are tuning their pipes to celebrate their victory, they shall be made to laugh on the other side of their mouths. They are all too sure, and too boastful; they reckon without their host: little do they dream of the end which will be put to their scheming.

---

67. Court

Their bird shall be flown, and they themselves shall be in the trap. The prayer of this text is a promise. Even before the lips of the wicked can frame a speech of exultation, they shall be disappointed; their heart speech shall be forestalled, their wishes frustrated, their knavish tricks exposed.

Psalm 35:26 *Let them be ashamed and brought to confusion together that rejoice at mine hurt: let them be clothed with shame and dishonour that magnify themselves against me.*

EXPOSITION: Verse 26. Here is the eternal result of all the laborious and crafty devices of the Lord's enemies. God will make little of them, though they magnified themselves; He will shame them for shaming His people, bring them to confusion for making confusion, pull off their fine apparel and give them a beggarly suit of dishonor, and turn all their rejoicing into weeping and wailing, and gnashing of teeth. Truly, the saints can afford to wait.

Psalm 35:27 *Let them shout for joy, and be glad, that favour my righteous cause: yea, let them say continually, Let the Lord be magnified, which hath pleasure in the prosperity of his servant.*

EXPOSITION: Verse 27. *Let them shout for joy, and be glad, that favour my righteous cause.* Even those who could not render him active aid, but in their hearts favored him, David would have the Lord reward most abundantly. Men of tender heart set great store by the good wishes and prayers of the Lord's people. Jesus also prizes those whose hearts are with His cause. The day is coming when shouts of victory shall be raised by all who are on Christ's side, for the battle will turn, and the foes of truth shall be routed.

Yea, let them say continually, Let the Lord be magnified.
He would have their gladness contributory to the divine
glory; they are not to shout to David's praise, but for the
honor of Jehovah. Such acclamations may fitly be continued
throughout time and eternity.

Which hath pleasure in the prosperity of his servant.
They recognized David as the Lord's servant, and saw with
pleasure the Lord's favor to him. We can have no nobler title
than "servant of God," and no greater reward than for our
Master to delight in our prosperity. What true prosperity
may be we are not always best able to judge. We must leave
that in Jesus' hand; He will not fail to rule all things for our
highest good. "For by his saints it stands confessed, That
what he does is always best."

Psalm 35:28 *And my tongue shall speak of thy
righteousness and of thy praise all the day long.*

EXPOSITION: **Verse 28.** Unceasing praise is here
vowed to the just and gracious God. From morning until
evening the grateful tongue would talk and sing, and glorify
the Lord. O for such a resolve carried out by us all!

Psalm 36
Psalm 36:1–Psalm 36:12

Psalm 36:1 *The transgression of the wicked saith within my heart, that there is no fear of God before his eyes.*

EXPOSITION: Verse 1. *The transgression of the wicked.* His daring and wanton sin; and his breaking the bounds of law and justice. *Saith within my heart, that there is no fear of God before his eyes.* Men's sins have a voice to godly ears. They are the outer index of an inner evil. It is clear that men who dare to sin constantly and presumptuously cannot respect the great Judge of all. Despite the professions of unrighteous men, when we see their unhallowed actions our heart is driven to the conclusion that they have

no religion whatever. Unholiness is clear evidence of ungodliness. Wickedness is the fruit of an atheistic root.

This may be made clear to the candid head by cogent[68]

---

68. Persuasive.

reasoning, but it is clear already and intuitively to the pious heart. If God be everywhere, and I fear Him, how can I dare to break His laws in His very presence? He must be a desperate traitor who will rebel in the monarch's own halls. Whatever theoretical opinions bad men may avow, they can only be classed with atheists, since they are such practically. Those eyes which have no fear of God before them now, shall have the terrors of hell before them forever.

Psalm 36:2 *For he flattereth himself in his own eyes, until his iniquity be found to be hateful.*

EXPOSITION: Verse 2. *For.* Here is the argument to prove the proposition laid down in the former verse. David here runs over the process of reasoning by which he had become convinced that wicked men have no proper idea of God or respect for Him. God fearing men see their sins and bewail them, where the reverse is the case we may be sure there is no fear of God.

He flattereth himself in his own eyes. He counts himself a fine fellow, worthy of great respect. He quiets his conscience, and so deceives his own judgment as to reckon himself a pattern of excellence; if not for morality, yet for having sense enough not to be enslaved by rules which are bonds to others. He is the free thinker, the man of strong mind, the hater of cant[69], the philosopher; and the servants of God are, in his esteem, mean spirited and narrow minded. Of all flatteries this is the most absurd and dangerous. Even the silliest bird will not set traps for itself; the most pettifogging [legal deception or trickery] attorney will not cheat himself. To smooth over one's own conduct to one's conscience (which is the meaning of the Hebrew) is to smooth one's own path to hell. The

---

69. Insincere talk about religion or morals.

descent to eternal ruin is easy enough, without making a glissade [gliding or slipping step] of it, as self flatters do.

Until his iniquity be found to be hateful. At length he is found out and detested, despite his self conceit. Rottenness smells sooner or later too strong to be concealed. There is a time when the leprosy cannot be hidden. At last the old house can no longer be propped up, and falls around the tenant's ears: so there is a limit to a man's self flattery; he is found out amid general scorn, and can no longer keep up the farce which he played so well. If this happens not in this life, the hand of death will let light in upon the coveted character, and expose the sinner to shame and contempt. The self flattering process plainly proves the atheism of sinners, since the bare reflection that God sees in them would render such self flatteries extremely difficult, if not impossible. Belief in God, like light reveals, and then our sin and evil are perceived; but wicked men are in the dark, for they cannot see what is so clearly within them and around them that stares them in the face.

Psalm 36:3 *The words of his mouth are iniquity and deceit: he hath left off to be wise, and to do good.*

EXPOSITION: Verse 3. *The words of his mouth are iniquity and deceit.* This pair of hell dogs generally hunts together, and what one does not catch the other will; if iniquity cannot win by oppression, deceit will gain by chicanery. When the heart is so corrupt as to flatter itself, the tongue follows suit. The open sepulcher of the throat reveals the foulness of the inner nature. God fearing men make a conscience of their words, and if they sin through infirmity they do not invent excuses, or go about to boast of their wickedness: but because wicked men think little of evil and artful speeches, we may be clear that God rules not in their souls. The original by declaring that the words of the wicked are falsehood and deceit is peculiarly strong; as if they were not only false in quality, but actual falseness itself. *He hath left off to be wise, and to do good.* From the good way he has altogether gone aside. Men who fear God proceed from strength to strength in the right path, but godless men soon forsake what little good they once knew. How could men apostatize if they had respect unto the supreme Judge? Is it not because they grow more and more forgetful of God, that in due season they relinquish even that hypocritical reverence of Him which in former days they maintained in order to flatter their souls?

Psalm 36:4 *He deviseth mischief upon his bed; he setteth himself in a way that is not good; he abhorreth not evil.*

EXPOSITION: **Verse 4.** *He deviseth mischief upon his bed.* His place of rest becomes the place for plotting. His bed is a hot bed for poisonous weeds. God fearing men meditate upon God and His service; but when men turn all their thoughts and inventive faculties towards evil, their godlessness is proved to a demonstration. He has the devil for his bed fellow who lies in bed and schemes how to sin. God is far from him. *He setteth himself in a way that is not good.* When he gets up he resolutely and persistently pursues the mischief which he planned. The worst of ways he prefers for his walking, for he has taught his heart to love filthiness, having accustomed himself to revel in it in imagination.

He abhorreth not evil. So far from having a contempt and abhorrence for evil, he even rejoices in it, and patronizes it. He never hates a wrong thing because it is wrong, but he meditates on it, defends it, and practices it. What a portrait of a graceless man these few verses afford us! His jauntiness of conscience, his licentiousness of speech, his intentness upon wrong doing, his deliberate and continued preference of iniquity, and withal his atheistic heart, are all photographed to the life. Lord, save us from being such.

Psalm 36:5 *Thy mercy, O Lord, is in the heavens; and thy faithfulness reacheth unto the clouds.*

EXPOSITION: **Verse 5.** *Thy mercy, O Lord, is in the heavens.* Like the ethereal blue, it encompasses the whole Earth, smiling upon universal nature, acting as a canopy for all the creatures of Earth, surmounting the loftiest peaks of human provocations, and rising high above the mists of mortal transgression. Clear sky is evermore above, and mercy calmly smiles above the din and smoke of this poor world. Darkness and clouds are but of Earth's lower atmospheres: the heavens are ever more serene, and bright with innumerable stars. Divine mercy abides in its vastness of expanse, and matchless patience, all unaltered by the rebellions of man. When we can measure the heavens, then we shall abound in the mercy of the Lord.

Towards His own servants especially, in the salvation of the Lord Jesus, He has displayed grace higher than the Heaven of heavens, and wider than the universe. O that the atheist could but see this, how earnestly would he long to become a servant of Jehovah! *And thy faithfulness reacheth unto the clouds.* Far, far above all comprehension is the truth and faithfulness of God. He never fails, nor forgets, nor falters, nor forfeits His Word. Afflictions are like clouds, but the divine truthfulness is all around them. While we are under the cloud we are in the region of God's faithfulness; when we mount above it we shall not need such an assurance. To every word of threat, or promise, prophecy or covenant, the Lord has exactly adhered, "for he is not a man that he should lie, nor the son of man that he should repent." [See Numbers 23:19.]

Psalm 36:6 *Thy righteousness is like the great mountains; thy judgments are a great deep: O Lord, thou preservest man and beast.*

EXPOSITION: **Verse 6.** *Thy righteousness is like the great mountains.* Firm and unmoved, lofty and sublime. As winds and hurricanes shake not an Alp, so the righteousness of God is never in any degree affected by circumstances; He is always just. Who can bribe the Judge of all the Earth, or who can, by threatening, compel Him to pervert judgment? Not even to save His elect would the Lord suffer His righteousness to be set aside. No awe inspired by mountain scenery can equal that which fills the soul when it beholds the Son of God slain as a victim to vindicate the justice of the Inflexible Lawgiver. Right across the path of every unholy man who dreams of Heaven stand the towering Andes of divine righteousness, which no unregenerate sinner can ever climb. Among great mountains lie slumbering avalanches, and there the young lightning tries its young wings until the storm rushes down at full speed from the awful peaks. So against the great day of the Lord's wrath the Lord has laid up in the mountains of His righteousness dreadful ammunition of war with which to overwhelm His adversaries.

Thy judgments are a great deep. God's dealings with men are not to be fathomed by every boaster who demands to see a why for every wherefore. The Lord is not to be questioned by us as to why this and why that. He has reasons, but He does not choose to submit them to our foolish consideration. Far and wide, terrible and irresistible like the ocean are the providential dispensations of God: at one time they appear as peaceful as the smooth sea of glass; at another tossed with tempest and whirlwind, but evermore most glorious and full of mystery. Who shall discover the springs of the sea? He who shall do this may hope to comprehend the providence of the Eternal.

> "Undiscovered sea!
> Into thy dark, unknown, mysterious caves,
> And secret haunts unfathomably deep,
> Beneath all visible retired, none went
> And came again to tell the wonders there."[70]

Yet as the deep mirrors the sky, so the mercy of the Lord is to be seen reflected in all the arrangements of His government on Earth, and over the profound depth the covenant rainbow casts its arch of comfort, for the Lord is faithful in all that He does. *O Lord, thou preservest man and beast.* All the myriads of creatures, rational and irrational, are fed by Jehovah's hand. The countless beasts, the innumerable birds, the inconceivable abundance of fishes, the all but infinite armies of insects, all owe their continuance of life to the unceasing outgoings of the divine power. What a view of God this presents to us! What a debased creature must he be who sees no trace of such a God, and feels no awe of Him!

Psalm 36:7 *How excellent is thy lovingkindness, O God! therefore the children of men put their trust under the shadow of thy wings.*

EXPOSITION: Verse 7. *How excellent is thy lovingkindness, O God.* Here we enter into the Holy of Holies. Benevolence, and mercy, and justice, are everywhere, but the excellence of that mercy only those have known whose

---

70. *"The Course of Time:"* A poem written by Robert Pollock, Book 7, page 173.

faith has lifted the veil and passed into the brighter presence of the Lord; these behold the excellency of the Lord's mercy. The word translated excellent may be rendered "precious;" no gem or pearl can ever equal in value a sense of the Lord's love. This is of such brilliance as angels wear. King's regalia are a beggarly collection of worthless pebbles when compared with the tender mercies of Jehovah. David could not estimate it, and therefore, after putting a note of admiration, he left our hearts and imagination, and, better still, our experience, to fill up the rest. He writes how excellent because he cannot tell us the half of it!

Therefore the children of men put their trust under the shadow of thy wings. The best of reasons for the best of courses. The figure is very beautiful. The Lord overshadows His people as a hen protects her brood, or as an eagle covers its young; and we as the little ones run under the blessed shelter and feel at rest. To cower down under the wings of God is so sweet. Although the enemy is far too strong for us, we have no fear, for we nestle under the Lord's wing. O that more of Adam's race knew the excellency of the heavenly shelter! It made Jesus weep to see how they refused it: our tears may well lament the same evil.

Psalm 36:8 *They shall be abundantly satisfied with the fatness of thy house; and thou shalt make them drink of the river of thy pleasures.*

EXPOSITION: **Verse 8.** *They shall be abundantly satisfied with the fatness of thy house.* Those who learn to put their trust in God shall be received into His house, and shall share in the provision laid up therein. The dwelling place of the Lord is not confined to any place, and hence reside where we may, we may regard our dwelling, if we be believers, as one room in the Lord's great house. We shall, both in providence and grace, find a soul contenting store supplied to us as the result of living by faith in nearness to the Lord. If we regard the assembly of the saints as being peculiarly the house of God, believers shall, indeed, find in sacred worship the richest spiritual food. Happy is the soul that can drink in the sumptuous dainties of the gospel—nothing can so completely fill the soul.

And thou shalt make them drink of the river of thy pleasures. As they have the fruits of Eden to feed on, so shall they have the river of Paradise to drink from. God's everlasting love bears to us a constant and ample comfort, of which grace makes us to drink by faith, and then our pleasure is of the richest kind. The Lord not only brings us to this river, but makes us drink: herein we see the condescension of divine love. Heaven will, in the fullest sense, fulfill these words; but they who trust in the Lord enjoy the foretaste even here. The happiness given to the faithful is that of God himself; purified spirits joy with the same joy as the Lord himself. "That my joy may be in you, that your joy may be full." [See John 15:11.]

Psalm 36:9 *For with thee is the fountain of life: in thy light shall we see light.*

EXPOSITION: **Verse 9.** *For with thee is the fountain of life.* This verse is made of simple words, but like the first chapter of John's Gospel, it is very deep. From the Lord, as from an independent self-sufficient spring, all creature life proceeds, by Him is sustained, through Him alone can it be perfected. Life is in the creature, but the fountain of it is only in the Creator. Of spiritual life, this is true in the most emphatic sense; "it is the Spirit that quickeneth," [See John 6:63.] "and we are dead, and our life is hid with Christ in God." [See Colossians 3:3.]

In thy light shall we see light. Light is the glory of life. Life in the dark is misery, and rather death than life. The Lord alone can give natural, intellectual, and spiritual life; He alone can make life bright and lustrous. In spiritual things the knowledge of God sheds a light on all other subjects. We need no candle to see the sun, we see it by its own radiance, and then see everything else by the same luster. We never see Jesus by the light of self, but self in the light of Jesus. No inward intelligence of ours leads us to receive the Spirit's light, but rather, it often helps to quench the sacred beam. Purely and only by His own illumination, the Holy Ghost lights up the dark recesses of our heart's ungodliness. Vain are they who look to learning and human wit, one ray from the throne of God is better than the noonday splendor of created wisdom. Lord, give me the sun, and let those who will delight in the wax candles of superstition and the phosphorescence of corrupt philosophy. Faith derives both light and life from God, and hence she neither dies nor darkens.

Psalm 36:10 *O continue thy lovingkindness unto them that know thee; and thy righteousness to the upright in heart.*

EXPOSITION: **Verse 10.** *O continue thy lovingkindness unto them that know thee.* We ask no more than a continuance of the past mercy. Lord, extend this grace of yours to all the days of all who have been taught to know your faithful love, your tenderness, your immutability and omnipotence. As they have been taught of the Lord to know the Lord, so go on to instruct them and perfect them. This prayer is the heart of the believer asking precisely that which the heart of his God is prepared to grant. It is well when the petition is but the reflection of the promise. *And thy righteousness to the upright in heart.* As you have never failed the righteous, so abide in the same manner their defender and avenger. The worst thing to be feared by the man of God is to be forsaken of Heaven, hence this prayer; but the fear is groundless, hence the peace which faith brings to us. Learn from this verse, that although a continuance of mercy is guaranteed in the covenant, we are yet to make it a matter of prayer. For this good thing will the Lord be enquired of.

Psalm 36:11 *Let not the foot of pride come against me, and let not the hand of the wicked remove me.*

EXPOSITION: **Verse 11.** *Let not the foot of pride come against me.* The general prayer is here turned into a particular and personal one for himself. Pride is the devil's sin. Good men may well be afraid of proud men, for the serpent's seed will never cease to bite the heel of the godly. Gladly would proud scoffers spurn the saints or trample them under foot: against their malice prayer lifts up her voice. No foot shall come upon us; no hand shall prevail against us, while Jehovah is on our side. *And let not the hand of the wicked remove me.* Suffer me not to be driven about as a fugitive, nor torn from my place like an uprooted tree. Violence with both hand and foot, with means fair and means foul, strove to overthrow the psalmist, but he resorts to his great Patron, and sings a song of triumph in anticipation of the defeat of his foes.

Psalm 36:12 *There are the workers of iniquity fallen: they are cast down, and shall not be able to rise.*

EXPOSITION: **Verse 12.** *There are the workers of iniquity fallen.* Faith sees them scattered on the plain. There before our very eyes sin, death, and hell, lies prostrate! Behold the vanquished foes! *They are cast down.* Providence and grace have dashed them from their vantage ground. Jesus has already thrown all the foes of His people upon their faces, and in due time all sinners shall find it so. *And shall not be able to rise.* The defeat of the ungodly and of the powers of evil is final, total, and irretrievable. Glory be to God, however high the powers of darkness may carry it, time hastens on when God shall defend the right. He shall give to evil such a fall as shall for ever crush the hopes of hell; while those who trust in the Lord shall eternally praise Him and rejoice in His holy name.

PSALM 37
PSALM 37:1–PSALM 37:40

Psalm 37:1 *Fret not thyself because of evildoers, neither be thou envious against the workers of iniquity.*

EXPOSITION: Verse 1. The Psalm opens with the first precept. Unfortunately it is too common for believers in their hours of adversity to think themselves harshly dealt with when they see persons utterly destitute of religion and honesty rejoicing in abundant prosperity. Much needed is the command; *Fret not thyself because of evildoers.* To fret is to worry, fume and become vexed which leads to heartburn. Nature is very apt to kindle a fire of jealousy when it sees lawbreakers riding on horses, and obedient subjects walking in the mire: it is a lesson learned only in the school of grace, when one comes to view the most paradoxical providences with the devout complacency of one who is sure that the Lord is righteous in all His acts. It seems hard to carnal judgments that the best meat should go to the dogs, while loving children pine for want of it.

Neither be thou envious against the workers of iniquity. The same advice under another shape. When one is poor, despised, and in deep trial, our old Adamic nature becomes envious of the rich and great; and when we are conscious that we have been more righteous than they, the devil is sure to be at hand with blasphemous reasonings. Stormy weather may curdle even the cream of humanity. Instead of being envied, evil men are to be viewed with horror and aversion; yet their loaded tables, and gilded trappings, are too apt to fascinate our poor half opened eyes. Who envies the fat bullock the ribbons and garlands which decorate him as he is led to the butcher shop? Yet the case is a parallel one; for ungodly rich men are but as beasts fattened for the slaughter.

Psalm 37:2 *For they shall soon be cut down like the grass, and wither as the green herb.*

EXPOSITION: **Verse 2.** *For they shall soon be cut down like the grass.* The scythe of death is sharpening. Green grows the grass, but quick comes the scythe. The destruction of the ungodly will be speedy, sudden, sure, overwhelming, irretrievable. The grass cannot resist or escape the mower. *And wither as the green herb.* The beauty of the herb dries up at once in the heat of the sun, and so all the glory of the wicked shall disappear at the hour of death. Death kills the ungodly man like grass, and wrath withers him like hay; he dies, and his name rots. How complete an end is made of the man whose boasts had no end! Is it worthwhile to waste ourselves in fretting about the insect of an hour, an ephemeral which in the same day is born and dies? Within believers there is a living and incorruptible seed which lives and abides for ever; why should they envy mere flesh, and the glory of it, which are but as grass, and the flower thereof?

Psalm 37:3 *Trust in the Lord, and do good; so shalt thou dwell in the land, and verily thou shalt be fed.*

EXPOSITION: **Verse 3.** *Trust in the Lord.* Here is the second precept and one appropriate to the occasion. Faith cures fretting. Sight is cross-eyed, and views things only as they seem, hence her envy: faith has clearer optics to behold things as they really are, hence her peace. *And do good.* True faith is actively obedient. Doing good is a fine remedy for fretting. There is a joy in holy activity which drives away the rust of discontent. *So shalt thou dwell in the land.* In "the land" which flows with milk and honey; the Canaan of the covenant. You will not wander in the wilderness of murmuring, but abide in the promised land of content and rest. "We which have believed do enter into rest." [See Hebrews 4:3.] Very much of our outward depends upon the inward: where there is Heaven in the heart there will be Heaven in the house. *And verily thou shalt be fed,* or shepherded. To integrity and faith necessaries are guaranteed. The good shepherd will exercise His pastoral care over all believers. In truth they shall be fed, and fed on truth. The promise of God shall be their perpetual banquet; they shall neither lack in spiritual nor in temporal. Some read this as an exhortation, "Feed on truth;" certainly this is good cheer, and banishes forever the hungry heart burnings of envy.

Psalm 37:4 *Delight thyself also in the Lord: and he shall give thee the desires of thine heart.*

EXPOSITION: Verse 4. There is an ascent in this third precept. He, who was first bidden not to fret, was then commanded to actively trust, and now is told with holy desire to delight in God. *Delight thyself also in the Lord.* Make Jehovah the joy and rejoicing of your spirit. Bad men delight in carnal objects; do not envy them if they are allowed to take their fill in such vain idols; look to your better delight, and fill yourself to the full with a more sublime portion. In a certain sense imitate the wicked; they delight in their portion—take care to delight in yours, and so far from envying you will pity them. There is no room for fretting if we remember that God is ours, but there is every incentive to sacred enjoyment of the most elevated and ecstatic kind.

Every name, attribute, word, or deed of Jehovah, should be delightful to us, and in meditating thereon our souls should be as glad as is the gourmet who feeds delicately with a profound relish for his dainties. *And he shall give thee the desires of thine heart.* A pleasant duty is here rewarded with another pleasure. Men who delight in God desire or ask for nothing but what will please God; hence it is safe to give them carte blanche. Their will is subdued to God's will, and now they may have what they will. Our innermost desire does not mean our casual wishes. There are many things that nature might desire which grace would never permit us to ask for. The deep, prayerful, asking desires are those to which the promise is made.

Psalm 37:5 *Commit thy way unto the Lord; trust also in him; and he shall bring it to pass.*

EXPOSITION: Verse 5. *Commit thy way unto the Lord.* Roll the whole burden of life upon the Lord. Leave with Jehovah not only your present fretfulness, but all your cares; in fact, submit the whole course of your way to Him. Cast away anxiety, resign your will, submit your judgment, and leave all with the God of all. What a medicine this is for expelling envy! What a high attainment this fourth precept indicates! How blessed must he be who lives every day in obedience to it! *Trust also in him; and he shall bring it to pass.* Our destiny shall be joyfully accomplished if we confidently trust all to our Lord. We may serenely sing—

"Thy way, not mine, O Lord,
However dark it be;
O lead me by thine own right hand,
Choose out the path for me."

"Smooth let it be or rough,
It will be still the best;
Winding or straight, it matters not,
It leads me to thy rest."

"I dare not choose my lot,
I would not if I might;
But choose Thou for me, O my God,
So shall I walk aright."

"Take thou my cup, and it
With joy or sorrow fill;
As ever best to thee may seem,
Choose thou my good and ill."[71]

The ploughman sows and harrows, and then leaves the harvest to God. What can he do else? He cannot cover the heavens with clouds, or command the rain, or bring forth the sun or create the dew. He does well to leave the whole matter with God; and so to all of us it is truest wisdom, having obediently trusted in God, to leave results in His hands, and expect a blessed issue.

Psalm 37:6 *And he shall bring forth thy righteousness as the light, and thy judgment as the noonday.*

EXPOSITION: **Verse 6.** *And he shall bring forth thy righteousness as the light.* In the matter of personal reputation

---

71. Hymn: *"Thy Way, Not Mine, O Lord."* Written by Horatius Bonar in 1857, music by J.T. Cooper

we may especially be content to be quiet, and leave our vindication with the Judge of all the Earth. The more we fret in this case the worse for us. Our strength is to sit still. The Lord will clear the slandered. If we look to His honor, he will see to ours. It is wonderful how, when faith learns to endure calumny [slander] with composure, the filth does not defile her, but falls off like snowballs from a wall of granite. Even in the worst cases, where a good name is for awhile darkened, Providence will send a clearing like the dawning light, which shall increase until the man once censured shall be universally admired. *And thy judgment as the noonday.* No shade of reproach shall remain. The man shall be in his meridian of splendor. The darkness of his sorrow and his ill repute shall both flee away.

Psalm 37:7 *Rest in the Lord, and wait patiently for him: fret not thyself because of him who prospereth in his way, because of the man who bringeth wicked devices to pass.*

EXPOSITION: **Verse 7.** *Rest in the Lord.* This fifth is a most divine precept, and requires much grace to carry it out. To hush the spirit, to be silent before the Lord, to wait in holy patience the time for clearing up the difficulties of Providence—that is what every gracious heart should aim at. "Aaron held his peace." [See Leviticus 10:3.] "I opened not my mouth; because thou didst it." [See Psalm 39:9.] A silent tongue in many cases not only shows a wise head, but a holy heart. *And wait patiently for him.* Time is nothing to him; let it be nothing to you. God is worth waiting for. "He never is before his time, he never is too late." In a story we wait for the end to clear up the plot; we ought not to prejudge the great drama of life, but stay until the closing scene, and see what the finish brings.

Fret not thyself because of him who prospereth in his way, because of the man who bringeth wicked devices to pass. There is no good, but much evil, in worrying your heart about the present success of graceless plotters: be not enticed into premature judgments—they dishonor God, and weary yourself. Determine to let the wicked succeed as they may, will treat the matter with indifference, and never allow a question to be raised as to the righteousness and goodness of the Lord. What if wicked devices succeed and your own plans are defeated . . . there is more of the love of God in your defeats than in the successes of the wicked.

Psalm 37:8 *Cease from anger, and forsake wrath: fret not thyself in any wise to do evil.*

EXPOSITION: **Verse 8.** *Cease from anger and forsake wrath.* Especially anger against the arrangements of Providence, and jealousies of the temporary pleasures of those who are so soon to be banished from all comfort. Anger anywhere is madness, here it is aggravated insanity. Yet since anger will try to keep us company, we must resolvedly forsake it. *Fret not thyself in any wise to do evil.* By no reasonings and under no circumstances be led into such a course. Fretfulness lies upon the verge of great sin. Many who have indulged a murmuring disposition have at last come to sin, in order to gain their fancied [imagined] rights. Beware of carping [criticizing] others, study to be found in the right way yourself; and as you would dread outward sin, tremble at inward repining.

Psalm 37:9 *For evildoers shall be cut off: but those that wait upon the Lord, they shall inherit the earth.*

EXPOSITION: **Verse 9.** *For evil doers shall be cut off.* Their death shall be a penal judgment; not a gentle removal to a better state, but an execution in which the axe of justice will be used. *But those that wait upon the Lord*—those who in patient faith expect their portion in another life—*they shall inherit the earth.* Even in this life they have the most of real enjoyment, and in the ages to come theirs shall be the glory and the triumph. Passion, according to Bunyan's parable, has his good things first, and they are soon over; Patience has his good things last, and they last forever.

Psalm 37:10 *For yet a little while, and the wicked shall not be: yea, thou shalt diligently consider his place, and it shall not be.*

EXPOSITION: **Verse 10.** *For yet a little while, and the wicked shall not be.* When bad men reach to greatness, the judgments of God frequently sweep them away; their riches melt, their power decays, their happiness turns to wretchedness; they themselves cease any longer to be numbered with the living. The shortness of life makes us see that the glitter of the wicked great is not true gold. O why, tried believer, do you envy one who in a little while will lie lower than the dust? *Yea, thou shalt diligently consider his place, and it shall not be.* His house shall be empty, his chair of office vacant, his estate without an owner; he shall be utterly blotted out, perhaps cut off by his own debauchery, or brought to a deathbed of penury by his own extravagance. Gone like a passing cloud—forgotten as a dream—where are his boastings and bullying, and where is the pomp which made poor mortals think the sinner was blest?

Psalm 37:11 *But the meek shall inherit the earth; and shall delight themselves in the abundance of peace.*

EXPOSITION: **Verse 11.** *But the meek shall inherit the earth.* Above all others they shall enjoy life. Even if they suffer, their consolations shall overcome their tribulations. By inheriting the land is meant obtaining covenant privileges and the salvation of God. Such as are truly humble shall take their lot with the rest of the heirs of grace, to whom all good things come by a sacred birthright. *And shall delight themselves in the abundance of peace.* Peace they love and peace they shall have. If they find not abundance of gold, abundance of peace will serve their turn far better. Others find joy in strife, and thence arises their misery in due time, but peace leads on to peace, and the more a man loves it the more shall it come to him. In the halcyon[72] period of the latter days, when universal peace shall make glad the Earth, the full prophetic meaning of words like these will be made plain.

Psalm 37:12 *The wicked plotteth against the just, and gnasheth upon him with his teeth.*

EXPOSITION: **Verse 12.** *The wicked plotteth against the just.* Why can he not let the good man alone? Because there is enmity between the serpent's seed and the seed of the woman. Why not attack him fairly? Why plot and scheme? Because it is according to the serpent's nature to be very subtle. Plain sailing does not suit those who are on board of "The Apollyon."[73] *And gnashed upon him with his teeth.*

---

72. Peace and prosperity.
73. The Destroyer-name used for the angel in the bottomless pit, answering to the Hebrew Abbadon.

The wicked show by their gestures what they would do if they could; if they cannot gnaw they will gnash; if they may not bite they will at least bark. This is precisely what the graceless world did with "that just One," the Prince of Peace. Yet He took no vengeance upon them, but like a silent lamb received injuries in patience.

Psalm 37:13 *The Lord shall laugh at him: for he seeth that his day is coming."*

EXPOSITION: Verse 13. *The Lord shall laugh at him.* The godly man needs not trouble himself, but leave well deserved vengeance to be dealt out by the Lord, who will utterly deride the malice of the good man's enemies. Let the proud scorner gnash his teeth and foam at the mouth; he has one to deal with who will look down upon him and his ravings with serene contempt. *For he seeth that his day is coming.* The evil man does not see how close his destruction is upon his heels; he boasts of crushing others when the foot of justice is already uplifted to trample him as the mire of the streets. Sinners, in the hand of an angry God, and yet plotting against his children! Poor souls, thus to run upon the point of Jehovah's spear.

Psalm 37:14 *The wicked have drawn out the sword, and have bent their bow, to cast down the poor and needy, and to slay such as be of upright conversation.*

EXPOSITION: Verse 14. *The wicked have drawn out the sword.* They hold their weapon out of its sheath, and watch for a time to use it. *And have bent their bow.* One weapon is not enough; they carry another ready for action. They carry so strong a bow that they have trodden upon it to bend it—they will lose nothing for want of force or readiness. *To cast down the poor and needy.* These are their game, the objects of their accursed malice. These cowards attack not their equals, but seek out those excellent ones who, from the gentleness of their spirits and the poverty of their estates, are not able to defend themselves. Note how our meek and lowly Lord was beset by cruel foes, armed with all manner of weapons to slay Him. *And to slay such as be of upright conversation.* Nothing short of the overthrow and death of the just will content the wicked. The sincere and straightforward are hated by the crafty schemers who delight in unrighteousness. See, then, the enemies of the godly doubly armed, and learn how true were our Lord's words, "If ye were of the world, the world would love its own: but because ye are not of this world, but I have chosen you out of the world, therefore the world hateth you." [See John 15:19.]

Psalm 37:15 *Their sword shall enter into their own heart, and their bows shall be broken.*

EXPOSITION: Verse 15. *Their sword shall enter into their own heart.* Like Haman they shall be hanged upon the gallows they built themselves for Mordecai. Hundreds of times has this been the case. Saul, who sought to slay David, fell on his own sword; and the bow, his favorite weapon, the use of which he taught the children of Israel, was not able to deliver him on Gilboa. *And their bows shall be broken.* Their inventions of evil shall be rendered useless. Malice outwits itself. It drinks the poisoned cup which it mixed for another, and burns itself in the fire which it kindled for its neighbor. Why need we fret at the prosperity of the wicked when they are so industriously ruining themselves while they fancy they are injuring the saints? The next nine verses mainly describe the character and blessedness of the godly, and the

light is brought out with a few black touches descriptive of
the wicked and their doom.

Psalm 37:16 *A little that a righteous man hath is
better than the riches of many wicked.*

EXPOSITION: Verse 16. *A little that a righteous man
hath is better than the riches of many wicked.* This is a fine
proverb. The little of one good man is contrasted with the
riches of many wicked, and so the expression is rendered
the more forcible. There is more happiness in the godly
dinner of herbs than in the stalled ox of profane rioters.
[See Proverbs 15:17.] In the original there is an allusion to
the noise of a multitude, as if to hint at the turmoil and
hurly burly of riotous wealth, and to contrast it with the
quiet of the humbler portion of the godly. We would sooner
hunger with John than feast with Herod; better feed on
scant fare with the prophets in Obadiah's cave than riot
with the priests of Baal. A man's happiness consists not
in the heaps of gold which he has in store. Content finds
multum in parvo,[74] while for a wicked heart the whole world
is too little.

Psalm 37:17 *For the arms of the wicked shall be
broken: but the Lord upholdeth the righteous.*

EXPOSITION: Verse 17. *For the arms of the wicked
shall be broken.* Their power to do mischief shall be effectually
taken away, for the arms which they lifted up against God
shall be crushed even to the bone. God often makes implacable
men incapable men. What is a more contemptible sight than
toothless malice, armless malevolence! *But the Lord upholdeth
the righteous.* Their cause and course shall be safe, for they

---

74. Latin: Much in little.

are in good keeping. The sword of two edges smites the wicked and defends the just.

Psalm 37:18 *The Lord knoweth the days of the upright: and their inheritance shall be for ever.*

EXPOSITION: Verse 18. *The Lord knoweth the days of the upright.* His foreknowledge made him laugh at the proud, but in the case of the upright he sees a brighter future, and treats them as heirs of salvation. Ever is this our comfort, that all events are known to our God, and that nothing in our future can take Him unawares. No arrow can pierce us by accident, no danger smite us by stealth; neither in time nor eternity can any unforeseen ill occur to us. For those of us in the future, it shall be but a continual development of the good things which the Lord has laid up in store for us. *And their inheritance shall be forever.* Their inheritance fades not away. It is entailed, [bequeathed] so that none can deprive them of it, and preserved, so that none shall destroy it. Eternity is the peculiar attribute of the believer's portion: what they have on Earth is safe enough, but what they shall have in Heaven is theirs without end.

Psalm 37:19 *They shall not be ashamed in the evil time: and in the days of famine they shall be satisfied.*

EXPOSITION: Verse 19. *They shall not be ashamed in the evil time.* Calamities will come, but deliverances will come also. As the righteous never reckoned upon immunity from trouble, they will not be disappointed when they are called to take their share of it, but rather they will cast themselves anew upon their God, and prove again His faithfulness and love. God is not a friend in the sunshine only; He is a friend indeed and a friend in need. *And in the days of famine they* *shall be satisfied*. Their barrel of meal and cruse of oil shall last out the day of distress, [See 1 Kings 17:12-16.], and if ravens do not bring them bread and meat, [See 1 Kings 17:4-6.] the supply of their needs shall come in some other way, for their bread shall be given them. Our Lord stayed himself upon this when He hungered in the wilderness, and by faith He repelled the tempter; we too may be enabled not to fret ourselves in any wise to do evil by the same consideration. If God's providence is our inheritance, we need not worry about the price of wheat. Mildew, and smut, and bent,[75] are all in the Lord's hands. Unbelief cannot save a single ear from being blasted,[76] but faith, if it does not preserve the crop, can do what is better, namely, preserve our joy in the Lord.

Psalm 37:20 *But the wicked shall perish, and the enemies of the Lord shall be as the fat of lambs: they shall consume; into smoke shall they consume away.*

EXPOSITION: **Verse 20.** *But the wicked shall perish.* Whatever phantom light may mock their present, their future is black with dark, substantial night. Judgment has been given against them, they are but reserved for execution. Let them flaunt their scarlet and fine linen, and fare sumptuously every day; the sword of Damocles[77] is above their heads, and if their wits were a little more awake, their mirth would turn to misery. *The enemies of the Lord shall be as the fat of lambs.* As the sacrificial fat was all consumed upon the altar, so shall the ungodly utterly vanish from the place of their

---

75. Pasture and lawn grass.

76. Withered

77. A 4th-century BC Greek courtier to Dionysius the Elder who (according to legend) was condemned to sit in the King's throne under a sword suspended by a single horsehair above his hear in order to demonstrate to him that being a king was not the happy state that Damocles said it was.

honor and pride. How can it be otherwise? If the stubble dares to contend with the flame, to what end can it hope to come? They shall be consumed. As dry wood, as heaps of leaves, as burning coals, they shall soon be gone, and gone altogether, for "into smoke shall they consume away." Sic transit gloria mundi[78]. A puff is the end of all their puffing. Their fuming ends in smoke. They made themselves fat, and perished in their own grease. Consumers of the good they tried to be, and consumed they shall be.

Psalm 37:21 *The wicked borroweth, and payeth not again: but the righteous sheweth mercy, and giveth.*

EXPOSITION: Verse 21. *The wicked borroweth, and payeth not again.* Partly because he will not, but mainly because he cannot. Want follows upon waste, and debt remains unpaid. Often are the wicked thus impoverished in this life. Their wanton extravagance brings them down to the usurer's door and to the bankrupt's suit. *But the righteous sheweth mercy, and giveth.* Mercy has given to him, and therefore he gives in mercy. He is generous and prosperous. He is not a borrower, but a giver. So far as the good man can do it, he lends an ear to the requests of need, and instead of being impoverished by what he imparts, he grows richer, and is able to do more. He does not give to encourage idleness, but in real mercy, which supposes real need. The text suggests to us how much better it generally is to give than to lend. Generally, lending comes to giving in the end, and it is as well to anticipate the fact, and by a little liberality forestall the inevitable. If these two sentences describe the wicked and the righteous, the writer of these lines has reason to

---

78. Latin: So passes away the glory of the world.

know that in and about the city of London the wicked are very numerous.

Psalm 37:22 *For such as be blessed of him shall inherit the earth; and they that be cursed of him shall be cut off.*

EXPOSITION: Verse 22. *For such as be blessed of him shall inherit the earth.* God's benediction is true wealth after all. True happiness, such as the covenant secures to all the chosen of Heaven, lies wrapped up in the divine favor. *And they that be cursed of him shall be cut off.* His frown is death; no more than that, it is hell.

Psalm 37:23 *The steps of a good man are ordered by the Lord: and he delighteth in his way.*

EXPOSITION: Verse 23. *The steps of a good man are ordered by the Lord.* All his course of life is graciously ordained, and in lovingkindness all is fixed, settled, and maintained. No reckless fate, no fickle chance rules us; our every step is the subject of divine decree. *And he delighteth in his way.* As parents are pleased with the tottering footsteps of their babes. All that concerns a saint is interesting to His heavenly Father. God loves to view the holy strivings of a soul pressing forward to the skies. In the trials and the joys of the faithful, Jesus has fellowship with them, and delights to be their sympathizing companion.

Psalm 37:24 *Though he fall, he shall not be utterly cast down: for the Lord upholdeth him with his hand.*

EXPOSITION: Verse 24. *Though he fall.* Disasters and reverses may lay him low; he may, like Job, be stripped of everything; like Joseph, be put in prison; like Jonah, be cast into the deep. *He shall not be utterly cast down.* He shall not be altogether prostrate. He shall be brought on his knees, but not on his face; or, if laid prone for a moment, he shall be up again before long. No saint shall fall finally or fatally. Sorrow may bring us to the earth, and death may bring us to the grave, but lower we cannot sink, and out of the lowest of all we shall arise to the highest of all. *For the Lord upholdeth him with his hand.* Condescendingly, with His own hand, God upholds His saints; He does not leave them to mere delegated agency, He gives personal assistance. Even in our falls the Lord gives a measure of sustaining. Where grace does not keep from going down, it shall save from keeping down. Job had double wealth at last, Joseph reigned over Egypt, and Jonah was safely landed. It is not that the saints are strong, or wise, or meritorious, that therefore they rise after every fall, but because God is their helper, and therefore none can prevail against them.

Psalm 37:25 *I have been young, and now am old; yet have I not seen the righteous forsaken, nor his seed begging bread.*

EXPOSITION: **Verse 25.** This was David's observation, I *have been young, and now am old; yet have I not seen the righteous forsaken, nor his seed begging bread.* It is not my observation just as it stands, for I have relieved the children of undoubtedly good men, who have appealed to me as common mendicants [beggars]. But this does not cast a doubt upon the observation of David. He lived under a dispensation more outward, and more of this world than the present rule of personal faith. Never are the righteous forsaken; that is a rule without exception. Seldom indeed do their seed beg bread; and although it does occasionally occur, through dissipation, idleness, or some other causes on the part of their sons, yet doubtless it is so rare a thing that there are many alive who never saw it. Go into the union house and see how few are the children of godly parents; enter the gaol[79] and see how much rarer still is the case. Poor minster's sons often become rich. I am not old, but I have seen families of the poor godly become rich, and have seen the Lord reward the faithfulness of the father in the success of the son, so that I have often thought that the best way to endow one's seed with wealth is to become poor for Christ's sake. In the Indian mission of the "Baptist Missionary Society," this is abundantly illustrated.

Psalm 37:26 *He is ever merciful, and lendeth; and his seed is blessed.*

EXPOSITION: Verse 26. *He is ever merciful, and lendeth.* The righteous are constantly under generous impulses; they do not prosper through parsimony, but through bounty. Like the bounteous giver of all good, of whom they are the beloved sons, they delight in doing good. How stingy covetous professors can hope for salvation is a marvel to those who read such verses as this in the Bible. *And his seed is blessed.* God pays back with interest in the next generation. Where the children of the righteous are not godly, there must be some reason for it in parental neglect, or some other guilty cause. The friend of the father is the friend of the family. The God of Abraham is the God of Isaac and of Jacob.

Psalm 37:27 *Depart from evil, and do good; and dwell for evermore.*

---

79. Jail

EXPOSITION: **Verse 27.** *Depart from evil, and do good.* We must not envy the doers of evil, but depart altogether from their spirit and example. As Lot left Sodom without casting a look behind, so must we leave sin. No truce or parley is to be held with sin; we must turn away from it without hesitation, and set ourselves practically to work in the opposite direction. He who neglects to do good will soon fall into evil. *And dwell for evermore.* Obtain an abiding and quiet inheritance. Short lived are the gains and pleasures of evil, but eternal are the rewards of grace.

Psalm 37:28 *For the Lord loveth judgment, and forsaketh not his saints; they are preserved for ever: but the seed of the wicked shall be cut off.*

EXPOSITION: **Verse 28.** *For the Lord loveth judgment.* The awarding of honor to whom honor is due is God's delight, especially when the upright man has been slandered by his fellow men. It must be a divine pleasure to right wrongs, and to defeat the machinations of the unjust. The great Arbiter of human destinies is sure to deal out righteous measure both to rich and po*or, to good and evil, for such judgment is His delight. And forsaketh not his saints.* This would not be right, and, therefore, shall never be done. God is as faithful to the objects of His love as He is just towards all mankind. *They are preserved for ever.* By covenant engagements their security is fixed, and by suretyship fulfillments that safety is accomplished; come what may, the saints are preserved in Christ Jesus, and because He lives, they shall live also. A king will not lose his jewels, nor will Jehovah lose His people. As the manna in the golden pot, to keep from melting was preserved in the Ark of the Covenant beneath the mercy seat, so shall the faithful be preserved in the covenant by the power of Jesus their propitiation. *But the seed of the* *wicked shall be cut off.* Like the house of Jeroboam and Ahab, of which not a dog was left. Honor and ill gotten wealth seldom reach the third generation; the curse grows ripe before many years have passed, and falls upon the evil house. Among the legacies of wicked men the surest entail is a judgment on their family.

Psalm 37:29 *The righteous shall inherit the land, and dwell therein for ever.*

EXPOSITION: **Verse 29.** *The righteous shall inherit the land.* As heirs with Jesus Christ, the Canaan above, which is the antitype of "the land," shall be theirs with all covenant blessing.

And dwell therein for ever. Tenures differ, but none can match the holding which believers have of Heaven. Paradise is theirs forever by inheritance, and they shall live forever to enjoy it. Who would not be a saint on such terms? Who would fret concerning the fleeting treasures of the godless?

Psalm 37:30 *The mouth of the righteous speaketh wisdom, and his tongue talketh of judgment.*

EXPOSITION: **Verse 30.** *The mouth of the righteous speaketh wisdom.* Where the whole Psalm is dedicated to a description of the different fates of the just and the wicked, it was right to give a test by which they could be known. A man's tongue is no ill index of his character. The mouth betrays the heart. Good men, as a rule, speak that which is to edifying, sound speech, religious conversation, consistent with the divine illumination which they have received. Righteousness is wisdom in action, hence all good men are practically wise men, and well may the speech be wise. *And his tongue talketh of judgment.* He advocates

180

justice, gives an honest verdict on things and men, and he foretells that God's judgments will come upon the wicked, as in the former days. His talk is neither foolish nor ribald, neither lacking significance nor corrupt. Our conversation is of far more consequence than some men imagine.

Psalm 37:31 *The law of his God is in his heart; none of his steps shall slide.*

EXPOSITION: Verse 31. *The law of his God is in his heart; none of his steps shall slide.* The best thing in the best place, producing the best results. Well might the man's talk be so admirable when his heart was so well stored. To love holiness, to have the motives and desires sanctified, to be in one's inmost nature obedient to the Lord—this is the surest method of making the whole run of our life efficient for its great ends, and even for securing the details of it, our steps from any serious mistake. To keep the even tenor of one's way, in such times as these, is given only to those whose hearts are sound towards God, who can, as in the text, call God their God. Policy slips and trips, it twists and tacks, and after all is defeated in the long run, but sincerity plods on its plain pathway and reaches the goal.

Psalm 37:32 *The wicked watcheth the righteous, and seeketh to slay him.*

EXPOSITION: Verse 32. *The wicked watcheth the righteous, and seeketh to slay him.* If it were not for the laws of the land, we should soon see a massacre of the righteous. Jesus was watched by His enemies, who were thirsting for His blood: His disciples must not look for favor where their Master found hatred and death.

Psalm 37:33 *The Lord will not leave him in his hand, nor condemn him when he is judged.*

EXPOSITION: **Verse 33.** *The Lord will not leave him in his hand.* God often appears to deliver His servants, and when He does not do so in this life as to their bodies, He gives their souls such joy and peace that they triumphantly rise beyond their tormentors' power. We may be in the enemy's hand for awhile, as Job was, but we cannot be left there.

Nor condemn him when he is judged. Time shall reverse the verdict of haste, or else eternity shall clear away the condemnation of time. In due season just men will be justified. Temporary injustices are tolerated, in the order of Providence, for purposes most wise; but the bitter shall not always be called sweet, nor light for ever be denigrated as darkness; the right shall appear in due season; the fictitious and pretentious shall be unmasked, and the real and true shall be revealed. If we have done faithfully, we may appeal from the petty sessions of society to the solemn court of the great day.

Psalm 37:34 *Wait on the Lord, and keep his way, and he shall exalt thee to inherit the land: when the wicked are cut off, thou shalt see it.*

EXPOSITION: **Verse 34.** *Wait on the Lord.* We have here the eighth precept, and it is a lofty eminence to attain to. Tarry in the Lord's leisure. Wait in obedience as a servant, in hope as an heir, in expectation as a believer. This little word "wait" is easy to say, but hard to carry out, yet faith must do it. *And keep his way.* Continue in the narrow path; let no haste for riches or ease cause unholy action. Let your motto be, "On, on, on." Never falter or dream of turning aside. "He that endureth to the end, the same shall be saved." [See Matthew 10:22.] *And he shall exalt thee to inherit the land.* Thou shalt have all of earthly good which is really good, and of heavenly good there shall be no stint. Exaltation shall be the lot of the excellent. *When the wicked are cut off, thou shalt see it.* A sight how terrible and how instructive! What a rebuke for fretfulness! What an incentive to gratitude! My soul, be still, as you foresee the end, the awful end of the Lord's enemies.

Psalm 37:35 *I have seen the wicked in great power, and spreading himself like a green bay tree.*

EXPOSITION: Verse 35. A second time David turns to his diary, and this time in poetic imagery tells us of what he had observed. It would be well if we too took notes of divine providences. *I have seen the wicked in great power.* The man was terrible to others, ruling with much authority, and carrying things with a high hand, a Caesar in might, a Croesus[80] in wealth. *And spreading himself like a green bay tree.* Adding house to house and field to field, rising higher and higher in the state. He seemed to be ever verdant like a laurel; he grew as a tree in its own native soil, from which it had never been transplanted. No particular tree is here meant, a spreading beech or a wide expanding oak may serve us to realize the picture; it is a thing of earth, whose roots are in the clay; its honors are fading leaves; and though its shadow dwarfs the plants which are condemned to pine beneath it, yet it is itself a dying things as the feller's axe shall prove. In the noble tree, which claims to be king of the forest, behold the grandeur of the ungodly today; wait awhile and wonder at the change, as the timber is carried away, and the very root torn from the ground.

---

80. A rich king and the last king of Lydia. Died 547 BC.

Psalm 37:36 *Yet he passed away, and, lo, he was not: yea, I sought him, but he could not be found.*

EXPOSITION: **Verse 36.** *Yet he passed away.* Tree and man both gone, the son of man as surely as the child of the forest. What clean sweeps death makes! *And, lo, he was not.* To the surprise of all men the great man was gone, his estates sold, his business bankrupt, his house alienated, his name forgotten, and all in a few months. *Yea, I sought him, but he could not be found.* Moved by curiosity, if we enquire for the ungodly, they have left no trace; like birds of ill omen none desire to remember them. Some of the humblest of the godly are immortalized, their names are imperishably fragrant in the Church, while of the ablest of infidels and blasphemers hardly their names are remembered beyond a few years. Men who were in everybody's mouths but yesterday are forgotten tomorrow, for only virtue is immortal.

Psalm 37:37 *Mark the perfect man, and behold the upright: for the end of that man is peace.*

EXPOSITION: **Verse 37.** *Mark the perfect man, and behold the upright.* After having watched with surprise the downfall of the wicked, give your attention to the sincerely godly man, and observe the blessed contrast. Good men are men of distinguishing notice, and are worth our study. Upright men are marvels of grace, and worth beholding. *For the end of that man is peace.* The man of peace has an end of peace. Peace without end comes in the end to the man of God. His way may be rough, but it leads home. With believers it may rain in the morning, thunder at midday, and pour in torrents in the afternoon, but it must clear up before the sun goes down. War may last until our last hour, but then we shall hear the last of it.

Psalm 37:38 *But the transgressors shall be destroyed together: the end of the wicked shall be cut off.*

EXPOSITION: **Verse 38.** *But the transgressors shall be destroyed together.* A common ruin awaits those who are joined in common rebellion. *The end of the wicked shall be cut off.* Their time shall be shortened, their happiness shall be ended, their hopes forever blasted, their execution hastened on. Their present is shortened by their sins; they shall not live out half their days. They have no future worth having, while the righteous count their future as their true heritage.

Psalm 37:39 *But the salvation of the righteous is of the Lord: he is their strength in the time of trouble.*

EXPOSITION: **Verse 39.** *But the salvation of the righteous is of the Lord.* This is sound doctrine. The very marrow of the gospel of free grace. By salvation is meant deliverance of every kind; not only the salvation which finally lands us in glory, but all the minor rescues of the way; these are all to be ascribed unto the Lord, and to Him alone. Let Him have glory from those to whom He grants salvation. *He is their strength in the time of trouble.* While trouble overthrows the wicked, it only drives the righteous to their strong Helper, who rejoices to uphold them.

Psalm 37:40 *And the Lord shall help them, and deliver them: he shall deliver them from the wicked, and save them, because they trust in him.*

EXPOSITION: **Verse 40.** *And the Lord shall help them.* In all future time Jehovah will stand up for His chosen. Our Great Ally will bring up His forces in the heat of the battle. *He shall deliver them from the wicked.* As He rescued Daniel from the lions, so will He preserve His beloved from their enemies; they need not therefore fret, nor be discouraged. *And save them, because they trust in him.* Faith shall ensure the safety of the elect. It is the mark of the sheep by which they shall be separated from the goats. Not their merit, but their believing, shall distinguish them. Who would not try the walk of faith? Whoever truly believes in God will be no longer fretful against the apparent irregularities of this present life, but will rest assured that what is mysterious is nevertheless just, and what seems hard, is, beyond a doubt, ordered in mercy. So the Psalm ends with a note which is the death knell of the unhallowed disquietude with which the Psalm commenced. Happy are they who can thus sing themselves out of ill frames into gracious conditions.

PSALM 38

PSALM 38:1–PSALM 38:22

Psalm 38:1 *O Lord, rebuke me not in thy wrath: neither chasten me in thy hot displeasure.*

EXPOSITION: **Verse 1.** *O LORD, rebuke me not in thy wrath.* Rebuked I must be, for I am an error prone child and you a careful Father, but throw not too much anger into the tones of your voice; deal gently although I have sinned grievously. The anger of others I can bear, but not yours. As your love is most sweet to my heart, so your displeasure is most cutting to my conscience. *Neither chasten me in thy hot displeasure.* Chasten me if you will, it is a Father's prerogative, and to endure it obediently is a child's duty; but, O turn not the rod into a sword, strike not to kill. True, my sins might well inflame you, but let your mercy and longsuffering quench the glowing coals of your wrath. O let me not be treated as an enemy or dealt with as a rebel. Bring to remembrance your covenant, your fatherhood, and my feebleness, and spare your servant.

Psalm 38:2 *For thine arrows stick fast in me, and thy hand presseth me sore.*

EXPOSITION: **Verse 2.** *For thine arrows stick fast in me.* By this he means both bodily and spiritual griefs, but we may suppose, especially the latter, for these are most piercing and stick securely. God's law applied by the Spirit to the conviction of the soul of sin, wounds deeply and chafes long; it is an arrow not lightly to be brushed out by careless mirthfulness, or to be extracted by the flattering hand of self-righteousness. The Lord knows how to shoot so that His bolts not only strike but stick. He can make convictions sink into the innermost spirit like arrows driven in up to the head. It seems strange that the Lord should shoot at His own beloved ones, but in truth He shoots at their sins rather than them, and those who feel His sin killing shafts in this life, shall not be slain with His hot thunderbolts in the next world. *And thy hand presseth me sore.* The Lord had come to close dealings with him, and pressed him down with the weight of His hand, so that he had no rest or strength left. By these two expressions we are taught that conviction of sin is a piercing and a pressing thing, sharp and sore, smarting and crushing. Those who know by experience "the terror of the Lord," [See 2 Corinthians 5:11.], will be best able to vouch for the accuracy of such descriptions; they are true to the life.

Psalm 38:3 *There is no soundness in my flesh because of thine anger; neither is there any rest in my bones because of my sin.*

EXPOSITION: Verse 3. *There is no soundness in my flesh because of thine anger.* Mental depression tells upon the bodily frame; it is enough to create and foster every disease, and is in itself the most painful of all diseases. Soul sickness tells upon the entire frame; it weakens the body, and then bodily weakness reacts upon the mind. One drop of divine anger sets the whole of our blood boiling with misery. *Neither is there any rest in my bones because of my sin.* Deeper still the malady penetrates, until the bones, the more solid parts of the system, are affected. No soundness and no rest are two sad deficiencies; yet these are both consciously gone from every awakened conscience until Jesus gives relief. God's anger is a fire that dries up the very marrow; it searches the secret parts of the belly. A man who has pain in his bones tosses to and fro in search of rest, but he finds none; he becomes worn out with agony, and in so many cases a sense of sin creates in the conscience a horrible unrest which cannot be exceeded in anguish except by hell itself.

Psalm 38:4 *For mine iniquities are gone over mine head: as an heavy burden they are too heavy for me.*

EXPOSITION: **Verse 4.** *For mine iniquities are gone over mine head.* Like waves of the deep sea; like black mire in which a man utterly sinks. Above my hopes, my strength, my life itself, my sin rises in its terror. Unawakened sinners think their sins to be mere shallows, but when conscience is aroused they find out the depth of iniquity. *As an heavy burden they are too heavy for me.* It is well when sin is an intolerable load, and when the remembrance of our sins burdens us beyond endurance. This verse is the genuine cry of one who feels himself undone by his transgressions and as yet sees not the great sacrifice.

Psalm 38:5 *My wounds stink and are corrupt because of my foolishness.*

EXPOSITION: **Verse 5.** *My wounds stink and are corrupt because of my foolishness.* Apply this to the body, and it pictures a sad condition of disease; but read it of the soul, and it is to the life. Conscience lays on stripe after stripe until the swelling becomes a wound and festers, and the corruption within grows offensive. What a horrible creature man appears to be in his own consciousness when his depravity and vileness are fully opened up by the Law of God, applied by the Holy Spirit!

It is true there are diseases which are correctly described in this verse, when in the worst stage; but we prefer to receive the expressions as instructively figurative, since the words "because of my foolishness" point rather at a moral than a physical malady. Some of us know what it is to stink in our own nostrils, so as to loathe ourselves. Even the filthiest diseases cannot be as foul as sin. No ulcers, cancers, or putrefying sores, can match the unutterable vileness and pollution of iniquity. Our own perceptions have made us feel this. We write what we do know, and testify what we have seen [See John 3:11.]; and even now we shudder to think that so much of evil should lie festering deep within our nature.

Psalm 38:6 *I am troubled; I am bowed down greatly; I go mourning all the day long.*

EXPOSITION: **Verse 6.** *I am troubled.* I am wearied with distress, writhing with pain, in sore travail on account of sin revealed within me. *I am bowed down greatly.* I am brought very low, grievously weakened and frightfully depressed. Nothing so pulls a man down from all loftiness as a sense of sin and of divine wrath concerning it. *I go mourning all the day long.* The mourner's soul sorrow knew no intermission, even when he went about such business as he was able to attend, he went forth like a mourner who goes to the tomb, and his words and manners were like the lamentations of those who follow the corpse. The whole verse may be the more clearly understood if we picture the Oriental mourner, covered with sackcloth and ashes, bowed as in a heap, sitting amid squalor and dirt, performing contortions and writhing expressive of his grief; such is the awakened sinner, not in outward guise, but in very deed.

Psalm 38:7 *For my loins are filled with a loathsome disease: and there is no soundness in my flesh.*

EXPOSITION: Verse 7. *For my loins are filled with a loathsome disease*—a hot, dry, parching disorder, probably accompanied by loathsome ulcers. Spiritually, the fire burns within when the evil of the heart is laid bare. Note the emphatic words, the evil is loathsome, it is in the loins, its seat is deep and vital—the man is filled with it. Those who have passed through the time of conviction understand all this. And there is no soundness in my flesh. This he had said before, and thus the Holy Spirit brings humiliating truth again and again to our memories, tears away every ground of glorying, and makes us know that in us, that is, in our flesh, there "dwelleth no good thing." [See Romans 7:18.]

Psalm 38:8 *I am feeble and sore broken: I have roared by reason of the disquietness of my heart.*

EXPOSITION: Verse 8. *I am feeble.* The original is "benumbed or frozen, such strange incongruities and contradictions meet in a distracted mind and a sick body—it appears to itself to be alternately parched with heat and pinched with cold. Like souls in the Popish fabled Purgatory, tossed from burning furnaces into thick ice, so tormented hearts rush from one extreme to the other, with equal torture in each. A heat of fear, a chill of horror, a flaming desire, a horrible insensibility—by these successive miseries a convinced sinner is brought to death's door. *And sore broken.* Crushed as in a mill, pounded as in a mortar. The body of the sick man appears to be all out of joint and smashed into a palpitating pulp, and the soul of the desponding is in an equally wretched case; as a victim crushed under the car of

Juggernaut,[81] such is a soul over whose conscience the wheels of divine wrath have forced their awful way.

I have roared by reason of the disquietness of my heart. Deep and hoarse is the voice of sorrow, and often inarticulate and terrible. The heart learns "groanings which cannot be uttered [See Romans 8:26.]," and the voice fails to tone and tune itself to human speech. When our prayers appear to be rather animal than spiritual, they are none the less prevalent with the pitiful Father of mercy. He hears the murmur of the heart and the roaring of the soul because of sin, and in due time He comes to relieve His afflicted. The more closely the preceding portrait of an awakened soul is studied in the light of experience, the more will its striking accuracy appear. It cannot be a description of merely outward disorder, graphic as it might then be; it has a depth and pathos in it which only the soul's mysterious and awful agony can fully match.

Psalm 38:9 *Lord, all my desire is before thee; and my groaning is not hid from thee.*

EXPOSITION: Verse 9. *Lord, all my desire is before thee.* If unuttered, yet perceived. Blessed be God, He reads the longings of our hearts; nothing can be hidden from Him; what we cannot tell to Him He perfectly understands. The psalmist is conscious that he has not exaggerated, and therefore appeals to Heaven for a confirmation of his words. The good Physician understands the symptoms of our diseases and sees the hidden evil which they reveal; hence our case is safe in His hands. *And my groaning is not hid from thee.* "He takes the meaning of our tears, / The language of our groans." Sorrow and anguish hide themselves from the observation of man, but God spies them out. None more lonely than the

---

81. Steamroller

broken hearted sinner, yet he has the Lord for his companion.

Psalm 38:10 *My heart panteth, my strength faileth me: as for the light of mine eyes, it also is gone from me.*

EXPOSITION: **Verse 10.** *My heart panteth.* Here begins another tale of woe. He was so dreadfully pained by the unkindness of friends that his heart was in a state of perpetual palpitation. Sharp and quick were the beatings of his heart; he was like a hunted deer, filled with distressing alarms, and ready to fly out of itself with fear. The soul seeks sympathy in sorrow, and if it finds none, its sorrowful heart throbs are incessant. *My strength faileth me.* What with disease and distraction, he was weakened and ready to expire. A sense of sin, and a clear perception that none can help us in our distress, is enough to bring a man to death's door, especially if there be none to speak a gentle word, and point the broken spirit to the beloved Physician. *As for the light of mine eyes, it also is gone from me.* Sweet light departed from his bodily eye, and consolation vanished from his soul. Those who were the very light of his eyes forsook him. Hope, the last lamp of night, was ready to go out. What a plight was the poor convicted one in! Yet here, we have some of us been; and here should we have perished had not infinite mercy interposed. Now, as we remember the loving-kindness of the Lord, we see how good it was for us to find our own strength fail us, since it drove us to the strong for strength; and how right it was that our light should all be quenched, that the Lord's light should be all in all to us.

Psalm 38:11 *My lovers and my friends stand aloof from my sore; and my kinsmen stand afar off.*

EXPOSITION: **Verse 11.** *My lovers and my friends stand aloof from my sore.* Whatever affection they might pretend to, they kept out of his company, lest as a sinking vessel often draws down boats with it, they might be made to suffer through his calamities. It is very hard when those who should be the first to come to the rescue, are the first to desert us. In times of deep soul trouble, even the most affectionate friends cannot enter into the sufferer's case; let them be as anxious as they may, the sores of a tender conscience they cannot bind up. Oh, the loneliness of a soul passing under the convincing power of the Holy Ghost! *And my kinsmen stand afar off.* As the women and others of our Lord's acquaintances from afar gazed on His Cross, so a soul wounded for sin sees all mankind as distant spectators, and in the whole crowd finds none to aid. Often relatives hinder seekers after Jesus, oftener still they look on with unconcern, and seldom do they endeavor to lead the penitent to Jesus.

Psalm 38:12 *They also that seek after my life lay snares for me: and they that seek my hurt speak mischievous things, and imagine deceits all the day long.*

EXPOSITION: **Verse 12.** *They also that seek after my life lay snares for me.* Alas for us when in addition to inward griefs, we are beset by outward temptations. David's foes endeavored basely to ensnare him. If fair means would not overthrow him, foul should be tried. This snaring business is a vile one, the devil's own poachers alone condescend to it; but prayer to God will deliver us, for the craft of the entire college of tempters can be met and overcome by those who are led by the Spirit. *And they that seek my hurt speak mischievous things.* Lies and slanders poured from them like water from the town pump. Their tongue was forever going, and their heart forever inventing lies.

And imagine deceit all the day long. They were never done; their forge was going from morning to night. When they could not act they talked, and when they could not talk they imagined, and schemed, and plotted. Restless is the activity of malice. Bad men never have enough of evil. They travel sea and land to injure a saint; no labor is too severe, no cost too great if they may utterly destroy the innocent. Our comfort is that our glorious Head knows the stubborn and persistent malignity of our foes, and will in due season put an end to it, as He even now sets a boundary around it.

Psalm 38:13 *But I, as a deaf man, heard not; and I was as a dumb man that openeth not his mouth.*

EXPOSITION: Verse 13. *But I, as a deaf man, heard not.* Well and bravely this was done. A sacred indifference to the slanders of malevolence is true courage and wise policy. It is well to be as if we could not hear or see. Perhaps the psalmist means that this deafness on his part was unavoidable because he had no power to answer the taunts of the cruel, but felt much of the truth of their ungenerous accusations. *And I was as a dumb man that openeth not his mouth.* David was bravely silent, and herein was eminently typical of our Lord Jesus, whose marvelous silence before Pilate was far more eloquent than words. To abstain from self-defense is often most difficult, and frequently most wise.

Psalm 38:14 *Thus I was as a man that heareth not, and in whose mouth are no reproofs.*

EXPOSITION: Verse 14. *Thus I was as a man that heareth not, and in whose mouth are no reproofs.* He repeats the fact of his silence that we may note it, admire it, and

195

imitate it. We have an advocate, and need not therefore plead our own cause. The Lord will rebuke our foes, for vengeance belongs to Him; we may therefore wait patiently and find it our strength to sit still.

Psalm 38:15 *For in thee, O Lord, do I hope: thou wilt hear, O Lord my God.*

EXPOSITION: Verse 15. David committed himself to Him that judges righteously, and so in patience was able to possess his soul. Hope in God's intervention, and belief in the power of prayer, are two most blessed stays to the soul in time of adversity. Turning right away from the creature to the sovereign Lord of all and to Him as our own covenant God, we shall find the richest solace in waiting upon Him. Reputation like a fair pearl may be cast into the mire, but in due time when the Lord makes up His jewels, the godly character shall shine with unclouded splendor. Rest then, O slandered one, and let not thy soul be tossed to and fro with anxiety.

Psalm 38:16 *For I said, Hear me, lest otherwise they should rejoice over me: when my foot slippeth, they magnify themselves against me.*

EXPOSITION: Verse 16. *For I said, hear me, lest otherwise they should rejoice over me.* The good man was not insensible, he dreaded the sharp stings of taunting malice; he feared lest either by his conduct or his condition, he should give occasion to the wicked to triumph. This fear his earnest desires used as an argument in prayer as well as an incentive to prayer. *When my foot slippeth, they magnify themselves against me.* The least flaw in a saint is sure to be noticed; long before it comes to a fall the enemy begins to rail, the merest trip of the foot sets all the dogs of hell barking. How careful ought we to be, and how persistent in prayer for upholding grace! We do not wish, like blind Samson, to make sport for our enemies; let us then beware of the treacherous Delilah of sin, by whose means our eyes may soon be put out.

Psalm 38:17 *For I am ready to halt, and my sorrow is continually before me.*

EXPOSITION: **Verse 17.** *For I am ready to halt.* Like one who limps, or a person with tottering footsteps, in danger of falling. How well this befits us all. "Let him that thinketh he standeth, take heed lest he fall." [See 1 Corinthians 10:12.] How small a thing will lame a Christian, how insignificant a stumbling block may cause him to fall! This passage refers to a weakness caused by pain and sorrow; the sufferer was ready to give up in despair; he was so depressed in spirit that he stumbled at a straw. Some of us painfully know what it is to be like dry tinder for the sparks of sorrow; ready to doubt and waver, ready to mourn, and sigh and cry upon any occasion, and for any cause. *And my sorrow is continually before me.* He did not need to look out the window to find sorrow, he felt it within, and groaned under a body of sin which was an increasing plague to him. Deep conviction continues to irritate the conscience; it will not endure a patched up peace; but cries war to the knife until the enmity is slain. Until the Holy Ghost applies the precious blood of Jesus, a truly awakened sinner is covered with raw wounds which cannot be healed nor bound up, nor soothed with ointment.

Psalm 38:18 *For I will declare mine iniquity; I will be sorry for my sin.*

EXPOSITION: Verse 18. *For I will declare mine iniquity.* The slander of his enemies he repudiates, but the accusations of his conscience he admits. Open confession is good for the soul. When sorrow leads to hearty and penitent acknowledgment of sin it is blessed sorrow, a thing to thank God for most devoutly. *I will be sorry for my sin.* My confession will be salted with briny tears. It is well not so much to bewail our sorrows as to denounce the sins which lie at the root of them. To be sorry for sin is no atonement for it, but it is the right spirit in which to go to Jesus, who is the reconciliation and the Savior. A man is near to the end of his trouble when he comes to an end with his sins.

Psalm 38:19 *But mine enemies are lively, and they are strong: and they that hate me wrongfully are multiplied.*

EXPOSITION: Verse 19. *But mine enemies are lively, and they are strong.* However weak and dying the righteous man may be, the evils which oppose him are sure to be lively enough. Neither the world, the flesh, nor the devil, are ever afflicted with debility or inertness; this trinity of evils labor with mighty unremitting energy to overthrow us. If the devil were sick, or our lusts feeble, or Madame Bubble[82] infirm, we might slacken prayer; but with such lively and vigorous enemies we must not cease to cry mightily unto our God. *And they that hate me wrongfully are multiplied.* Here is another misery, that as we are no match for our enemies in strength, so also they outnumber us as a hundred to one. Wrong as the cause of evil is, it is a popular one. More and

---

82. Madam Bubble is the witch who enchants the Enchanted Grounds in the book *Pilgrim's Progress*. She represents the world's temptations, but with Great-Heart as their guide, she is unable to sway Christiana and her group of pilgrims.

more the kingdom of darkness grows. Oh, misery of miseries, that we see the professed friends of Jesus forsaking Him, and the enemies of His Cross and His cause mustering in increasing bands!

Psalm 38:20 *They also that render evil for good are mine adversaries; because I follow the thing that good is.*

EXPOSITION: **Verse 20.** *They also that render evil for good are mine adversaries.* Such would a wise man wish his enemies to be. Why should we seek to be beloved of such graceless souls? It is a fine plea against our enemies when we can without injustice declare them to be like the devil, whose nature it is to render evil for good. *Because I follow the thing that good is.* If men hate us for this reason we may rejoice to bear it: their wrath is the unconscious homage which vice renders to virtue. This verse is not inconsistent with the writer's previous confession; we may feel equally guilty before God, and yet be entirely innocent of any wrong to our fellow men. It is one sin to acknowledge the truth, quite another thing to submit to contradiction. The Lord may strike me justly, and yet I may be able to say to my fellow man, "Why do you strike me?"

Psalm 38:21 *Forsake me not, O Lord: O my God, be not far from me.*

EXPOSITION: **Verse 21.** *Forsake me not, O Lord.* Now is the time I need you most. When sickness, slander, and sin, all beset a saint, he requires the especial aid of Heaven, and he shall have it too. He is afraid of nothing while God is with him, and God is with him evermore. *O my God, be not far from me.* Withhold not the light of your near and dear love. Reveal yourself to me. Stand at my side. Let me feel that though friendless besides, I have a most gracious and all sufficient friend in you.

Psalm 38:22 *Make haste to help me, O LORD my salvation.*

EXPOSITION: **Verse 22.** *Make haste to help me.* Delay would prove destruction. The poor pleader was far gone and ready to expire; only speedy help would serve his turn. See how sorrow quickens the importunity of prayer! Here is one of the sweet results of affliction, it gives new life to our pleading, and drives us with eagerness to our God. *O Lord my salvation.* Not my Savior only, but my salvation. He who has the Lord on his side has salvation in present possession. Faith foresees the blessed issue of all her pleas and in this verse begins to ascribe to God the glory of the expected mercy. We shall not be left of the Lord. His grace will help us most opportunely, and in Heaven we shall see that we had not one trial too many, or one pang too severe. A sense of sin shall melt into the joy of salvation; grief shall lead on to gratitude, and gratitude to joy unspeakable and full of glory.

PSALM 39

PSALM 39:1–PSALM 39:13

Psalm 39:1 *I said, I will take heed to my ways, that I sin not with my tongue: I will keep my mouth with a bridle, while the wicked is before me.*

EXPOSITION: **Verse 1.** *I said.* I steadily resolved and registered a determination. In his great perplexity his greatest fear was lest he should sin; and, therefore, he cast about for the most likely method for avoiding it, and he determined to be silent. It is right excellent when a man can strengthen himself in a good course by the remembrance of a well and wisely formed resolve. "What I have written I have written," or what I have spoken I will perform, may prove a good strengthener to a man in a fixed course of right. *I will take heed to my ways.* To avoid sin one had need be very circumspect, and keep one's actions as with a guard or garrison. Unguarded ways are generally unholy ones. Heedless is another word for graceless. In times of sickness or other trouble we must watch against the sins peculiar to such trials, especially against murmuring and repining.

That I sin not with my tongue. Tongue sins are great sins; like sparks of fire ill words spread, and do great damage. If believers utter hard words of God in times of depression, the ungodly will take them up and use them as a justification for their sinful courses. If a man's own children rail at him, no wonder if his enemies' mouths are full of abuse. Our tongue always wants watching, for it is restive as an ill broken horse; but especially must we hold it in when the sharp cuts of the

Lord's rod excite it to rebel.

I will keep my mouth with a bridle, or more accurately, with a muzzle. The original does not so much mean a bridle to check the tongue as a muzzle to stop it altogether.

David was not quite so wise as our translation would make him; if he had resolved to be very guarded in his speech, it would have been altogether commendable; but when he went so far as to condemn himself to entire silence, "even from good," there must have been at least a little sullenness in his soul. In trying to avoid one fault, he fell into another. To use the tongue against God is a sin of commission, but not to use it at all involves an evident sin of omission. Commendable virtues may be followed so eagerly that we may fall into vices; to avoid Scylla[83] we run into Charybdis.[84]

While the wicked is before me. This qualifies the silence, and almost screens it from criticism, for bad men are so sure to misuse even our holiest speech, that it is as well not to cast any of our pearls before such swine; but what if the psalmist meant, "I was silent while I had the prosperity of the wicked in my thoughts," then we see the discontent and questioning of his mind, and the muzzled mouth indicates much that is not to be commended. Yet, if we blame we must also praise, for the highest wisdom suggests that when good men are bewildered with skeptical thoughts, they should not hasten to repeat them, but should fight out their inward battle upon its own battlefield. The firmest believers are exercised with unbelief, and it would be doing the devil's work with a vengeance if they were to publish abroad all their questionings and suspicions. If I have the fever myself, there is no reason why I should communicate it to my neighbors. If any on board the vessel of my soul are diseased, I will put my heart

---

83. Greek mythical being said to drown sailors.
84. In Greek mythology, said to be a shipwrecking whirlpool.

in quarantine, and allow none to go on shore in the boat of speech until I have a clean bill of health.

Psalm 39:2 *I was dumb with silence, I held my peace, even from good; and my sorrow was stirred.*

EXPOSITION: **Verse 2.** *I was dumb with silence.* He was as strictly speechless as if he had been tongue less—not a word escaped him. He was as silent as the dumb. *I held my peace, even from good.* Neither bad nor good escaped his lips. Perhaps he feared that if he began to talk at all, he would be sure to speak amiss, and, therefore, he totally abstained. It was an easy, safe, and effectual way of avoiding sin, if it did not involve a neglect of the duty which he owed to God to speak well of His name. Our divine Lord was silent before the wicked, but not altogether so, for before Pontius Pilate He witnessed a good confession, and asserted His kingdom. A sound course of action may be pushed to the extreme, and become a fault.

And my sorrow was stirred. Inward grief was made to work and ferment by want of vent. The pent up floods are swollen and agitated. Utterance is the natural outlet for the heart's anguish, and silence is, therefore, both an aggravation of the evil and a barrier against its cure. In such a case the resolve to hold one's peace needs powerful backing and even this is most likely to give way when grief rushes upon the soul. Before a flood gathering in force and foaming for outlet the strongest banks are likely to be swept away. Nature may do her best to silence the expression of discontent, but unless grace comes to her rescue, she will be sure to succumb.

Psalm 39:3 *My heart was hot within me, while I was musing the fire burned: then spake I with my tongue,*

EXPOSITION: **Verse 3.** *My heart was hot within me.* The friction of inward thoughts produced an intense mental heat. The door of his heart was shut, and with the fire of sorrow burning within, the chamber of his soul soon grew unbearable with heat. Silence is an awful thing for a sufferer; it is the surest method to produce madness. Mourner, tell your sorrow; do it first and most fully to God, but even to pour it out before some wise and godly friend is far from being wasted breath. *While I was musing the fire burned.* As he thought upon the ease of the wicked and his own daily affliction, he could not unravel the mystery of providence, and therefore he became greatly agitated. While his heart was musing it was fusing, for the subject was confusing. It became harder every moment to be quiet; his volcanic soul was tossed with an inward ocean of fire, and heaved to and fro with a mental earthquake; and eruption was imminent, the burning lava must pour forth in a fiery stream. *Then spake I with my tongue.* The original is grandly laconic. "I spake." The muzzled tongue burst all its bonds. The gag was hurled away. Misery, like murder, will out. You can silence praise, but anguish is clamorous. Resolve or no resolve, heed or no heed, sin or no sin, the impetuous torrent forced for itself a channel and swept away every restraint.

Psalm 39:4 *Lord, make me to know mine end, and the measure of my days, what it is: that I may know how frail I am.*

EXPOSITION: **Verse 4.** *Lord.* It is well that the vent of his soul was toward God and not towards man. Oh! if my swelling heart must speak, Lord let it speak with you; even if there is too much of natural heat in what I say, you will be more patient with me than man, and upon your purity it can cast no stain; whereas if I speak to my fellows, they may harshly rebuke me or else learn evil from my petulance. *Make me to know mine end.* Did he mean the same as Elias in his agony, "Let me die, I am no better than my father?" Perhaps so. At any rate, he rashly and petulantly desired to know the end of his wretched life that he might begin to reckon the days until death would put a finish to his woe. Impatience would pry between the folded leaves. As if there were no other comfort to be had, unbelief would hide itself in the grave and sleep itself into oblivion.

David was neither the first nor the last who have spoken unadvisedly in prayer. Yet, there is a better meaning: the psalmist wanted to know more of the shortness of life that he might better bear its transient ills, and herein we may safely kneel with him, uttering the same petition. That there is no end to its misery is the hell of hell; that there is an end to life's sorrow is the hope of all who have a hope beyond the grave. God is the best teacher of the divine philosophy which looks for an expected end. They, who see death through the Lord's glass, see a fair sight, which makes them forget the evil of life in foreseeing the end of life. *And the measure of my days.* David wanted to be assured that his days would be soon over and his trials with them; he wanted to be taught anew that life is measured out to us by wisdom, and is not a matter of chance. As the trader measures his cloth by inches, and ells,[85] and yards, so with scrupulous accuracy is life measured out to man.

That I may know how frail I am, or when I shall cease to be. Alas, poor human nature, dear as life is, man quarrels with God at such a rate that he would sooner cease to be than bear the Lord's appointment. Such pettishness in a saint! Let us wait until we are in a like position, and we shall do

---

85. About 45 inches.

no better. The ship on the stocks wonders that the barque[86] springs a leak, but when it has tried the high seas, it marvels that its timbers hold together in such storms. David's case is not recorded for our imitation, but for our learning.

Psalm 39:5 *Behold, thou hast made my days as an handbreadth; and mine age is as nothing before thee: verily every man at his best state is altogether vanity. Selah.*

EXPOSITION: **Verse 5.** *Behold, thou hast made my days as an handbreadth.* Upon consideration, the psalmist finds little room to bewail the length of life, but rather to bemoan its shortness. What changeful creatures we are! One moment we cry to be rid of existence, and the next instant beg to have it prolonged! A handbreadth is one of the shortest natural measures, being the breadth of four fingers; such is the brevity of life, by divine appointment; God has made it so, fixing the period in wisdom. The "behold" calls us to attention; to some the thoughts of life's hastiness will bring the most acute pain, to others the most solemn earnestness. How well should those live who are to live so little! Is my earthly pilgrimage so brief? Then let me watch every step of it so that in the little of time there may be much of grace.

And mine age is as nothing before thee. So short as not to amount to an entity. Think of eternity, and an angel is as a newborn babe, the world a fresh blown bubble, the sun a spark just fallen from the fire, and man a nullity.[87] Before the Eternal, all the age of frail man is less than one ticking of a clock. *Verily, every man at his best state is altogether vanity.* This is the surest truth, that nothing about man is either sure or true. Take man at his best, he is but a man,

---

86. Boat
87. Nothingness

and a man is a mere breath, unsubstantial as the wind. Man is settled, as the margin has it, and by divine decree it is settled that he shall not be settled. He is constant only in inconstancy. His vanity is his only verity; his best, of which he is vain, is but vain; and this is verily true of every man, that everything about him is every way fleeting. This is sad news for those whose treasures are beneath the moon; those whose glorying is in themselves may well hang the flag half mast; but those whose best estate is settled upon them in Christ Jesus in the land of unfading flowers, may rejoice that it is no vain thing in which they trust.

Psalm 39:6 *Surely every man walketh in a vain shew: surely they are disquieted in vain: he heapeth up riches, and knoweth not who shall gather them.*

EXPOSITION: **Verse 6.** *Surely every man walketh in a vain shew.* Life is but a passing pageant. This alone is sure, that nothing is sure. All around us shadows mock us; we walk among them, and too many live for them as if the mocking images were substantial; acting their borrowed parts with zeal fit only to be spent on realities, and lost upon the phantoms of this passing scene. Worldly men walk like travelers in a mirage, deluded, duped, deceived, soon to be filled with disappointment and despair. *Surely they are disquieted in vain.* Men fret, and fume, and worry, and all for mere nothing. They are shadows pursuing shadows, while death pursues them. He who toils and contrives, and wearies himself for gold, for fame, for rank, even if he wins his desire, finds at the end his labor is lost. It all vanished when he awakes to the world of reality, for like the treasure of the miser's dream, it is not real.

Read well this text, and then listen to the clamor of the market, the hum of the exchange, the din of the city streets, and remember that all this noise (for so the word means), this breach of quiet, is made about unsubstantial, fleeting vanities. Broken rest, anxious fear, over worked brain, failing mind, lunacy, these are the steps in the process of disquieting with many, and all to be rich, or, in other words, to load one's self with the thick clay; clay, too, which a man must leave so soon.

He heapeth up riches, and knoweth not who shall gather them. He misses often the result of his ventures, for there are many slips between the cup and the lips. His wheat is sheaved, but an interloping robber bears it away—as so often happens with the poor Eastern husbandman; or, the wheat is even stored, but the invader feasts thereon. Many work for others all unknown to them. This verse especially refers to those who work the fields and gather the crops for their livelihood only to have them given to the rich who gather but give stingily. We know not our heirs, for our children die, and strangers fill the old ancestral halls; estates change hands, and entail, though riveted with a thousand bonds, yields to the corroding power of time. Men rise up early and sit up late to build a house, and then the stranger tramps along its passages, laughs in its chambers, and forgetful of its first builder, calls it all his own. Here is one of the evils under the sun for which no remedy can be prescribed.

Psalm 39:7 *And now, Lord, what wait I for? my hope is in thee.*

EXPOSITION: Verse 7. *And now, Lord, what wait I for?"* What is there in these phantoms to enchant me? Why should I linger where the prospect is so uninviting, and the present so trying? It would be worse than vanity to linger in the abodes of sorrow to gain a heritage of emptiness. The psalmist, therefore, turns to his God, in disgust of all things else; he has thought on the world and all things in it, and is relieved by knowing that such vain things are all passing away; he has cut all cords which bound him to Earth, and is ready to sound "Boot and saddle, up and away."

My hope is in thee. The Lord is self existent and true, and therefore worthy of the confidence of men; He will live when all the creatures die, and His fullness will abide when all second causes are exhausted; to Him, therefore, let us direct our expectation, and on Him let us rest our confidence. Away from sand to rock let all wise builders turn themselves, for if not today, yet surely before long, a storm will rise before which nothing will be able to stand but that which has the lasting element of faith in God to cement it. David had but one hope, and that hope entered within the veil, hence he brought his vessel to safe anchorage, and after a little drifting all was peace.

Psalm 39:8 *Deliver me from all my transgressions: make me not the reproach of the foolish.*

EXPOSITION: Verse 8. *Deliver me from all my transgressions.* How fair a sign it is when the psalmist no longer harps upon his sorrows, but begs freedom from his sins! What is sorrow when compared with sin! Let but the poison of sin be gone from the cup, and we need not fear its gall, for the bitter will act medicinally. None can deliver a man from his transgression but the blessed One who is called Jesus, because He saves His people from their sins; and when He once works this great deliverance for a man from the cause, the consequences are sure to disappear too. The thorough cleansing desired is well worthy of note: to be saved from some transgressions would be of small benefit; total and perfect deliverance is needed. *Make me not the reproach of the foolish.* The wicked are the foolish here meant: such are always on the watch for the faults of saints, and at once make them the theme of ridicule. It is a wretched thing for a man to be suffered to make himself the butt of unholy scorn by apostasy from the right way. Alas, how many have thus exposed themselves to well deserved reproach! Sin and shame go together, and from both David desires to be preserved.

Psalm 39:9 *I was dumb, I opened not my mouth; because thou didst it.*

EXPOSITION: **Verse 9.** *I was dumb, I opened not my mouth; because thou didst it.* This would have been far clearer if it had been rendered, "I am silenced, I will not open my mouth." Here we have a nobler silence, purged of all sullenness, and sweetened with submission. Nature failed to muzzle the mouth, but grace achieved the work in the worthiest manner. How like in appearance may two very different things appear! Silence is ever silence, but it may be sinful in one case and saintly in another. What a reason for hushing every murmuring thought is the reflection, "because thou didst it."! It is His right to do as He wills, and He always wills to do that which is wisest and kindest; why should I then arraign His dealings? No, if it is indeed the Lord, let Him do what seems good to Him.

Psalm 39:10 *Remove thy stroke away from me: I am consumed by the blow of thine hand.*

EXPOSITION: **Verse 10.** *Remove thy stroke away from me.* Silence from all repining did not prevent the voice of prayer, which must never cease. In all probability the Lord would grant the psalmist's petition, for He usually removes affliction when we are resigned to it; if we kiss the rod, our

Father always burns it. When we are still, the rod is soon still. It is quite consistent with resignation to pray for the removal of a trial. David was fully acquiescent in the divine will, and yet found it in his heart to pray for deliverance; indeed, it was while he was rebellious that he was prayerless about his trial, and only when he became submissive did he plead for mercy. *I am consumed by the blow of thine hand.* Good pleas may be found in our weakness and distress. It is well to show our Father the bruises which His scourge has made, for peradventure His fatherly pity will bind His hands, and move Him to comfort us in His bosom. It is not to consume us, but to consume our sins, that the Lord aims at in His chastisements.

Psalm 39:11 *When thou with rebukes dost correct man for iniquity, thou makest his beauty to consume away like a moth: surely every man is vanity. Selah.*

EXPOSITION: **Verse 11.** *When thou with rebukes dost correct man for iniquity.* God does not trifle with His rod; He uses it because of sin, and with a view to whip us from it; hence He means His strokes to be felt, and felt they are. *Thou makest his beauty to consume away like a moth.* As the moth tears the substance of the fabric, mars all its beauty, and leaves it worn out and worthless, so do the chastisements of God show to us our folly, weakness, and nothingness, and make us feel ourselves to be as worn out vestures, worthless and useless. Beauty must be a poor thing when a moth can consume it and a rebuke can mar it. All our desires and delights are wretched moth eaten things when the Lord visits us in His anger. *Surely every man is vanity.* He is as Joseph Trapp[88] wittily says "a curious picture

---

88. English clergyman.

of nothing." He is unsubstantial as his own breath, a vapor which appears for a little while, and then vanishes away. *Selah*. Well may this truth bring us to a pause, like the dead body of Amasa, which, lying in the way, stopped the hosts of Joab. [See 2 Samuel 20:10-12.]

Psalm 39:12 *Hear my prayer, O Lord, and give ear unto my cry; hold not thy peace at my tears: for I am a stranger with thee, and a sojourner, as all my fathers were.*

EXPOSITION: **Verse 12.** *Hear my prayer, O Lord.* Drown not my pleadings with the sound of your strokes. You have heard the clamor of my sins, Lord; hear the laments of my prayers. *And give ear unto my cry.* Here is an advance in intensity: a cry is more vehement, pathetic, and impassioned, than a prayer. The main thing was to have the Lord's ear and heart. *Hold not thy peace at my tears.* This is a yet higher degree of importunate pleading. Who can withstand tears, which are the irresistible weapons of weakness? How often women, children, beggars, and sinners, have taken themselves to tears as their last resort, and therewith have won the desire of their hearts! "This shower, blown up by tempest of the soul,"[89] falls not in vain. Tears speak more eloquently than ten thousand tongues; they act as keys upon tender hearts, and mercy denies them nothing, if through them the weeper looks to richer drops, even to the blood of Jesus. When our sorrows pull up the sluices [tears] of our eyes, God will before long interpose and turn our mourning into joy. Long may He be quiet as though He regarded not, but the hour of deliverance will come, and come like the morning when the dewdrops are plentiful. *For I am a stranger with thee.*

---

89. From Act 5 of "The Tempest" by William Shakespeare

Not to you, but with you. Like you, my Lord, a stranger among the sons of men, an alien from my mother's children. God made the world, sustains it, and owns it, and yet men treat Him as though He were a foreign intruder; and as they treat the Master, so do they deal with the servants. It is no surprising thing that we should be unknown. These words may also mean, I share the hospitality of God like a stranger entertained by a generous host. Israel was bidden to deal tenderly with the stranger, and the God of Israel has in much compassion treated us poor aliens with unbounded liberality.

And a sojourner, as all my fathers were. They knew that this was not their rest; they passed through life in pilgrim fashion, they used the world as travelers use an inn, and even so do we. Why should we dream of rest on Earth when our fathers' sepulchers are before our eyes? If they had been immortal, their sons would have had an abiding city this side of the tomb; but as the sires were mortal, so must their offspring pass away. All of our lineage, without exception, was passing pilgrims, and such are we. David uses the fleeting nature of our life as an argument for the Lord's mercy, and it is such a one as God will regard. We show pity to poor pilgrims, and so will the Lord.

Psalm 39:13 *O spare me, that I may recover strength, before I go hence, and be no more.*

EXPOSITION: Verse 13. *O spare me.* Put away your rod. Turn away your angry face. Give me breathing time. Do not kill me. *That I may recover strength.* Let me have sufficient cessation from pain, to be able to take repose and nourishment, and so aid my wasted frame. He expects to die soon, but begs a little respite from sorrow, so as to be able to rally and once more enjoy life before its close. *Before I go hence, and be no more.* So far as this world is concerned, death is a being no more; such a state awaits us, we are hurrying onward towards it. May the short interval which divides us from it be gilded with the sunlight of our heavenly Father's love. It is sad to be an invalid from the cradle to the grave, far worse to be under the Lord's chastisements month after month, but what are these compared with the endurance of the endless punishment threatened to those who die in their sins!

PSALM 40
PSALM 40:1–PSALM 40:17

Psalm 40:1 *I waited patiently for the Lord; and he inclined unto me, and heard my cry.*

EXPOSITION: Verse 1. *I waited patiently for the Lord.* Patient waiting upon God was a special characteristic of our Lord Jesus. Impatience never lingered in His heart, much less escaped His lips. All through His agony in the Garden of Gethsemane, His trial of cruel mocking before Herod and Pilate, and His passion on the Cross, He waited in omnipotence of patience. No glance of wrath, no word of murmuring, no deed of vengeance came from God's patient Lamb; He waited and waited on; was patient, and patient to perfection, far excelling all others who have according to their measure glorified God in the fires. Job on the dunghill does not equal Jesus on the Cross. The Christ of God wears the imperial crown among the patient. Did the Only Begotten wait, and shall we be petulant and rebellious?

And he inclined unto me, and heard my cry. Neither Jesus the head, nor any one of the members of His body, shall ever wait upon the Lord in vain. Mark the figure of inclining, as though the suppliant cried out of the lowest depression, and condescending love stooped to hear His feeble moans. What a marvel is it that our Lord Jesus should have to cry as we do, and wait as we do, and should receive the Father's help after the same process of faith and pleading as must be gone through by ourselves! The Savior's prayers among the midnight mountains and in Gethsemane expound this verse.

The Son of David was brought very low, but He rose to victory; and here He teaches us how to conduct our conflicts so as to succeed after the same glorious pattern of triumph. Let us arm ourselves with the same mind; a multitude of patience, the armor of prayer, and girded with faith, and let us maintain the Holy War.

Psalm 40:2 *He brought me up also out of an horrible pit, out of the miry clay, and set my feet upon a rock, and established my goings.*

EXPOSITION: Verse 2. *He brought me up also out of an horrible pit.* When our Lord bore in His own person the terrible curse which was due to sin, He was so cast down as to be like a prisoner in a deep, dark, fearful dungeon, amid whose horrible glooms the captive heard a noise as of rushing torrents, while overhead resounded the tramp of furious foes. Our Lord in His anguish was like a captive in the oubliettes[90], forgotten of all mankind, immured amid horror, darkness, and desolation. Yet the Lord Jehovah made Him to ascend from all His abasement; He retraced His steps from that deep hell of anguish into which He had been cast as our substitute. He, who thus delivered our surety in extremis, will not fail to liberate us from our far lighter griefs.

Out of the miry clay. The sufferer was as one who cannot find a foothold, but slips and sinks. The figure indicates not only positive misery as in the former figure, but the absence of solid comfort by which sorrow might have been rendered supportable. Once give man a good foothold, and a burden is greatly lightened, but to be burdened and placed on slimy, slippery clay, is to be tried doubly. Reader, with humble gratitude, adore the dear Redeemer who, for your

---

90. A dungeon with the only exit being a trap door in the ceiling.

sake, was deprived of all consolation while surrounded with every form of misery; remark His gratitude at being born up amid His arduous labors and sufferings, and if you, too, have experienced the divine help, be sure to join your Lord in this song.

And set my feet upon a rock, and established my goings. The Redeemer's work is done. He reposes on the firm ground of His accomplished engagements; He can never suffer again; forever He does reign in glory. What a comfort to know that Jesus our Lord and Savior stands on a sure foundation in all that He is and does for us, and His goings forth in love are not liable to be cut short by failure in years to come, for God has fixed Him firmly. He is forever and eternally able to save unto the uttermost them that come unto God by Him, seeing that in the highest heavens He ever lives to make intercession for them. Jesus is the true Joseph taken from the pit to be Lord of all. It is something more than a "sip of sweetness" to remember that if we are cast like our Lord into the lowest pit of shame and sorrow, we shall by faith rise to stand on the same elevated, sure, and everlasting rock of divine favor and faithfulness.

Psalm 40:3 *And he hath put a new song in my mouth, even praise unto our God: many shall see it, and fear, and shall trust in the Lord.*

EXPOSITION: Verse 3. *And he hath put a new song in my mouth, even praise unto our God.* At the Passover, before His passion, our Lord sang one of the grand old Psalms of praise; but what is the music of His heart now, in the midst of His redeemed! What a song is that in which His glad heart forever leads the chorus of the elect! Not Miriam's tabor nor Moses' triumphant hymn over Miriam's chivalry can for a moment rival that ever new and exulting song. Justice magnified and grace victorious; hell subdued and Heaven glorified; death destroyed and immortality established; sin overthrown and righteousness resplendent; what a theme for a hymn in that day when our Lord drinks the red wine new with all of us in our heavenly Father's Kingdom!

Even on Earth, and before His great passion, He foresaw the joy which was set before Him, and was sustained by the prospect. Our God. The God of Jesus, the God of Israel, and as Jesus said "my God and your God." [See John 20:17.] How we will praise Him, but ah! Jesus will be the chief player on our stringed instruments; He will lead the solemn hallelujah which shall go up from the sacramental host redeemed by blood.

Many shall see it, and fear, and shall trust in the Lord. A multitude that no man can number shall see the griefs and triumphs of Jesus, shall tremble because of their sinful rejection of Him, and then through grace shall receive faith and shall trust in Jehovah. Here is our Lord's reward. Here is the assurance which makes preachers bold and workers persevering. Reader, are you one among the many? Note the way of salvation, a sight, a fear, a trust! Do you know what these mean by possessing and practicing them in your own soul? Trusting in the Lord is the evidence, in fact, the essence of salvation. He who is a true believer is evidently redeemed from the dominion of sin and Satan.

Psalm 40:4 *Blessed is that man that maketh the Lord his trust, and respecteth not the proud, nor such as turn aside to lies.*

EXPOSITION: Verse 4. *Blessed.* This is an exclamation similar to that of the first Psalm, "Oh, the happiness of the man." God's blessings are emphatic, "I wish that he whom you bless is blessed," indeed and in very truth.

Is that man that makes the Lord his trust. Faith obtains promises. A simple single-eyed confidence in God is the sure mark of blessedness. A man may be as poor as Lazarus, as hated as Mordecai, as sick as Hezekiah, as lonely as Elijah, but while his hand of faith can keep its hold on God, none of his outward afflictions can prevent his being numbered among the blessed. But the wealthiest and most prosperous man who has no faith is accursed, be he who he may.

And respecteth not the proud. The proud expect all men to bow down and do them reverence, as if the worship of the golden calves were again set up in Israel; but believing men are too noble to honor mere money bags, or cringe before bombastic dignity. The righteous pay their respect to humble goodness, rather than to inflated self-confidence. Our Lord Jesus was in this our bright example. No flattery of kings and great ones ever fell from His lips; He gave no honor to dishonorable men. The haughty were never His favorites. *Nor such as turn aside to lies.* Heresies and idolatries are lies, and so are avarice, worldliness, and pleasure seeking. Woe to those who follow such deceptions. Our Lord was ever both the truth and the lover of truth, and the father of lies had no part in Him. We must never pay deference to apostates, time servers[91], and false teachers; they are trouble makers, and the more we purge ourselves of them the better; God preserves from all error in creed and practice they who are blessed by Him. Judged by this verse, many apparently happy persons must be the reverse of blessed, for anything in the shape of a purse, a fine equipage, or a wealthy establishment, commands their reverence, whether the owner is a rogue or a saint, an idiot or a philosopher. Truly, if the arch fiend of hell was to have a carriage and

91. One who conforms to current ways and opinions to his own advantage.

pair of horses, and live like a lord, he would have thousands who would court his acquaintance.

Psalm 40:5 *Many, O Lord my God, are thy wonderful works which thou hast done, and thy thoughts which are to us-ward: they cannot be reckoned up in order unto thee: if I would declare and speak of them, they are more than can be numbered.*

EXPOSITION: Verse 5. *Many, O Lord my God, are thy wonderful works which thou hast done.* Creation, providence, and redemption, teem with wonders as the sea with life. Our special attention is called by this passage to the marvels which cluster around the Cross and flash from it. The accomplished redemption achieves many ends, and compasses a variety of designs; the outgoings of the atonement are not to be reckoned up, the influences of the Cross reach further than the beams of the sun. Wonders of grace beyond all enumeration take their rise from the Cross; adoption, pardon, justification, and a long chain of godlike miracles of love proceed from it. Note that our Lord here speaks of the Lord as "my God." The man Christ Jesus claimed for himself and us a covenant relationship with Jehovah. Let our interest in our God be ever to us our peculiar treasure.

And thy thoughts which are to us-ward. The divine thoughts march with the divine acts, for it is not according the God's wisdom to act without deliberation and counsel. All the divine thoughts are good and gracious towards His elect. God's thoughts of love are very many, very wonderful, and very practical! Muse on them, dear reader; no sweeter subject ever occupied your mind. God's thoughts of you are many; let not yours be few in return. *They cannot be reckoned up in order unto thee.* Their sum is so great as to forbid a like analysis and numeration. Human minds fail to measure, or to arrange in order, the Lord's ways and thoughts; and it must always be so, for He has said, "As the heavens are higher than the earth, so are my ways higher than your ways, and my thoughts than your thoughts." [See Isaiah 55:9.] No maze to lose oneself in like the labyrinth of love. How sweet to be outdone, overcome and overwhelmed by the astonishing grace of the Lord our God! *If I would declare and speak of them,* and surely this should be the occupation of my tongue at all seasonable opportunities, they *are more than can be numbered;* far beyond all human arithmetic they are multiplied; thoughts from all eternity, thoughts of my fall, my restoration, my redemption, my conversion, my pardon, my upholding, my perfecting, my eternal reward; the list is too long for writing, and the value of the mercies too great for estimation. Yet, if we cannot show forth all the works of the Lord, let us not make this an excuse for silence; for our Lord, who is in this our best example, often spoke of the tender thoughts of the great Father.

Psalm 40:6 *Sacrifice and offering thou didst not desire; mine ears hast thou opened: burnt offering and sin offering hast thou not required.*

EXPOSITION: Verse 6. Here we enter upon one of the most wonderful passages in the whole of the Old Testament, a passage in which the incarnate Son of God is seen not through a glass darkly, but as it were face to face. *Sacrifice and offering thou didst not desire.* In themselves considered, and for their own sakes, the Lord saw nothing satisfactory in the various offerings of the ceremonial law. Neither the victim pouring forth its blood, nor the fine flour rising in smoke from the altar, could yield content to Jehovah's mind; He cared not for the flesh of bulls or of goats, neither had He pleasure in corn and wine, and oil. Typically these offerings had their worth, but when Jesus, the Antitype, came into the world, they ceased to be of value, as candles are of no use when the sun has arisen. *Mine ears hast thou opened.* Our Lord was quick to hear and perform His Father's will; His ears were as if excavated down to His soul; they were not closed up like Isaac's wells, which the Philistines filled up, but clear passages down to the fountains of His soul. The prompt obedience of our Lord is here the first idea. There is, however, no reason whatever to reject the notion that the digging of the ear here intended may refer to the boring of the ear of the servant, who refused out of love to his master to take his liberty, at the year of jubilee; his perforated ear, the token of perpetual service, is a true picture of our blessed Lord's fidelity to His Father's business, and His love to His Father's children.

Jesus irrevocably gave himself up to be the servant of servants for our sake and God's glory. The Septuagint, from which Paul quoted, has translated this passage, "A body hast thou prepared me:" [See Hebrews 10:5.]: how this reading arose it is not easy to imagine, but since apostolical authority has sanctioned the variation, we accept it as no mistake, but as an instance of various readings equally inspired. In any case, the passage represents the Only Begotten as coming into the world equipped for service; and in a real and material body, by actual life and death, putting aside all the shadows of the Mosaic Law. *Burnt offering and sin offering hast thou not required.* Two other forms of offerings are here mentioned; tokens of gratitude and sacrifices for sin as typically presented are set aside; neither the general nor the private offerings are any longer demanded. What need of mere emblems when the substance itself is present? We learn from this verse that Jehovah values far more the obedience of the heart than all the imposing performances of ritualistic worship; and that our expiation from sin comes not to us as the result of an elaborate ceremonial, but as the effect of our great Substitute's obedience to the will of Jehovah.

Psalm 40:7 *Then said I, Lo, I come: in the volume of the book it is written of me,*

EXPOSITION: **Verse 7.** *Then said I,* that is to say, when it was clearly seen that man's misery could not be remedied by sacrifices and offerings. It being certain that the mere images of atonement and the bare symbols of propitiation were of no avail, the Lord Jesus, in propria persona,[92] intervened. O blessed "then said I." Lord, ever give us to hear and feed on such living words as these, so peculiarly and personally your own. *Lo, I come.* Behold, O heavens, and Earth, and you places under the Earth! Here is something worthy of your most intense gaze. Sit down and watch with earnestness, for the invisible God comes in the likeness of sinful flesh, and as an infant the Infinite hangs at a virgin's breast! Immanuel did not send but came; He came in His own personality, in all that constituted His essential self He came forth from the ivory palaces to the abodes of misery; He came promptly at the destined hour; He came with sacred alacrity as one freely offering himself.

In the volume of the book it is written of me. In the eternal decree it is thus recorded. The mystic roll of predestination which providence gradually unfolds contained within it, to the Savior's knowledge, a written covenant, that in the fullness of time, the divine I, should descend to Earth to accomplish a purpose which the catacombs of bullocks and rams could not achieve. What a privilege to find our names written in the Book of Life, and what an honor, since the name of Jesus heads the page! Our Lord had respect to His

---

92. On one's own person.

ancient covenant engagements, and herein He teaches us to be scrupulously just in keeping our word; have we so promised, it is so written in the book of remembrance? Then let us never be defaulters.

Psalm 40:8 *I delight to do thy will, O my God: yea, thy law is within my heart.*

EXPOSITION: **Verse 8.** *I delight to do thy will, O my God.* Our blessed Lord alone could completely do the will of God. The law is too broad for such poor creatures as we are to hope to fulfill it to the uttermost: but Jesus not only did the Father's will, but found a delight therein. From old eternity He had desired the work set before Him; in His human life He kept to His purpose until He reached the baptism of agony in which He magnified the law. He chose the Father's will, and set aside His own even in Gethsemane. Herein is the essence of obedience, namely, in the soul's cheerful devotion to God: and our Lord's obedience, which is our righteousness, is in no measure lacking in this eminent quality. Notwithstanding His measureless griefs, our Lord found delight in His work, and for "the joy that was set before him he endured the cross, despising the shame." [See Hebrews 12:2.] *Yea, thy law is within my heart.* No outward, formal devotion was rendered by Christ; His heart was in His work, holiness was His element, the Father's will His meat and drink. We must, each of us, be like our Lord in this, or we shall lack the evidence of being His disciples. Where there is no heart work, no pleasure, no delight in God's law, there can be no acceptance. Let the devout reader adore the Savior for the spontaneous and hearty manner in which He undertook the great work of our salvation.

Psalm 40:9 *I have preached righteousness in the great congregation: lo, I have not refrained my lips, O Lord, thou knowest.*

EXPOSITION: **Verse 9.** *I have preached righteousness in the great congregation.* The purest morality and the highest holiness were preached by Jesus. Righteousness divine was His theme. Our Lord's whole life was a sermon, eloquent beyond compare, and it is heard each day by myriads. Moreover, He never shunned in His ministry to declare the whole counsel of God; God's great plan of righteousness He plainly set forth. He taught openly in the temple, and was not ashamed to be a faithful and a true witness. He was the great evangelist; the master of itinerant preachers; the head of the clan of open air missionaries. O servants of the Lord, hide not your lights, but reveal to others what your God has revealed to you; and especially by your lives testify for holiness, be champions for the right, both in word and deed.

Lo, I have not refrained my lips, O Lord, thou knowest. Never either from love of ease, of fear of men, did the Great Teacher's lips become closed. He was instant in season and out of season. The poor listened to Him, and princes heard His rebuke; Publicans rejoiced at Him, and Pharisees raged, but to them both He proclaimed the truth from Heaven. It is well for a tried believer when he can appeal to God and call Him to witness that he has not been ashamed to bear witness for Him; for rest assured if we are not ashamed to confess our God, He will never be ashamed to own us. Yet what a wonder is here, that the Son of God should plead, just as we plead, and urge just such arguments as would befit the mouths of his diligent ministers! How truly is He "made like unto his brethren." [See Hebrews 2:17.]

Psalm 40:10 *I have not hid thy righteousness within my heart; I have declared thy faithfulness and thy salvation: I have not concealed thy lovingkindness and thy truth from the great congregation.*

EXPOSITION: **Verse 10.** *I have not hid thy righteousness within my heart.* On the contrary, "Never man spake like this man." [See John 7:46.] God's divine plan of making men righteous was well known to Him, and He plainly taught it. What was in our great Master's heart He poured forth in holy eloquence from His lips. The doctrine of righteousness by faith He spoke with great simplicity of speech. Law and gospel equally found in Him a clear expositor. *I have declared thy faithfulness and thy salvation.* Jehovah's fidelity to His promises and His grace in saving believers were declared by the Lord Jesus on many occasions, and are blessedly blended in the gospel which He came to preach. God, faithful to His own character, law and threatenings, and yet saving sinners, is a peculiar revelation of the gospel. God faithful to the saved ones evermore is the joy of the followers of Christ Jesus.

I have not concealed thy lovingkindness and thy truth from the great congregation. The tender as well as the stern attributes of God, our Lord Jesus fully unveiled. Concealment was far from the Great Apostle of our profession. Cowardice He never exhibited, hesitancy never weakened His language. He who as a child of twelve years spoke in the temple among the doctors, and afterward preached to five thousand at Gennesaret. [See Luke 5:1.] He spoke to the vast crowds at Jerusalem on that great day, the last day of the feast, He was always ready to proclaim the name of the Lord, and could never be charged with unholy silence. He could be silent when prophecy so demanded and patience suggested, but otherwise, preaching was His meat and His drink, and He kept back nothing which would be profitable to His disciples.

This in the day of His trouble, according to this Psalm, He used as a plea for divine aid. He had been faithful to His God, and now begs the Lord to be faithful to Him. Let every silent professor of Christianity, tongue tied by sinful shame, think to himself how little he will be able to plead after this fashion in the day of his distress.

Psalm 40:11 *Withhold not thou thy tender mercies from me, O Lord: let thy lovingkindness and thy truth continually preserve me.*

EXPOSITION: Verse 11. *Withhold not thou thy tender mercies from me, O Lord.* Alas! these were to be for awhile withheld from our Lord while on the accursed tree, but meanwhile in His great agony He seeks for gentle dealing; and the coming of the angel to strengthen Him was a clear answer to His prayer. He had been blessed aforetime in the desert, and now at the entrance of the valley of the shadow of death, like a true, trustful, and experienced man, He utters a holy, plaintive desire for the tenderness of Heaven. He had not withheld His testimony to God's truth, now in return He begs His Father not to withhold His compassion. This verse might more correctly be read as a declaration of His confidence that help would not be refused; but whether we view this utterance as the cry of prayer, or the avowal of faith, in either case it is instructive to us who take our suffering Lord for an example, and it proves to us how thoroughly He was made like unto His brethren. *Let thy lovingkindness and thy truth continually preserve me.* He had preached both of these, and now He asks for an experience of them, that He might be kept in the evil day and rescued from His enemies and His afflictions. Nothing endears our Lord to us more than to hear Him thus pleading with "strong crying and tears unto him who was able to save." [See Hebrews 5:6-8.] O

Lord Jesus, in our nights of wrestling we will remember you.

Psalm 40:12 *For innumerable evils have compassed me about: mine iniquities have taken hold upon me, so that I am not able to look up; they are more than the hairs of mine head: therefore my heart faileth me.*

EXPOSITION: Verse 12. *For innumerable evils have compassed me about.* On every side He was beset with evils; countless woes environed the great Substitute for our sins. Our sins were innumerable, and so were His griefs. There was no escape for us from our iniquities, and there was no escape for Him from the woes which we deserved. From every quarter evils accumulated around the blessed One, although in His heart evil found no place. *Mine iniquities have taken hold upon me, so that I am not able to look up.* He had no sin, but sins were laid on Him, and He took them as if they were His. "He was made sin for us." The transfer of sin to the Savior was real, and produced in Him as man the horror which forbade Him to look into the face of God, bowing Him down with crushing anguish and woe intolerable.

O my soul, what would your sins have done for you eternally if the Friend of sinners had not condescended to take them all upon himself? Oh, blessed Scripture! "The Lord hath made to meet upon him the iniquity of us all." [See Isaiah 53:6.] Oh, marvelous depth of love, which could lead the perfectly immaculate to stand in the sinner's place, and bear the horror of great trembling which sin must bring upon those conscious of it. *They are more than the hairs of mine head: therefore my heart faileth me.* The pains of the divine penalty were beyond compute, and the Savior's soul was so burdened with them, that He was sore amazed, and very heavy even unto a sweat of blood. His strength was gone, His spirits sank, and He was in an agony.

"Came at length the dreadful night.
Vengeance with its iron rod
Stood, and with collected might
Bruised the harmless Lamb of God,
See, my soul, thy Saviour see,
Prostrate in Gethsemane!"
"There my God bore all my guilt,
This through grace can be believed;
But the horrors which he felt
Are too vast to be conceived.
None can penetrate through thee,
Doleful, dark Gethsemane."

"Sins against a holy God;
Sins against his righteous laws;
Sins against his love, his blood;
Sins against his name and cause;
Sins immense as is the sea . . . Hide me,
O Gethsemane!"[93]

Psalm 40:13 *Be pleased, O Lord, to deliver me: O Lord, make haste to help me.*

EXPOSITION: Verse 13. *Be pleased, O Lord, to deliver me: O Lord, make haste to help me.* How touching! How humble! How plaintive! The words thrill us as we think that after this sort our Lord and Master prayed. His petition is not so much that the cup should pass away undrained, but that He should be sustained while drinking it, and set free from its power at the first fitting moment. He seeks deliverance and help; and He entreats that the help may not be slow in coming; this is after the manner of our pleadings. Is it not?

---

93. Hymn *"Gethsemane,"* written by Joseph Hart in 1750.

Note, reader, how our Lord was heard in that He feared, for there was after Gethsemane a calm endurance which made the fight as glorious as the victory.

Psalm 40:14 *Let them be ashamed and confounded together that seek after my soul to destroy it; let them be driven backward and put to shame that wish me evil.*

EXPOSITION: Verse 14. *Let them be ashamed and confounded together that seek after my soul to destroy it.* Whether we read this as a prayer or a prophecy it matters not, for the powers of sin, and death, and hell, may well be ashamed as they see the result of their malice for ever turned against themselves. It is to the infinite confusion of Satan that his attempts to destroy the Savior destroyed himself; the diabolical conclave who plotted in council are now all alike put to shame, for the Lord Jesus has met them at all points, and turned all their wisdom into foolishness. *Let them be driven backward and put to shame that wish me evil.* It is even so; the hosts of darkness are utterly put to the rout, and made a theme for holy derision forever and ever. How did they gloat over the thought of crushing the seed of the woman! But the Crucified has conquered, the Nazarene has laughed them to scorn, the dying Son of Man has become the death of death and hell's destruction. Forever blessed be His name.

Psalm 40:15 *Let them be desolate for a reward of their shame that say unto me, Aha, aha.*

EXPOSITION: Verse 15. *Let them be desolate,* or amazed; even as Jesus was desolate in His agony, so let His enemies be in their despair when He defeats them. The desolation caused in the hearts of evil spirits and evil men by envy, malice, chagrin, disappointment, and despair, shall be a fit recompense for their cruelty to the Lord when He was in their hands. *For a reward of their shame that say unto me, Aha, aha.* Did the foul fiend insult our Lord? Behold how shame is now his reward! Do wicked men today pour shame upon the name of the Redeemer? Their desolation shall avenge Him of His adversaries! Jesus is the gentle Lamb to all who seek mercy through His blood; but let despisers beware, for He is the Lion of the tribe of Judah, and "who shall rouse him up?" The Jewish rulers exulted and scornfully said, "Aha, aha;" but when the streets of Jerusalem ran like rivers deep with gore, "and the temple was utterly consumed," then their house was left unto them desolate, and the blood of the last of the prophets, according to their own desire, came upon themselves and upon their children. O ungodly reader, if such a person glance over this page, beware of persecuting Christ and His people, for God will surely avenge His own elect. Your "aha's" will cost you dearly. *It is hard for thee to kick against the pricks.* [See Acts 9:5.]

Psalm 40:16 *Let all those that seek thee rejoice and be glad in thee: let such as love thy salvation say continually, The Lord be magnified.*

EXPOSITION: Verse 16. *Let all those that seek thee, rejoice and be glad in thee.* We have done with Ebal and turn to Gerizim. Here our Lord pronounces benedictions on His people. Note who the blessed objects of His petition are: not all men, but some men, "I pray for them, I pray not for the world." [See John 17:9.] He pleads for seekers: the lowest in the kingdom, the babes of the family; those who have true desires, longing prayers, and consistent endeavors after God. Let seeking souls pluck up heart when they hear of this. What riches of grace that in His bitterest hour Jesus should remember the lambs of the flock! And what does He entreat for them? It is that they may be doubly glad, intensely happy, emphatically joyful, for such the repetition of terms implies. Jesus would have all seekers made happy, by finding what they seek after, and by winning peace through His grief. As deep as were His sorrows, so high would He have their joys. He groaned that we might sing, and was covered with a bloody sweat that we might be anointed with the oil of gladness.

Let such as love thy salvation say continually, The Lord be magnified. Another result of the Redeemer's passion is the promotion of the glory of God by those who gratefully delight in His salvation. Our Lord's desire should be our directory; we love with all our hearts His great salvation, let us then, with all our tongues proclaim the glory of God which is resplendent therein. Never let His praises cease. As the heart is warm with gladness let it incite the tongue to perpetual praise. If we cannot do what we would for the spread of the Kingdom of God, at least let us desire and pray for it. Be it ours to make God's glory the chief end of every breath and pulse. The suffering Redeemer regarded the consecration of His people to the service of Heaven as a grand result of His atoning death; it is the joy which was set before Him; that God is glorified as the reward of the Savior's travail.

Psalm 40:17 *But I am poor and needy; yet the Lord thinketh upon me: thou art my help and my deliverer; make no tarrying, O my God.*

EXPOSITION: Verse 17. *But I am poor and needy.* The man of sorrows closes with another appeal, based upon His affliction and poverty. *Yet the Lord thinketh upon me.* Sweet was this solace to the holy heart of the great sufferer. The Lord's thoughts of us are a cheering subject of meditation, for they are ever kind and never cease. His disciples forsook Him, and His friends forgot Him, but Jesus knew that Jehovah never turned away His heart from Him, and this upheld Him in the hour of need. *Thou art my help and my deliverer.* His unmoved confidence stayed itself alone on God. O that all believers would imitate more fully their great Apostle and High Priest in His firm reliance upon God, even when afflictions abounded and the light was veiled. *Make no tarrying, O my God.* The peril was imminent, the need urgent, the suppliant could not endure delay, nor was He made to wait, for the angel came to strengthen, and the brave heart of Jesus rose up to meet the foe. Lord Jesus, grant that in all our adversities we may possess like precious faith, and be found like you, more than conquerors.

PSALM 41
PSALM 41:1–PSALM 41:13

Psalm 41:1 *Blessed is he that considereth the poor: the Lord will deliver him in time of trouble.*

EXPOSITION: **Verse 1.** *Blessed is he that considereth the poor.* This is the third Psalm opening with a benediction, and there is a growth in it beyond the first two. To search the Word of God comes first, pardoned sin is second, and now the forgiven sinner brings forth fruit unto God available for the good of others. The word used is as emphatic as in the former cases, and so is the blessing which follows it. The poor intended, are such as are poor in substance, weak in bodily strength, despised in repute, and desponding in spirit. These are mostly avoided and frequently scorned. The worldly proverb bequeaths the hindmost to one who has no mercy. The sick and the sorry are poor company, and the world deserts them as the Amalekite left his dying servant. Such as have been made partakers of divine grace receive a more tender nature, and are not hardened against their own flesh and blood; they undertake the cause of the downtrodden, and turn their minds seriously to the promotion of their welfare. They do not toss them a penny and go on their way, but enquire into their sorrows, sift out their cause, study the best ways for their relief, and practically come to their rescue: such as these have the mark of the divine favor plainly upon them, and are as surely the sheep of the Lord's pasture as if they wore a brand upon their foreheads.

They are not said to have considered the poor years

235

ago, but they still do so. Stale benevolence, when boasted of, argues present churlishness. First and foremost, and far above all others put together in tender compassion for the needy is our Lord Jesus, who so remembered our low estate, that though He was rich, for our sakes He became poor. All His attributes were charged with the task of our uplifting. He weighed our case and came in the fullness of wisdom to execute the wonderful work of mercy by which we are redeemed from our destructions. Wretchedness brought forth His pity, misery moved His mercy, and thrice blessed is He both by His God and His saints for His attentive care and wise action towards us. He still considers us; His mercy is always in the present tense, and so let our praises be.

The Lord will deliver him in time of trouble. The compassionate lover of the poor thought of others, and therefore God will think of him. God measures to us with our own bushel. Days of trouble come even to the most generous, and they who have made the wisest provision for rainy days and have lent shelter to others when times were better with them. The promise is not that the generous saint shall have no trouble, but that he shall be preserved in it, and in due time brought out of it. How true was this of our Lord! Never trouble deeper nor triumph brighter than His, and glory be to His name, He secures the ultimate victory of all His blood bought ones. I wish that they all were more like Him in putting on bowels of compassion to the poor. Much blessedness they miss who stint their alms. The joy of doing good, the sweet reaction of another's happiness, the approving smile of Heaven upon the heart, if not upon the estate; all these the stingy soul knows nothing of. Selfishness bears in itself a curse, it is a cancer in the heart; while liberality is happiness, and makes fat the bones. In dark days we cannot rest upon the supposed merit of alms giving, but still the music of memory brings with it no mean solace when it tells of widows and orphans whom we have helped, and prisoners and sick folk to whom we have ministered.

Psalm 41:2 *The Lord will preserve him, and keep him alive; and he shall be blessed upon the earth: and thou wilt not deliver him unto the will of his enemies.*

EXPOSITION: Verse 2. *The Lord will preserve him, and keep him alive.* His noblest life shall be immortal, and even his mortal life shall be sacredly guarded by the power of Jehovah. Jesus lived on until His hour came, nor could the devices of crafty Herod take away His life until the destined hour had struck; and even then no man took His life from Him, but He laid it down of himself, to take it again. Here is the portion of all those who are made like their Lord, they bless and they shall be blessed, they preserve and shall be preserved, they watch over the lives of others and they themselves shall be precious in the sight of the Lord. The miser like the hog is of no use until he is dead—then let him die; the righteous like the ox is of service during life—then let him live. *And he shall be blessed upon the earth.* Prosperity shall attend him. His cruse of oil shall not be dried up because he fed the poor prophet. He shall cut from his roll of cloth and find it longer at both ends. "There was a man, and some did count him mad, / The more he gave away the more he had."[94]

If temporal gains be not given him, spirituals shall be doubled to him. His little shall be blessed; bread and water shall be a feast to him. The liberal are and must be blessed even here; they have a present as well as a future portion. Our Lord's real blessedness of heart in the joy that was set before him is a subject worthy of earnest thought, especially

---

94. *Pilgrim's Progress* by John Bunyan

237

as it is the picture of the blessing which all liberal saints may look for. *And thou wilt not deliver him unto the will of his enemies.* He helped the distressed, and now he shall find a champion in his God. What would not the good man's enemies do to him if they had him at their disposal? Better be in a pit with vipers than to be at the mercy of persecutors. This sentence sets before us a sweet negative, and yet it is not easy to have seen how it could be true of our Lord Jesus, if we did not know that although He was exempted from much of blessing, being made a curse for us, yet even He was not altogether nor forever left of God, but in due time was exalted above all His enemies.

Psalm 41:3 *The Lord will strengthen him upon the bed of languishing: thou wilt make all his bed in his sickness.*

EXPOSITION: **Verse 3.** *The Lord will strengthen him upon the bed of languishing.* The everlasting arms shall stay up his soul as friendly hands and downy pillows stay up the body of the sick. How tender and sympathizing is this image; how near it brings our God to our infirmities and sicknesses! Whoever heard this of the old heathen Jove[95], or of the gods of India or China? This is language peculiar to the God of Israel; He it is who deigns to become nurse and attendant upon good men. If He smites with one hand He sustains with the other. Oh, it is blessed fainting when one falls upon the Lord's own bosom, and is borne up thereby! Grace is the best of restoratives; divine love is the noblest stimulant for a languishing patient; it makes the soul strong as a giant, even when the aching bones are breaking through the skin. No physician like the Lord, no tonic like

---

95. Roman god, a counterpart of the Greek god, Zeus.

His promise, no wine like His love. *Thou wilt make all his bed in his sickness.* What? Does the Lord become bed maker to His sick children? Herein is love indeed. Who would not consider the poor if such be the promised reward? A bed soon grows hard when the body is weary with tossing to and fro upon it, but grace gives patience, and God's smile gives peace, and the bed is made soft because the man's heart is content; the pillows are downy because the head is peaceful.

Note that the Lord will make all his bed, from head to foot. What considerate and indefatigable kindness! Our dear and ever blessed Lord Jesus, though in all respects an inheritor of this promise, for our sakes condescended to forego the blessing, and died on a Cross and not upon a bed; yet, even there, He was after awhile upheld and cheered by the Lord His God, so that He died in triumph. We must not imagine that the benediction pronounced in these three verses belongs to all who casually give money to the poor, or leave it in their wills, or contribute to societies. Such do well, or act from mere custom, as the case may be, but they are not here alluded to. The blessing is for those whose habit it is to love their neighbor as themselves, and who for Christ's sake feed the hungry and clothe the naked. To imagine a man to be a saint who does not consider the poor as he has ability, is to conceive the fruitless fig tree to be acceptable; there will be sharp dealing with many professors on this point in the day when the King comes in His glory.

Psalm 41:4 *I said, Lord, be merciful unto me: heal my soul; for I have sinned against thee.*

EXPOSITION: **Verse 4.** *I said*— in earnest prayer— *Lord, be merciful unto me.* Prove now your gracious dealings with my soul in adversity, since you did in times before give me grace to act liberally in my prosperity. No appeal is made to justice; the petitioner but hints at the promised reward, but goes straightforward to lay his plea at the feet of mercy. How low was our Redeemer brought when such petitions could come from His reverend mouth, when His lips like lilies dropped such sweet smelling but bitter myrrh!

Heal my soul. My time of languishing is come, now do as you have said, and strengthen me, especially in my soul. We ought to be far more earnest for the soul's healing than for the body's ease. We hear much of the cure of souls, but we often forget to care about it.

For I have sinned against thee. Here was the root of sorrow. Sin and suffering are inevitable companions. Observe that by the psalmist sin was felt to be mainly evil because directed against God. This is of the essence of true repentance. The immaculate Savior could never have used such language as this unless there is here a reference to the sin which He took upon himself by imputation; and for our part we tremble to apply words so manifestly indicating personal rather than imputed sin. Applying the petition to David and other sinful believers, how strangely evangelical is the argument: heal me, not because I am innocent, but I have sinned. How contrary is this to all self righteous pleading! How in harmony with grace! How inconsistent with merit! Even the fact that the confessing penitent had remembered the poor, is but obliquely urged, but a direct appeal is made to mercy on the ground of great sin. O trembling reader, here is a divinely revealed precedent for you, be not slow to follow it.

Psalm 41:5 *Mine enemies speak evil of me, When shall he die, and his name perish?*

EXPOSITION: Verse 5. *Mine enemies speak evil of me.* It was their nature to do and speak evil; it was not possible that the child of God could escape them. The viper fastened on Paul's hand: the better the man the more likely and the more venomous the slander. Evil tongues are busy tongues, and never deal in truth. Jesus was maligned to the utmost, although no offence was in Him. *When shall he die, and his name perish?* They could not be content until He was away. The world is not wide enough for evil men to live in while the righteous remain, the bodily presence of the saints may be gone, but their memory is an offence to their foes. It was never merry England, say they, since men took to Psalm singing. In the Master's case, they cried, "Away with such a fellow from the Earth, it is not fit that He should live." [See Acts 22.] If persecutors could have their way, the Church should have but one neck, and that should be on the block. Thieves would gladly blow out all candles. The lights of the world are not the delights of the world. Poor blind bats, they fly at the lamp, and try to dash it down; but the Lord lives, and preserves both the saints and their names.

Psalm 41:6 *And if he come to see me, he speaketh vanity: his heart gathereth iniquity to itself; when he goeth abroad, he telleth it.*

EXPOSITION: Verse 6. *And if he come to see me, he speaketh vanity.* His visits of sympathy are visitations of mockery. When the fox calls on the sick lamb his words are soft, but he licks his lips in hope of the carcass. It is wretched work to have spies haunting one's bedchamber, calling in pretence of kindness, but with malice in their hearts. Hypocritical talk is always unpleasant and sickening to honest men, but especially to the suffering saint. Our divine Lord had much of this from the false hearts that watched His words. *His heart gathereth iniquity to itself.* Like will to like. The bird makes its nest of feathers. Out of the sweetest flowers chemists can distil poison, and from the purest words and deeds malice can gather groundwork for a slanderous report. It is perfectly marvelous how spite spins webs out of no materials whatever. It is no small trial to have base persons around you lying in wait for every word which they may pervert into evil.

The Master whom we serve was constantly subject to this affliction. *When he goeth abroad, he telleth it.* He makes his lies, and then vends them in open market. He is no sooner out of the house than he outs with his lie, and this against a sick man whom he called to see as a friend—a sick man to who's incoherent and random speeches pity should be showed. Ah, black hearted wretch! A devil's cub indeed. How far abroad men will go to publish their slanders! They would prefer to placard the sky with their falsehoods. A little fault is made much of; a slip of the tongue is a libel, a mistake a crime, and if a word can bear two meanings the worse is always fathered upon it. Tell it in Gath, publish it in Ashkelon that the daughters of the uncircumcised may triumph. It is degrading to strike a man when he is down, yet such is the meanness of mankind towards a Christian hero should he for awhile chance to be under a cloud.

Psalm 41:7 *All that hate me whisper together against me: against me do they devise my hurt.*

EXPOSITION: **Verse 7.** *All that hate me whisper together against me.* The spy meets his comrades in conclave and sets them all a whispering. Why could they not speak out? Were they afraid of the sick warrior? Or were their designs so treacherous that they must be hatched in secrecy? Mark the unanimity of the wicked—all. How heartily the dogs unite to hunt the stag! It would be good if we were even half as united in holy labor as persecutors are in their malicious projects, and if we were half as wise as they are crafty, for their whispering was craft as well as cowardice. *Against me do they devise my hurt.* They lay their heads together, and scheme and plot. So did Ahithophel and the rest of Absalom's counselors, so also did the chief priests and Pharisees. Evil men are good at devising; they are given to meditation, they are deep thinkers, but the mark they aim at is evermore the hurt of the faithful. Snakes in the grass are never there for a good end.

Psalm 41:8 *An evil disease, say they, cleaveth fast unto him: and now that he lieth he shall rise up no more.*

EXPOSITION: Verse 8. *An evil disease, say they, cleaveth fast unto him.* They whisper that some curse has fallen upon him, and is riveted to him. They insinuate that a foul secret stains his character, the ghost whereof haunts his house, and never can be caught. An air of mystery is cast around this doubly dark saying, as if to show how indistinct are the mutterings of malice. Even thus was our Lord accounted "smitten of God and afflicted." [See Isaiah 53:4.] His enemies conceived that God had forsaken Him, and delivered Him forever into their hands. *And now that He lieth He shall rise up no more.* His sickness they hoped was mortal, and this was fine news for them. No more would the good man's holiness chide their sin, they would now be free from the check of his godliness. Like the friars around Wycliffe's[96] bed, their prophesies were more jubilant than accurate, but they were a sore scourge to the sick man. When the Lord smites His people with His rod of affliction for a small moment, their enemies expect to see them capitally executed, and prepare their jubilates to celebrate

---

96. John Wycliffe, English theologian and translator of the Bible from the Latin Vulgate into English in the 1380's.

their funerals, but they are in too great a hurry, and have to alter their ditties and sing to another tune. Our Redeemer eminently foretold this, for out of His lying in the grave He has gloriously risen. Vain the watch, the stone, the seal! Rising He pours confusion on His enemies.

Psalm 41:9 *Yea, mine own familiar friend, in whom I trusted, which did eat of my bread, hath lifted up his heel against me.*

EXPOSITION: Verse 9. *Yea.* Here is the climax of the sufferer's woe, and he places before it the emphatic affirmation, as if he thought that such villainy would scarcely be believed. *Mine own familiar friend.* The man of my peace," so runs the original, with whom I had no differences, with whom I was in league, that had aforetime ministered to my peace and comfort. This was Ahithophel to David, and Iscariot with our Lord. Judas was an apostle, admitted to the privacy of the Great Teacher, hearing his secret thoughts, and, as it were, allowed to read his very heart. "Et tu Brute?"[97] said the expiring Caesar. The kiss of the traitor wounded our Lord's heart as much as the nail wounded His hand. *In whom I trusted.* Judas was the treasurer of the apostolic college. Where we place great confidence an unkind act is the more severely felt. *Which did eat of my bread.* Not only as a guest but as a dependant, a pensioner at my board. Judas dipped in the same dish with his Lord, and hence the more accursed was his treachery in his selling his Master for a slave's price.

Hath lifted up his heel against me. Not merely turned his back on me, but left me with a heavy kick such as a vicious horse might give. Hard is it to be spurned in our need by

---

97. Latin phrase meaning: "and you, Brut?" or "You too, Brutus?"

those who formerly fed at our table. It is noteworthy that the Redeemer applied only the last words of this verse to Judas; perhaps because, knowing his duplicity, he had never made a familiar friend of him in the fullest sense, and had not placed implicit trust in him. Infernal malice so planned it that every circumstance in Jesus' death should add wormwood to it; and the betrayal was one of the bitterest drops of gall. We are indeed, wretched when our former friend becomes our relentless foe, when confidence is betrayed, when all the rites of hospitality are perverted, and ingratitude is the only return for kindness; yet in so deplorable a case we may cast ourselves upon the faithfulness of God, who, having, delivered our Covenant Head, is in verity engaged to be the very present help of all for whom that covenant was made.

Psalm 41:10 *But thou, O Lord, be merciful unto me, and raise me up, that I may requite them."*

EXPOSITION: **Verse 10.** *But thou, O Lord, be merciful unto me.* How the hunted and frightened soul turns to her God! How she seems to take breath with a "but, thou!" How she clings to the hope of mercy from God when every chance of pity from man is gone! *And raise me up.* Recover me from my sickness, let me regain my position. Jesus was raised up from the grave; His descent was ended by an ascent. *That I may requite them.* This as it reads is a truly Old Testament sentence, and quite aside from the spirit of Christianity, yet we must remember that David was a person in magisterial office, and might without any personal revenge, desire to punish those who had insulted his authority and libeled his public character. Our great Apostle and High Priest had no personal animosities, but even He by His resurrection has requited the powers of evil, and avenged on death and hell all their base attacks upon His cause and person. Still the strained application of every sentence of this Psalm to Christ is not to our liking, and we prefer to call attention to the better spirit of the gospel beyond that of the old dispensation.

Psalm 41:11 *By this I know that thou favourest me, because mine enemy doth not triumph over me.*

EXPOSITION: **Verse 11.** We are all cheered by tokens for good, and the psalmist felt it to be an auspicious omen, that after all his deep depression he was not utterly given over to his foe. *By this I know that thou favourest me.* You have a special regard to me, I have the secret assurance of this in my heart, and, therefore, your outward dealings do not dismay me, for I know that you love me in them all. *Because mine enemy doth not triumph over me.* What if the believer has no triumph over his foes, he must be glad that they do not triumph over him. If we have not all we would like we should praise God for all we have. There is much in us over which the ungodly might exult, and if God's mercy keeps the dog's mouths closed when they might be opened, we must give Him our heartiest gratitude. What a wonder it is that when the devil enters the lists with a poor, erring, bedridden, deserted, slandered saint, and has a thousand evil tongues to aid him, yet he cannot win the day, but in the end slinks off without renown. "The feeblest saint shall win the day / Though death and hell obstruct the way."[98]

Psalm 41:12 *And as for me, thou upholdest me in mine integrity, and settest me before thy face for ever.*

EXPOSITION: **Verse 12.** *And as for me,* despite them

---

98. Hymn: Verse 4 of "Join All the Glorious Names" by Isaac Watts 1709.

all and in the sight of them all, *thou upholdest me in mine integrity*; your power enables me to rise above the reach of slander by living in purity and righteousness. Our innocence and consistency are the result of the divine upholding. We are like those glasses without feet, which can only be upright while they are held in the hand; we fall, and spill, and spoil all, if left to ourselves. The Lord should be praised every day if we are preserved from gross sin. When others sin they show us what we should do but for grace. "He today and I tomorrow," was the exclamation of a holy man, whenever he saw another falling into sin. Our integrity is comparative as well as dependent; we must therefore be humbled while we are grateful. If we are clear of the faults alleged against us by our slanderers, we have nevertheless quite enough of actual blame to render it shameful for us to boast. *And settest me before thy face for ever.* He rejoiced that he lived under the divine surveillance; tended, cared for, and smiled upon by his Lord; and yet more, that it would be so world without end. To stand before an earthly monarch is considered to be a singular honor, but what must it be to be a perpetual courtier in the palace of the King Eternal, Immortal, Invisible?

Psalm 41:13 *Blessed be the Lord God of Israel from everlasting, and to everlasting. Amen and Amen.*

EXPOSITION: **Verse 13.** The Psalm ends with a doxology. *Blessed be the Lord,* i.e., let Him be glorified. The blessing at the beginning from the mouth of God is returned from the mouth of His servant. We cannot add to the Lord's blessedness, but we can pour out our grateful wishes, and these He accepts, as we receive little presents of flowers from children who love us. Jehovah is the personal name of our God. *God of Israel* is His covenant title, and shows

247

His special relation to His elect people. *From everlasting and to everlasting.* The strongest way of expressing endless duration. We die, but the glory of God goes on and on without pause. "Amen and Amen." So let it surely, firmly, and eternally be. Thus the people joined in the Psalm by a double shout of holy affirmation; let us unite in it with all our hearts. This last verse may serve for the prayer of the universal Church in all ages, but none can sing it so sweetly as those who have experienced as David did the faithfulness of God in times of extremity.

PSALM 42

PSALM 42:1–PSALM 42:11

Psalm 42:1 *As the hart panteth after the water brooks, so panteth my soul after thee, O God.*

EXPOSITION: Verse 1. *As the hart panteth after the water brooks, so panteth my soul after thee, O God.* As after a long drought the poor fainting hind[99] longs for the streams, or rather as the hunted hart[100] instinctively seeks after the river to lave[101] its smoking flanks and to escape the dogs, even so my weary, persecuted soul pants after the Lord my God. Debarred from public worship, David was heartsick. Ease he did not seek, honor he did not covet, but the enjoyment of communion with God was an urgent need of his soul; he viewed it not merely as the sweetest of all luxuries, but as an absolute necessity, like water to a stag. Like the parched traveler in the wilderness, whose skin bottle is empty, and who finds the wells dry, he must drink or die—he must have his God or faint. His soul, his very self, his deepest life, was insatiable for a sense of the divine presence. As the hart brays so his soul prays. Give him his God and he is as content as the poor deer which at length slakes its thirst and is perfectly happy; but deny him his Lord, and his heart heaves, his bosom palpitates, his whole frame is convulsed, like one who gasps for breath, or pants with long running. Dear reader, do you know what this is,

---

99. A female deer, often an adult female red deer.
100. A male deer, often an adult male red deer.
101. Refresh and cool it flanks.

249

by personally having felt the same? It is a sweet bitterness. The next best thing to living in the light of the Lord's love is to be unhappy until we have it, and to pant hourly after it—hourly, did I say? Thirst is a perpetual appetite, and not to be forgotten and even thus continual is the heart's longing after God. When it is as natural for us to long for God as for an animal to thirst, it is well with our souls, however painful our feelings. We may learn from this verse that the eagerness of our desires may be pleaded with God, and the more so, because there are special promises for the importunate and fervent.

Psalm 42:2 *My soul thirsteth for God, for the living God: when shall I come and appear before God?*

EXPOSITION: **Verse 2.** *My soul.* All my nature, my inmost self. *Thirsteth.* Which is more than hungering; hunger you can palliate, but thirst is awful, insatiable, clamorous, and deadly. O to have the most intense craving after the highest good! This is no questionable mark of grace. For God. Not merely for the temple and the ordinances, but for fellowship with God himself. None but spiritual men can sympathize with this thirst. *For the living God.* Because He lives, and gives to men the living water; therefore we, with greater eagerness, desire Him. A dead God is a mere mockery; we loathe such a monstrous deity; but the ever living God, the perennial fountain of life and light and love, is our soul's desire. What are gold, honor, and pleasure, but dead idols? May we never pant for these. *When shall I come and appear before God?*

He who loves the Lord loves also the assemblies wherein His name is adored. Vain are all pretences to religion where the outward means of grace have no attraction. David was never so much at home as in the house of the Lord; he was not content with private worship; he did not forsake the place where saints assemble, as the manner of some is. See how pathetically he questions as to the prospect of his again uniting in the joyous gathering! How he repeats and reiterates his desire! After his God, his Elohim (his God to be worshipped, who had entered into covenant with him), he yearned even as the drooping flowers for the dew, or the moaning turtle for her mate. It would be well if all our resorting to public worship were viewed as appearances before God, it would then be a sure mark of grace to delight in them. Alas, how many appear before the minister, or their fellow men, and think that enough! "To see the face of God" is a nearer translation of the Hebrew; but the two ideas may be combined—he would see his God and be seen of Him: this is worth thirsting after!

Psalm 42:3 *My tears have been my meat day and night, while they continually say unto me, Where is thy God?*

EXPOSITION: Verse 3. *My tears have been my meat day and night.* Salt meats, but healthful to the soul. When a man comes to tears, constant tears, plenteous tears, tears that fill his cup and trencher[102], he is in earnest indeed. As the big tears stand in the stag's eyes in his distress, so did the salt drops glitter in the eyes of David. His appetite was gone, his tears not only seasoned his meat, but became his only meat, and he had no mind for other diet. Perhaps it was well for him that the heart could open the safety valves; there is a dry grief far more terrible than showery sorrows. His tears, since they were shed because God was blasphemed,

---

102. Platter

were "honorable dew," drops of holy water, such as Jehovah puts into His bottle. [See Psalm 56:8.]

While they continually say unto me, Where is thy God? Cruel taunts come naturally from coward minds. Surely they might have left the mourner alone; he could weep no more than he did—it was an act of cruelty and malice to pump more tears from a heart which already overflowed. Note how incessant was their jeer, and how artfully they framed it! It cut the good man to the bone to have the faithfulness of his God impugned. He would rather have needles thrust into his eyes than have darted insinuations against his God. Shimei may here be alluded to who after this fashion mocked David as he fled from Absalom. He bluntly asserted that David was a bloody man, and that God was punishing him for supplanting Saul and his house; his wish was father to his thought. The wicked know that our worst misfortune would be to lose God's favor; hence their diabolical malice leads them to declare that such is the case. Glory be to God, they lie in their throats, for our God is in the heavens, yes, and in the furnace too, helping His people.

Psalm 42:4 *When I remember these things, I pour out my soul in me: for I had gone with the multitude, I went with them to the house of God, with the voice of joy and praise, with a multitude that kept holyday.*

EXPOSITION: Verse 4. *When I remember these things, I pour out my soul in me.* When he harped upon his woes his heart melted into water and was poured out upon itself. God hidden, and foes raging, a pair of evils enough to bring down the stoutest heart! Yet why let reflections so gloomy engross us, since the result is of no value: merely to turn the soul on itself, to empty it from itself into itself is useless, how much better to pour out the heart before the

Lord! The prisoner's tread wheel might sooner land him in the skies than mere inward questioning raise us nearer to consolation. *For I had gone with the multitude, I went with them to the house of God.* Painful reflections were awakened by the memory of past joys; he had mingled in the pious throng, their numbers had helped to give him exhilaration and to awaken holy delight, their company had been a charm to him as with them he ascended the hill of Zion. Gently proceeding with holy ease, in comely procession, with frequent strains of song, he and the people of Jehovah had marched in reverent ranks up to the shrine of sacrifice, the dear abode of peace and holiness. Far away from such goodly company the holy man pictures the sacred scene and dwells upon the details of the pious march. *With the voice of joy and praise, with a multitude that kept holyday.* The festive noise is in his ears, and the solemn dance before his eyes. Perhaps he alludes to the removal of the ark and to the glorious gatherings of the tribes on that grand national holy day and holiday. How changed his present place! For Zion, a wilderness; for the priests in white linen, soldiers in garments of war; for the song, the sneer of blasphemy; for the festivity, lamentation; for joy in the Lord, a mournful dirge over his absence.

> "I sigh to think of happier days
> When thou, O God, wast nigh,
> When every heart was tuned to praise;
> And none more blest than I."[103]

When in a foreign land, amid the idolatries of Popery, we have felt just the same homesickness for the house of the Lord which is here described; we have said, "Ziona, Ziona,

---

103. Verse four of a hymn based on Psalm 42 and a poem in *The Spirit of the Psalms* by H.F. Lyte

our holy and beautiful house, when shall I see thee again? Thou church of the living God, my mother, my home, when shall I hear thy psalms and holy prayers, and once again behold the Lord in the midst of his people"[104] David appears to have had a peculiarly tender remembrance of the singing of the pilgrims, and assuredly it is the most delightful part of worship and that which comes nearest to the adoration of Heaven. What a degradation to supplant the intelligent song of the whole congregation by the theatrical prettiness of a quartet, the refined niceties of a choir, or the blowing off of wind from inanimate bellows and pipes! We might as well pray by machinery as praise by it.

Psalm 42:5 *Why art thou cast down, O my soul? and why art thou disquieted in me? hope thou in God: for I shall yet praise him for the help of his countenance.*

EXPOSITION: **Verse 5.** *Why art thou cast down, O my soul?* As though he were two men, the psalmist talks to himself. His faith reasons with his fears, his hope argues with his sorrows. These present troubles, are they to last forever? The rejoicings of my foes, are they more than empty talk? My absence from the solemn feasts, is that a perpetual exile? Why this deep depression, this faithless fainting, this chicken hearted melancholy? As Trapp[105] says, "David chides David out of the dumps;" and herein he is an example for all desponding ones. To search out the cause of our sorrow is often the best surgery for grief. Self- ignorance is not bliss; in this case it is misery. The mist of ignorance magnifies the causes of our alarm; a clearer view will make monsters dwindle

---

104. Taken from Sermon #2001, titled "A Little Sanctuary" by Charles Spurgeon on January 8, 1888.
105. Joseph Trapp, (1679-1747) English clergyman.

into trifles. *And why art thou disquieted within me?* Why is my quiet gone? If I cannot keep a public Sabbath, yet why do I deny my soul her indoor Sabbath? Why am I agitated like a troubled sea, and why do my thoughts make a noise like a tumultuous multitude? The causes are not enough to justify such utter yielding to despondency. Up, my heart! What ails you? Play the man, and your casting down shall turn to uplifting, and your disquietude to calm.

Hope thou in God. If every evil is let loose from Pandora's Box, yet is there hope at the bottom. This is the grace that swims, though the waves roar and are troubled. God is unchangeable, and therefore His grace is the ground for unshaken hope. If everything is dark, yet the day will come, and meanwhile hope carries stars in her eyes; her lamps are not dependent on oil from without, her light is fed by secret visitations of God, which sustain the spirit. For I shall yet praise him. Yet will my sighs give place to songs, my mournful ditties shall be exchanged for triumphal praise. A loss of the present sense of God's love is not a loss of that love itself; the jewel is there, though it gleams not on our breast; hope knows her title good when she cannot read it clear; she expects the promised boon though present providence stands before her with empty hands.

For I shall yet praise him for the help of his countenance. Salvations come from the propitious face of God, and He will yet lift up His countenance upon us. Note well that the main hope and chief desire of David rest in the smile of God. His face is what he seeks and hopes to see, and this will recover his low spirits, this will put to scorn his laughing enemies, this will restore to him all the joys of those holy and happy days around which memory lingers. This is grand cheer. This verse, like the singing of Paul and Silas, looses chains and shakes prison walls. He who can use such heroic language in his gloomy hours will surely conquer. In the garden of hope grow the laurels for future victories, the roses of coming joy, and the lilies of approaching peace.

Psalm 42:6 *O my God, my soul is cast down within me: therefore will I remember thee from the land of Jordan, and of the Hermonites, from the hill Mizar.*

EXPOSITION: **Verse 6.** *O my God, my soul is cast down within me.* Here the song begins again upon the bass. So sweet an ending deserves that for the sake of a second hopeful close the Psalm should even begin again. Perhaps the psalmist's dejection continued, the spasm of despondency returned; well, then, he will take down his harp again, and try again its power upon himself, as in his younger days, he saw its influence upon Saul when the evil spirit came upon him. With God the song begins a second time more nearly than at first. The singer was also a little more tranquil. Outward expression of desire was gone; there was no visible panting; the sorrow was not all restrained within doors. Within or upon himself he was cast down; and, truly, it may well be so, while our thoughts look more within than upward. If self were to furnish comfort, we would have but poor provision. There is no solid foundation for comfort in such fickle frames as our heart is subject to. It is good to tell the Lord how we feel, and the more plain the confession the better: David talks like a sick child to its mother, and we should learn to imitate him.

Therefore will I remember thee. It is good to fly to our God. Here is terra firma. Blessed down casting which drives us to so sure a rock of refuge as you, *O Lord! From the hill Mizar.* He recalls his seasons of choice communion by the river and among the hills, and especially that dearest hour upon the little hill, where love spoke her sweetest language and revealed her nearest fellowship. It is great wisdom to store up in memory our choice occasions of converse with Heaven; we may want them another day, when the Lord is slow in bringing back His banished ones, and our soul is aching with fear. "His love in times past"[106] has been a precious cordial to many a fainting one; like soft breath it has fanned the smoking flax into a flame, and bound up the bruised reed. Oh, never to be forgotten valley of Achor,[107] thou art a door of hope! Fair days, now gone, you have left a light behind you which cheers our present gloom. Or does David mean that even where he was he would think of his God; does he declare that, forgetful of time and place, he would count Jordan as sacred as Siloam, Hermon as holy as Zion, and even Mizar, that insignificant rising ground as glorious as the mountains which are round about Jerusalem! Oh! It is a heavenly heart which can sing:

> "To me remains nor place nor time;
> my country is in every clime;
> I can be calm and free from care
> On any shore, since God is there."
> "Could I be cast where thou art not,
> That were indeed a dreadful lot,
> But regions none remote I call,
> Secure of finding God in all."[108]

Psalm 42:7 *Deep calleth unto deep at the noise of thy waterspouts: all thy waves and thy billows are gone over me.*

---

106. Verse 3 in the hymn *"Begone Unbelief!"* by *John Newton 1779*
107. See Hosea 2:15
108. Verse 2 of the Hymn *"My Lord, How Full of Sweet Content." Words written by Madame Guyon in 1722 and translated from French to English by William Cowper in 1801. Music by Lowell Mason in 1824.*

EXPOSITION: **Verse 7.** *Deep calleth unto deep at the noise of thy waterspouts.* Your severe dealings with me seem to excite all creation to attack me; Heaven, and Earth, and hell, call to each other, stirring each other up in dreadful conspiracy against my peace. As in a waterspout, the deeps above and below clasp hands, so it seemed to David that Heaven and Earth united to create a tempest around him. His woes were incessant and overwhelming. Billow followed billow, one sea echoed the roaring of another; bodily pain aroused mental fear, Satanic suggestions chimed in with mistrustful forebodings. Outward tribulation thundered in awful harmony with inward anguish: his soul seemed drowned as in a universal deluge of trouble, over whose waves the providence of the Lord moved as a watery pillar, in dreadful majesty inspiring the utmost terror. As for the afflicted one he was like a lonely boat around which the fury of a storm is bursting, or a mariner floating on a mast, almost every moment submerged.

All thy waves and thy billows are gone over me. David thought that every trouble in the world had met in him, but he exaggerated, for all the breaking waves of Jehovah have passed over none but the Lord Jesus; there are griefs to which he makes his children strangers for his love's sake. Sorrow naturally states its case forcibly; the mercy is that the Lord after all has not dealt with us according to our fears. Yet what a plight to be in! Atlantic rollers sweeping in ceaseless succession over one's head, waterspouts coming nearer and nearer, and all the ocean in uproar around the weary swimmer; most of the heirs of Heaven can realize the description, for they have experienced the like. This is a deep experience unknown to babes in grace, but common enough to such as do business on great waters of affliction: to such it is some comfort to remember that the waves and billows are the Lord's, "thy waves and thy billows," says David, they are all sent, and directed by Him, and achieve His designs, and the child of God knowing this, is the more resigned.

Psalm 42:8 *Yet the Lord will command his lovingkindness in the day time, and in the night his song shall be with me, and my prayer unto the God of my life.*

EXPOSITION: Verse 8. *Yet the Lord will command his lovingkindness in the day time.* Come what may there shall be "a certain secret something" to sweeten all. Loving-kindness is a noble life belt in a rough sea. The day may darken into a strange and untimely midnight, but the love of God ordained of old to be the portion of the elect, shall be by sovereign decree meted out to them. No day shall ever dawn on an heir of grace and find him altogether forsaken of his Lord: the Lord reigns, and as a sovereign He will with authority command mercy to be reserved for His chosen. *And in the night.* Both divisions of the day shall be illuminated with special love, and no stress of trial shall prevent it. Our God is God of the nights as well as the days; none shall find His Israel unprotected, whatever the hour may be. *His song shall be with me.* Songs of praise for blessings received shall cheer the gloom of night. No music sweeter than this. The belief that we shall yet glorify the Lord for mercy given in extremity is a delightful stay to the soul. Affliction may put out our candle, but if it cannot silence our song we will soon light the candle again. *And my prayer unto the God of my life.* Prayer is yoked with praise. He, who is the living God, is the God of our life, from Him we derive it, with Him in prayer and praise we spend it, to Him we devote it, and in Him we shall prefect it. To be assured that our sighs and songs shall both have free access to our glorious Lord is to have reason for hope in the most deplorable condition.

Psalm 42:9 *I will say unto God my rock, Why hast thou forgotten me? why go I mourning because of the oppression of the enemy?*

EXPOSITION: **Verse 9.** *I will say unto God my rock, Why hast thou forgotten me?* Faith is allowed to enquire of her God the causes of His displeasure, and she is even permitted to reason with Him and put Him in mind of His promises, and ask why apparently they are not fulfilled. If the Lord is indeed our refuge, when we find no refuge, it is time to be raising the question, "Why is this?" Yet we must not let go our hold, the Lord must be my rock still; we must keep to Him alone as our confidence, and never forego our interest in Him. *Why go I mourning because of the oppression of the enemy?* He who condescends to be pleaded with by Abraham, His friend, allows us to put to Him the question that we may search out the causes of His severity towards us. Surely He can have no pleasure in seeing the faces of His servants stained and soiled with their tears; He can find no content in the harshness with which their foes assail them. He can never take pleasure in the tyranny with which Satan vexes them. Why then does He leave them to be mocked by His enemies and theirs? How can the strong God, who is as firm and abiding as a rock, be also as hard and unmoved as a rock towards those who trust in Him? Such enquiries humbly pressed often afford relief to the soul. To know the reason for sorrow is in part to know how to escape it, or at least to endure it. Want of attentive consideration often makes adversity appear to be more mysterious and hopeless than it really is. It is a pitiable thing for any man to have a limb amputated, but when we know that the operation was needful to save life, we are glad to hear that it has been successfully performed; even thus as trial unfolds, the design of the Lord sending it becomes far more easy to bear.

Psalm 42:10 *As with a sword in my bones, mine enemies reproach me; while they say daily unto me, Where is thy God?*

EXPOSITION: Verse 10. *As with a sword in my bones, mine enemies reproach me.* Cruel mockeries cut deeper than the flesh; they reach the soul as though a rapier were introduced between the ribs to prick the heart. If reproaches kill not, yet they are killing, the pain caused is excruciating. The tongue cuts to the bone and its wounds are hard to cure. *While they say daily unto me, Where is thy God?* This is the most unkind cut of all, reflecting as it does both upon the Lord's faithfulness and His servant's character. Such was the malice of David's foes, that having thought of the cruel question, they said it, said it daily, repeated it to him, and that for a length, of time; surely the continual yapping of these curs at his heel was enough to madden him, and perhaps would have done so had he not resorted to prayer and made the persecutions of his enemies a plea with his Lord.

Psalm 42:11 *Why art thou cast down, O my soul? and why art thou disquieted within me? hope thou in God: for I shall yet praise him, who is the health of my countenance, and my God.*

EXPOSITION: Verse 11. *Why art thou cast down, O my soul? and why art thou disquieted within me?* In the rehearsal of his sorrow, he finds after all no sufficient ground for being disquieted. Looked in the face, his fears were not as overwhelming as they seemed when shrouded in obscurity. *Hope thou in God.* Let the anchor still keep its hold. God is faithful, God is love, therefore there is room and reason for hope. *He, who is the health of my countenance, and my God.* This is the same hopeful expression as that contained in verse five, but the addition of and my God shows that the writer was growing in confidence, and was able defiantly to reply to the question, "Where is thy God?" Here, even here, He is, ready to deliver me. I am not ashamed to own Him amid your sneers and taunts, for He will rescue me out of your hands. Thus faith closes the struggle, a victor in fact by anticipation and in heart by firm reliance. The saddest countenance shall yet be made to shine, if there is a taking of God at His word and an expectation of His salvation. For I know I shall praise Him, who graciously to me *the health is of my countenance,* Yea, mine own God is He. [See Psalm 43:5.]

PSALM 43

PSALM 43:1–PSALM 43:5

Psalm 43:1 *Judge me, O God, and plead my cause against an ungodly nation: O deliver me from the deceitful and unjust man.*

EXPOSITION: **Verse 1.** *Judge me, O God.* Others are unable to understand my motives, and unwilling to give me a just verdict. My heart is clear as to intent and therefore I bring my case before you, content that you will impartially weigh my character, and right my wrongs. If you will judge, your acceptance of my conduct will be enough for me; I can laugh at human misrepresentation if my conscience knows that you are on my side; you are the only one I care for; and besides, your verdict will not sleep, but you will see practical justice done to your slandered servant.

And plead my cause against an ungodly nation. One such advocate as the Lord will more than suffice to answer a nation of brawling accusers. When people are ungodly, no wonder that they are unjust; those who are not true to God himself cannot be expected to deal rightly with His people. Hating the King they will not love His subjects. Popular opinion weighs with many, but divine opinion is far more weighty with the gracious few. One good word from God outweighs ten thousand railing speeches of men. He bears a brazen shield before him whose reliance in all things is upon his God; the arrows of calumny fall harmlessly from such a buckler.

O deliver me from the deceitful and unjust man. Deceit

and injustice are boon companions: he who fawns will not fear to slander. From two such devils none can deliver us but God. His wisdom can outwit the craft of the vilest serpent, and His power can over match the most raging lion. Whether this was Doeg[109] or Ahithophel[110] is small matter, such double distilled villains are plentiful, and the only way of dealing with them is to refer the matter to the righteous Judge of all; if we try to fight them with their own weapons, we shall suffer more serious injury from ourselves than from them. O child of God, leave your enemies in better hands, remembering that vengeance belongs not to you, but to your Lord. Turn to Him in prayer, crying, "O deliver me," and before long you shall publish abroad the remembrance of His salvation.

Psalm 43:2 *For thou art the God of my strength: why dost thou cast me off? why go I mourning because of the oppression of the enemy?*

EXPOSITION: **Verse 2.** *For.* Here is argument, which is the very sinew of prayer. If we reasoned more with the Lord would have more victories in supplication. *Thou art the God of my strength.* All my strength belongs to you—I will not, therefore, use it on my own behalf against my personal foes. All my strength comes from you; I therefore seek help from you, who are able to bestow it. All my strength is in you, I leave therefore this task of combating my foes entirely in your hands. Faith which leaves such things alone is wise faith. Note the assurance of David, thou art, not I hope and trust so, but I know it is so; we shall find confidence to be our consolation.

Why dost thou cast me off? Why am I treated as if

---

109. Doeg was a Chief herdsman to King Saul.
110. Ahithophel was a counselor to King David, and was known for his judgment. He later turned against King David and sided with David's son, Absalom, in his revolt.

you loathe me? Have I become an offence unto you? There are many reasons why the Lord might cast us off, but no reason shall prevail to make Him do so. He has not cast off His people, though He for awhile treats them as cast offs. Learn from this question that it is well to enquire into dark providences, but we must enquire of God, not of our own fears. He who is the author of a mysterious trial can best expound it to us.

> "Blind unbelief is sure to err,
> And scan his work in vain;
> God is his own interpreter,
> And he will make it plain."[111]

Why go I mourning because of the oppression of the enemy? Why do I wander hither and thither like a restless spirit? Why do I wear the clothes of sorrow on my body and the lines of grief on my face? Oppression makes a wise man mad; why, Lord, am I called to endure so much of it for so long a time? Here again is a useful question, addressed to the right quarter. The answer will often be because we are saints, and must be made like our Head, and because such sorrow is chastening to the spirit, and yields comfortable fruit. We are not to cross-examine the Lord in peevishness, but we may ask of Him in humility; God help us to observe the distinction so as not to sin through stress of sorrow.

Psalm 43:3 *O send out thy light and thy truth: let them lead me; let them bring me unto thy holy hill, and to thy tabernacles.*

EXPOSITION: Verse 3. *O send out thy light and thy truth.* The joy of your presence and the faithfulness of your

---

111. Quote by William Cowper.

heart; let both of these be manifest to me. Reveal my true character by your light, and reward me your truthful promise. As the sun darts forth his beams, so does the Lord send forth His favor and His faithfulness towards all His people; and as all nature rejoices in the sunshine, even so the saints triumph in the manifestation of the love and fidelity of their God, which, like the golden sunbeam, lights up even the darkest surroundings with delightful splendor. *Let them lead me.* Be these my star to guide me to my rest. Be these my Alpine guides to conduct me over mountains and precipices to the abodes of grace. *Let them bring me unto thy holy hill, and to thy tabernacles.* First in your mercy bring me to your earthly courts, and end my weary exile, and then in due time admit me to your celestial palace above. We seek not light to sin by, nor truth to be exalted by it, but that they may become our practical guides to the nearest communion with God. Only such light and truth as are sent us from God will do this, common light is not strong enough to show the road to Heaven, nor will mere moral or physical truths assist to the holy hill. But the light of the Holy Spirit, and the truth as it is in Jesus, these are elevating, sanctifying, perfecting; and hence their virtue in leading us to the glorious presence of God. It is beautiful to observe how David's longing to be away from the oppression of man always leads him to sigh more intensely for communion with God.

Psalm 43:4 *Then will I go unto the altar of God, unto God my exceeding joy: yea, upon the harp will I praise thee, O God my God.*

EXPOSITION: Verse 4. *Then will I go unto the altar of God.* If David might but be favored with such a deliverance as would permit his return, it would not be his own house or heritage which would be his first resort, but to the altar of God his willing feet would conduct him. His whole heart would go as sacrifice to the altar, he himself counting it his greatest happiness to be permitted to lie as a burnt offering wholly dedicated to the Lord. With what exultation should believers draw near unto Christ, who is the antitype of the altar! Clearer light should give greater intensity of desire.

Unto God my exceeding joy. It was not the altar as such that the psalmist cared for, he was no believer in the heathenism of ritualism: his soul desired spiritual fellowship, fellowship with God himself in very deed. What are all the rites of worship unless the Lord is in them; what, indeed, but empty shells and dry husks? Note the holy rapture with which David regards his Lord! He is not his joy alone, but his exceeding joy; not the fountain of joy, the giver of joy, or the maintainer of joy, but that joy itself. The margin has it, "The gladness of my joy," i.e., the soul, the essence, the very bowels of my joy. To draw near to God, who is such a joy to us, may well be the object of our hungering and thirsting.

Yea, upon the harp will I praise thee. His best music for his best love. When God fills us with joy we ought ever to pour it out at His feet in praise, and all the skill and talent we have should be laid under contribution to increase the divine revenue of glory. *O God, my God.* How he dwells upon the name which he loves so well! He already harps on it as though his harp music had begun. What sweeter sounds can music know than these four words? To have God in possession, and to know it by faith, is the heart's Heaven—a fullness of bliss lies therein.

Psalm 43:5 *Why art thou cast down, O my soul? and why art thou disquieted within me? hope in God: for I shall yet praise him, who is the health of my countenance, and my God.*

EXPOSITION: **Verse 5.** *Why art thou cast down, O my soul?* If God is thine, why this dejection? If He uplifts are you so near the ground? The dew of love is falling, O withering heart, revive. *And why art thou disquieted within me?* What cause is there to break the repose of your heart? Wherefore indulge unreasonable sorrows, which benefit no one, fret yourself, and dishonor your God? Why overburden yourself with forebodings? *Hope in God,* or wait for God. There is need of patience, but there is ground for hope. The Lord cannot but avenge His own elect. The heavenly Father will not stand by and see His children trampled on forever; as surely as the sun is in the heavens, light must arise for the people of God, though for awhile they may walk in darkness. Why, then, should we not be encouraged, and lift up our head with comfortable hope?

For I shall yet praise Him. Times of complaint will soon end, and seasons of praise will begin. Come, my heart, look out of the window, borrow the telescopic glass, forecast a little, and sweeten your chamber with sprigs of the sweet herb of hope. He is the health of my countenance, and my God. My God will clear the furrows from my brow, and the tear marks from my cheek; therefore will I lift up my head and smile in the face of the storm. The Psalm has a blessed ending, such as we would gladly imitate when death puts an end to our mortal existence.

PSALM 44

PSALM 44:1–PSALM 44:26

Psalm 44:1 *We have heard with our ears, O God, our fathers have told us, what work thou didst in their days, in the times of old.*

EXPOSITION: Verse 1. *We have heard with our ears, O God.* Your mighty acts have been the subjects of common conversation; not alone in books have we read your famous deeds, but in the ordinary talk of the people we have heard of them. Among the godly Israelites the biography of their nation was preserved by oral tradition, with great diligence and accuracy. This mode of preserving and transmitting history has its disadvantages, but it certainly produces a more vivid impression on the mind than any other; to hear with the ears affects us more sensitively than to read with the eyes; we ought to note this, and seize every possible opportunity of telling abroad the gospel of our Lord Jesus via voice, since this is the most telling mode of communication. The expression, "heard with our ears," may denote the pleasure with which they listened, the intensity of their interest, the personality of their hearing, and the lively remembrance they had of the romantic and soul stirring narrative. Too many have ears but hear not; happy are they who, having ears, have learned to hear.

Our fathers have told us. They could not have had better informants. Schoolmasters are good enough, but godly fathers are, both by the order of nature and grace, the best instructors of their sons, nor can they delegate the sacred duty. It is to be feared that many children of Christians could plead very little before God of what their fathers have told them. When fathers are tongue-tied religiously with their offspring, need they wonder if their children's hearts remain sin-tied? Just as in all free nations men delight to gather around the hearth, and tell the deeds of valor of their sires "in the brave days of old," so the people of God under the old dispensation made their families cheerful around the table, by rehearsing the wondrous doings of the Lord their God. Religious conversation need not be dull, and indeed it could not be if, as in this case, it dealt more with facts and less with opinions.

What work thou didst in their days, in the times of old. They began with what their own eyes had witnessed, and then passed on to what were the traditions of their youth. Note that the main point of the history transmitted from father to son was the work of God; this is the core of history, and therefore no man can write history rightly who is a stranger to the Lord's work. It is delightful to see the footprints of the Lord on the sea of changing events, to behold Him riding on the whirlwind of war, pestilence, and famine, and above all to see His unchanging care for His chosen people. Those who are taught to see God in history have learned a good lesson from their fathers, and no son of believing parents should be left in ignorance of so holy an art. A nation tutored as Israel was in a history as marvelous as their own, always had an available argument in pleading with God for aid in trouble, since He who never changes gives in every deed of grace a pledge of mercy yet to come. The traditions of our past experience are powerful pleas for present help.

Psalm 44:2 *How thou didst drive out the heathen with thy hand, and plantedst them; how thou didst afflict the people, and cast them out.*

EXPOSITION: **Verse 2.** *How thou didst drive out the heathen with thy hand.* The destruction of the Canaanites from the Promised Land is the work here brought to remembrance. A people numerous, warlike, gigantic and courageous, firmly established and strongly fortified, were driven out by a far feebler nation, because the Lord was against them in the fight. It is clear from Scripture that God sent a plague (so that the land ate up the inhabitants thereof), and also a visitation of hornets against the Canaanites, and by other means dispirited them, so that the easy victories of Joshua were but the results of God's having worked beforehand against the idolatrous nation. *And plantedst them.* The tribes of Israel were planted in the places formerly occupied by the heathen. Hivites[112] and Jebusites[113] were chased from their cities to make room for Ephraim and Judah. The Great Wonder worker tore up by the roots the oaks of Bashan, that He might plant instead thereof His own chosen "vineyard of red wine." *How thou didst afflict the people.* The condemned nations were harassed by fire and sword and were hunted to death until they were all expelled, and the enemies of Israel were banished far away.

And cast them out. This most probably refers to Israel and should be read, "caused them to increase." He who troubled His enemies smiled on His friends; He meted out vengeance to the ungodly nations, but He reserved His mercy for the chosen tribes. How fair is mercy when she stands by the side of justice! Bright beams the star of grace amid the night of wrath! It is a solemn thought that the greatness of divine love has its counterpart in the greatness of His indignation. The weight of mercy bestowed on Israel

---

112. The Hivites were descendants of Canaan the son of Ham, who was the son of Noah.
113. The Jebusites are said to be descendants of Jebus, also a son of Ham.

is balanced by the tremendous vengeance which swept the thousands of Amorites and Hittites down to hell with the edge of the sword. Hell is as deep as Heaven is high, and the flame of Tophet [hell] is as everlasting as the blaze of the celestial glory. God's might, as shown in deeds both of mercy and justice, should be called to mind in troublesome times as a strong tower to our fainting faith.

Psalm 44:3 *For they got not the land in possession by their own sword, neither did their own arm save them: but thy right hand, and thine arm, and the light of thy countenance, because thou hadst a favour unto them.*

EXPOSITION: **Verse 3.** *For they got not the land in possession by their own sword.* Behold how the Lord alone was exalted in bringing His people to the land which flows with milk and honey! He, in His distinguishing grace, had put a difference between Canaan and Israel, and therefore, by His own effectual power, He wrought for His chosen and against their adversaries. The tribes fought for their allotments, but their success was wholly due to the Lord who wrought with them. The warriors of Israel were not inactive, but their valor was secondary to that mysterious, divine working by which Jericho's walls fell down, and the hearts of the heathen failed them for fear. The efforts of all the men at arms were employed, but as these would have been futile without divine help, all the honor is ascribed unto the Lord. The passage may be viewed as a beautiful parable of the work of salvation; men are not saved without prayer, repentance, etc., but none of those save a man, salvation is altogether of the Lord. Canaan was not conquered without the armies of Israel, but it is equally true that it was not conquered by them; the Lord was the conqueror, and the people were but instruments in His hands.

Neither did their own arm save them. They could not ascribe their memorable victories to themselves; He who made sun and moon stand still for them was worthy of all their praise. A negative is put both upon their weapons and themselves as if to show us how ready men are to ascribe success to second causes.

But thy right hand, and thine arm, and the light of thy countenance. The divine hand actively fought for them, the divine arm powerfully sustained them with more than human energy, and the divine smile inspired them with dauntless courage. Who could not win with such triple help, though Earth, death, and hell should rise in war against him? What mattered the tallness of the sons of Anak, or the terror of their chariots of iron, they were as nothing when Jehovah arose for the avenging of Israel.

Because thou hadst a favour unto them. Here is the fountain from whence every stream of mercy flows. The Lord's delight in His people, His peculiar affection, His distinguishing regard—this is the mainspring which moves every wheel of a gracious providence. Israel was a chosen nation, hence their victories and the scattering of their foes; believers are an elect people, hence their spiritual blessings and conquests. There was nothing in the people themselves to secure them success, the Lord's favor alone did it, and it is ever so in our case, our hope of final glory must not rest on anything in ourselves, but on the free and sovereign favor of the Lord of Hosts.

Psalm 44:4 *Thou art my King, O God: command deliverances for Jacob.*

EXPOSITION: **Verse 4.** *Thou art my King, O God.* Knowing right well your power and grace my heart is glad to own you for her sovereign prince. Who among the mighty are as illustrious as you are? To whom, then, should I yield my homage or turn for aid? God of my fathers in the olden time, you are my soul's monarch and liege Lord. *Command deliverances for Jacob.* To whom should a people look but to their king? He it is who, by virtue of His office, fights their battles for them. In the case of our King, how easy it is for Him to scatter all our foes!

O Lord, the King of kings, with what ease you can rescue your people; a word of yours can do it, give but the command and your persecuted people shall be free. Jacob's long life was crowded with trials and deliverances, and his descendants are here called by his name, as if to typify the similarity of their experience to that of their great forefather. He who would win the blessings of Israel must share the sorrows of Jacob. This verse contains a personal declaration and an intercessory prayer; those can pray best who make most sure of their personal interest in God, and those who have the fullest assurance that the Lord is their God should be the foremost to plead for the rest of the tried family of the faithful.

Psalm 44:5 *Through thee will we push down our enemies: through thy name will we tread them under that rise up against us.*

EXPOSITION: **Verse 5.** *Through thee will we push down our enemies.* The fight was very close, bows were of no avail, and swords failed to be of service, it came to daggers drawing, and hand to hand wrestling, pushing and tugging. Jacob's God was renewing in the seed of Jacob their father's wrestling. And how did it fare with faith then? Could she stand foot to foot with her foe and hold her own? Yes, truly, she came forth victorious from the encounter, for she is great at a close push, and overthrows all her adversaries, the Lord being her helper.

Through thy name will we tread them under that rise up against us. The Lord's name served instead of weapons, and enabled those who used it to leap on their foes and crush them with jubilant valor. In union and communion with God, saints work wonders; "if God be for us, who can be against us?" [See Romans 8:31.] Mark well that all the conquests of these believers are said to be "through thee," "through thy name:" never let us forget this, lest going at warfare at our own charges, we fail most ignominiously.[114] Let us not, however, fall into the equally dangerous sin of distrust, for the Lord can make the weakest of us equal to any emergency. Though today we are timid and defenseless as sheep, He can by His power make us strong as the firstling of His bullock, and cause us to push as with the horns of unicorns, until those who rose up against us shall be so crushed and battered as never to rise again. Those who of themselves can scarcely keep their feet, but like little babes totter and fall, are by divine assistance made to overthrow their foes, and set their feet upon their necks. Read Christian's fight with Apollyon, and see how "The man so bravely played the man, He made the fiend to fly."[115]

Psalm 44:6 *For I will not trust in my bow, neither shall my sword save me.*

EXPOSITION: **Verse 6.** *For I will not trust in my bow, neither shall my sword save me.* Your people Israel, under your guidance, shouldered out the heathen, and gained their land, not by skill of weapons or prowess of arms, but

---

114. Dishonorably
115. Excerpt from Pilgrim's Progress, pg. 204. Written by John Bunyan

by your power alone; therefore will we renounce forever all reliance upon outward confidences, of which other men make such boast, and we will cast ourselves upon the omnipotence of our God. Bows having been newly introduced by King Saul were regarded as very formidable weapons in the early history of Israel, but they are here laid aside together with the all conquering sword, in order that there may be room for faith in the living God. This verse, in the first person singular, may serve as the confession of faith of every believer renouncing his own righteousness and strength, and looking alone to the Lord Jesus. O for grace to stand to this self renunciation, for alas, our proud nature is all too apt to fix its trust on the puffed up and supposititious [supposed] power of the creature! Arm of flesh, how dare I trust you? How dare I bring upon myself the curse of those who rely upon man?

Psalm 44:7 *But thou hast saved us from our enemies, and hast put them to shame that hated us.*

EXPOSITION: Verse 7. *But thou hast saved us from our enemies.* In ages past all our rescues have been due to you, O God. Never have you failed us. Out of every danger you have brought us. *And hast put them to shame that hated us.* With the back of your saving hand you hast given them a cuff which has made them hide their faces; you have defeated them in such a manner as to make them ashamed of themselves to be overthrown by such puny adversaries as they thought the Israelites to be. The double action of God in blessing His people and confounding His enemies is evermore to be observed; Pharaoh is drowned, while Israel passes through the sea; Amalek is smitten, while the tribes rejoice; the heathen are chased from their abodes, while the sons of Jacob rest beneath their vine and fig tree.

Psalm 44:8 *In God we boast all the day long, and praise thy name for ever. Selah.*

EXPOSITION: Verse 8. *In God we boast all the day long.* We have abundant reason for doing so while we recount His mighty acts. What blessed boasting is this! It is the only sort of boasting that is bearable. All other manna bred worms and stank except that which was laid up before the Lord, and all other boasting is loathsome save this glorying in the Lord, which is laudable and pleasing. *And praise thy name for ever.* Praise should be perpetual. If there were no new acts of love, yet ought the Lord to be praised for what He has done for His people. Let the song be lifted up high as we bring to remembrance the eternal love which chose us, predestinated us to be sons, redeemed us with a price, and then enriched us with all the fullness of God. *Selah.* A pause comes in fitly here, when we are about to descend from the highest to the lowest key. No longer are we to hear Miriam's timbrel, but rather Rachel's weeping.

Psalm 44:9 *But thou hast cast off, and put us to shame; and goest not forth with our armies.*

EXPOSITION: Verse 9. *But thou hast cast off, and put us to shame.* Here the patriot bard begins to contrast the past glories of the nation's history with its present sadness and distress; which he does not ascribe to the death of some human champion, or to the accidents of war, but solely and alone to the withdrawal of Israel's God. It seemed to the mourner that Jehovah had grown weary of His people and put them away in abhorrence, as men lay aside leprous garments, loathing the sight of them. To show His displeasure He had made His people to be ridiculed by the heathen, whose easy victories over their largest armies covered Israel with disgrace.

Alas! For a church and people when the Lord in the active energy of His Spirit withdraws from them, they want no greater shame or sorrow. He will not cast away His people finally and totally, but many a church has been left to defeat and disgrace on account of sin, and therefore all churches should be exceedingly watchful lest the same should happen to them. Poverty and distress bring no shame on a people, but the Lord's absence takes from a church everything which can exalt and ennoble.

And goest not forth with our armies. If the Lord is not the leader, of what avail are strong battalions? Vain are the combined efforts of the most zealous workers if God's arm is not revealed. May none of us in our churches have to mourn over the ministry, the Sabbath school, the missionary work, the visiting, or the street preaching, all left to be carried out without the divine aid. If our great ally will not go with us our defeat is inevitable.

Psalm 44:10 *Thou makest us to turn back from the enemy: and they which hate us spoil for themselves.*

EXPOSITION: Verse 10. *Thou makest us to turn back from the enemy.* The humiliating consciousness that the Lord has left them soon makes men cowards. Flight closes the fight of those who have not the Lord in the van. *And they which hate us spoil for themselves.* After defeat and retreat, comes spoliation. The poor, vanquished nation paid a terrible penalty for being overcome; plunder and murder desolated the conquered land, and the invaders loaded themselves with every precious thing which they could carry away. In spiritual experience we know what it is to be ravaged by our enemies; doubts and fears rob us of our comforts, and terrible forebodings spoil our hopes; and all because the Lord, for wise purposes, sees fit to leave us to ourselves. Alas! For the deserted soul; no calamity can equal the sorrow of being left of God, though it is but for a small moment.

> **Psalm 44:11** *Thou hast given us like sheep appointed for meat; and hast scattered us among the heathen.*

EXPOSITION: Verse 11. *Thou hast given us like sheep appointed for meat.* As sheep are slaughtered for food, so were the people slain in flocks, with ease, and frequency. Not with dignity of sacrifice, but with the cruelty of the shambles, they were put to death. God appeared to give them up like sheep allotted to the butcher, to abandon them as the hireling abandons the flock to wolves. The complaint is bitterly eloquent. *And hast scattered us among the heathen.* Many were carried into captivity, far off from the public worship of the temple of God, to pine as exiles among idolaters. All this is ascribed to the Lord, as being allowed by Him, and even appointed by His decree. It is well to trace the hand of God in our sorrows, for it is surely there.

> **Psalm 44:12** *Thou sellest thy people for nought, and dost not increase thy wealth by their price.*

EXPOSITION: Verse 12. *Thou sellest thy people for nought.* As men sell merchandise to anyone who cares to have it, so the Lord seemed to hand over His people to any nation who might choose to make war upon them. Meanwhile no good result was perceptible from all the miseries of Israel; so far as the psalmist could discover, the Lord's name received no honor from the sorrows of His people; they were given away to their foes as if they were so little valued as not to be worth the ordinary price of slaves, and the Lord did not care to gain by them so long as they did but suffer. The woe expressed in this line is as vinegar mingled with gall: the expression is worthy of the weeping prophet.

And dost not increase thy wealth by their price. If Jehovah had been glorified by all this wretchedness it could have been borne patiently, but it was the reverse; the Lord's name had, through the nation's calamities, been despised by the insulting heathen, who counted the overthrow of Israel to be the defeat of Jehovah himself. It always lightens a believer's trouble when he can see that God's great name will be honored thereby, but it is a grievous aggravation of misery when we appear to be tortured in vain. For our comfort let us rest satisfied that in reality the Lord is glorified, and when no revenue of glory is manifestly rendered to Him, He none the less accomplishes His own secret purposes, of which the grand result will be revealed in due time. We do not suffer for nothing, nor are our griefs without result.

Psalm 44:13 *Thou makest us a reproach to our neighbours, a scorn and a derision to them that are round about us.*

EXPOSITION: **Verse 13.** *Thou makest us a reproach to our neighbours.* Scorn is always an intensely bitter ingredient in the cup of the oppressed. The taunts and jeers of the victors pain the vanquished almost as much as their swords and spears. It was a mystery indeed that God should suffer His royal nation, His peculiar people, to be taunted by all who dwelt near them. *A scorn and a derision to them that are round about us.* The downtrodden people had become a common jest; "as base as Israel" cried the cruel tongue of the tyrant: so ordinary had the scorn become that the neighboring nations, though perhaps equally oppressed, borrowed the language of the conquerors, and joined in the common mockery. To be a derision to both strong and weak, superiors, equals, and inferiors, is hard to bear. The tooth of scoffing bites to the bone.

The psalmist sets forth the brutality of the enemy in many words, in order to move the pity of the Lord, to whose just anger he traced all the sorrows of His people. He used the very best of arguments, for the sufferings of His chosen touch the heart of God far more readily than any other reasonings. Blessed be His name, our great Advocate above knows how to avail himself of this powerful plea, and if we are at this hour enduring reproach for truth's sake, He will urge it before the eternal throne; and "shall not God avenge His own elect?" [See Luke 18:7.] A father will not long endure to see his children despitefully entreated; he may put up with it for a little, but his love will speedily arouse his anger, and then it will fare ill with the persecutor and reviler.

Psalm 44:14 *Thou makest us a byword among the heathen, a shaking of the head among the people.*

EXPOSITION: Verse 14. *Thou makest us a byword among the heathen, a shaking of the head among the people.* The lamentation is here repeated. They had sunk so low that none did them reverence, but universally and publicly they were treated as infamous and despicable. Those who reviled others dragged in Israel's name by the way as a garnish to their insults, and if perchance they saw one of the seed of Jacob in the street they used lewd gestures to annoy him. Those whose heads were emptiest wagged them at the separated people. They were the common butts of every fool's arrow. Such has been the lot of the righteous in ages past, such is their portion in a measure now, and such may be yet again their heritage in the worst sense. The world knows not its nobility; it has no eye for true excellence: it found a Cross for the Master, and cannot be expected to award crowns to His disciples.

Psalm 44:15 *My confusion is continually before me, and the shame of my face hath covered me,*

EXPOSITION: Verse 15. *My confusion is continually before me.* The poet makes himself the representative of his nation, and declares his own constant distress of soul. He is a man of ill blood who is unconcerned for the sorrows of the Church of which he is a member, or the nation of which he is a citizen; the better the heart the greater its sympathy. *And the shame of my face hath covered me.* One constant blush, like a crimson mantle, covered him both before God and man; he felt before God that the divine desertion was well deserved, and before man, that he and his people were despicable indeed now that heavenly help was gone. It is good for a nation when there still exists in it men who take to heart its sin and shame. God will have pity on His chastened ones, and it is a pledge thereof when He sends us choice ministers, men of tenderness, who make the people's case their own.

Psalm 44:16 *For the voice of him that reproacheth and blasphemeth; by reason of the enemy and avenger.*

EXPOSITION: Verse 16. *For the voice of him that reproacheth and blasphemeth.* It seems that from mocking the people of God, the adversaries advanced to reviling God himself, they proceeded from persecution to the sin which is next of kin, namely blasphemy. *By reason of the enemy and avenger.* The enemy boasted of avenging the defeats of their forefathers; they took revenge for the ancient victories of Israel, by insulting over the now fallen people. Here was a sad plight for a nation to be placed in, but it was by no means a hopeless case, for the Lord who brought all this evil upon them could with equal ease release them from it.

So long as Israel looked alone to her God, and not to her own arm, no foe could retain her beneath his foot; she must arise, for God was on her side.

Psalm 44:17 *All this is come upon us; yet have we not forgotten thee, neither have we dealt falsely in thy covenant.*

EXPOSITION: **Verse 17.** *All this is come upon us; yet have we not forgotten thee.* Here the psalmist urges that Israel had not turned away from her allegiance to Jehovah. When in the midst of many griefs we can still cling to God in loving obedience, it must be well with us. True fidelity can endure rough usage. Those who follow God for what they get will leave Him when persecution is stirred up, but not so the sincere believer; he will not forget his God, even though the worst come to the worst.

Neither have we dealt falsely in thy covenant. No idol was set up, the ordained worship was not relinquished, God was still nationally acknowledged, and therefore the psalmist is more earnest that the Lord should interpose. This and the succeeding verses are suitable for the lips of martyrs; indeed the entire psalm might be called the martyr's complaint. Not for sin but for righteousness did the saints suffer, not for falsehood but for truth, not for forsaking the Lord, but for following hard after Him. Sufferings of such a sort may be very terrible, but they are exceedingly honorable, and the comforts of the Lord shall sustain those who are accounted worthy to suffer for Christ's sake.

Psalm 44:18 *Our heart is not turned back, neither have our steps declined from thy way;*

EXPOSITION: **Verse 18.** *Our heart is not turned back,* *neither have our steps declined from thy way.* Heart and life were agreed, and both were true to the Lord's way. Neither within nor without had the godly sufferers offended; they were not absolutely perfect, but they were sincerely free from all willful transgression. It was a healthy sign for the nation that her prophet poet could testify to her uprightness before God, both in heart and act; far oftener the case would have worn quite another color, for the tribes were all too apt to set up other gods and forsake the rock of their salvation.

Psalm 44:19 *Though thou hast sore broken us in the place of dragons, and covered us with the shadow of death.*

EXPOSITION: **Verse 19.** *Though thou hast sore broken us in the place of dragons.* Though utterly crushed and rendered desolate and driven as it were to associate with creatures such as jackals, owls, serpents, which haunt deserted ruins, yet Israel remained faithful. To be true to a smiting God, even when the blows lay our joys in ruinous heaps, is to be such as the Lord delights in. Better to be broken by God than from God. Better to be in the place of dragons than of deceivers. *And covered us with the shadow of death.* The language is very strong. The nation is described as completely enveloped in the dense darkness of despair and death, covered up as though confined in hopelessness. Yet the claim is made that they still remained mindful of their God, and a glorious plea it is. Better death than false of faith. Those who are true to God shall never find Him false to them.

Psalm 44:20 *If we have forgotten the name of our God, or stretched out our hands to a strange god;*

EXPOSITION: Verse 20. An appeal is now made to the omniscience of God; He is himself called in to bear witness that Israel had not set up another God. *If we have forgotten the name of our God.* This would be the first step in apostasy; men first forget the true, and then adore the false. *Or stretched out our hands to a strange god.* Stretching out the hands was the symbol of adoration or of entreaty in prayer; this they had not offered to any of the idols of the heathens.

Psalm 44:21 *Shall not God search this out? for he knoweth the secrets of the heart.*

EXPOSITION: Verse 21. *Shall not God search this out?* Could such idolatry be concealed from Him? Would He not with holy indignation have detected unfaithfulness to itself, even had it been hidden in the heart and unrevealed in the life? *For he knoweth the secrets of the heart.* He is acquainted with the inner workings of the mind, and therefore this could not have escaped Him. Not the heart only which is secret, but the secrets of the heart, which are secrets of the most secret thing, is as open to God as a book to a reader. The reasoning is that the Lord himself knew the people to be sincerely His followers, and therefore was not visiting them for sin; hence, then, affliction evidently came from quite another cause.

Psalm 44:22 *Yea, for thy sake are we killed all the day long; we are counted as sheep for the slaughter.*

EXPOSITION: Verse 22. *Yea,* i.e., assuredly, certainly, *for thy sake,* not for our offences, but for obeying you; the trials of these suppliants came upon them because they were loyal to their God. *Are we killed all the day long.* Persecution never ceased to hound them to the death; they had no respite and found no door of escape; and all in God's behalf, because they would not forsake their covenant God and King. *We are counted as sheep for the slaughter;* as if we were only meant to be killed, and made on purpose to be victims; as if it were as easy and as innocent a thing to slay us as to slaughter sheep. In this and following verses we clearly hear the martyr's cry. From Piedmont[116] and Smithfield[117], from St. Bartholomew's massacre and the dragoonades of Claverhouse[118], this appeal goes up to Heaven, while the souls under the altar continue their solemn cry for vengeance. Not long shall the Church plead in this fashion, her shame shall be recompensed, and her triumph shall dawn.

Psalm 44:23 *Awake, why sleepest thou, O Lord? arise, cast us not off for ever.*

EXPOSITION: Verse 23. *Awake, why sleepest thou, O Lord.* God sleeps not, but the psalmist puts it so, as if on no other theory he could explain the divine inaction. He would gladly see the great Judge ending oppression and giving peace to the holy, therefore does he cry *Awake;* he cannot understand why the reign of tyranny and the oppression of virtue are permitted, and therefore he enquires "Why sleepest thou?" Arise. This is all you need to do; one move of yours will save us. *Cast us not off for ever.* Long enough have you deserted us; the terrible effects of your absence are destroying us; end our calamities, and let your anger be appeased. In persecuting times men are apt to cry, where is the God of Israel? At the thought of what the saints have endured from their haughty enemies, we join our voices in

---

116. Piedmont Massacre of the Waldensians of Italy , January 1655
117. Smithfield Massacre by burning of Martyrs in 1546.
118. Massacres of peasants by the Dragoonades of Claverhouse in Scotland

the great martyr cry and sing with the bard of Paradise: —

> "Avenge, O Lord, thy slaughtered saints,
>   whose bones
> Lie scattered on the Alpine mountains cold;
> Even those who kept thy truth so pure of old,
> When all our fathers worshipped stocks and stones,
> Forget not: in thy book record their groans
> Who were thy sheep."[119]

Psalm 44:24 *Wherefore hidest thou thy face, and forgettest our affliction and our oppression?*

EXPOSITION: Verse 24. *Wherefore hidest thou thy face, and forgettest our affliction and our oppression?* Not petulantly, but piteously and inquiringly, we may question the Lord when His dealings are mysterious. We are permitted to order our case with arguments, and plead the right before the face of the august Majesty. Why, Lord, have you become oblivious of your children's woes? This question is far more easily asked than answered; it is hard, indeed, in the midst of persecution to see the reason why we are left to suffer so severely.

Psalm 44:25 *For our soul is bowed down to the dust: our belly cleaveth unto the earth.*

EXPOSITION: Verse 25. *For our soul is bowed down to the dust.* Our heart is low as low can be, as low as the dust beneath the soles of men's feet. When the heart sinks, the man is down indeed. Heart sorrow is the very heart of sorrow. *Our belly cleaveth unto the earth.* The man is prone upon the ground, and he is not only down, but fastened

---

119. "Paradise Lost" by John Milton.

down on the ground and glued to it. It is misery; indeed, when the heart cannot escape from itself, is shut up in its own dejection, and bound with the cords of despondency. God's saints may be thus abject, they may be not only in the dust, but on the dunghill with Job and Lazarus, but their day cometh, and their tide will turn, and they shall have a brave summer after their bitter winter.

Psalm 44:26 *Arise for our help, and redeem us for thy mercies' sake.*

EXPOSITION: **Verse 26.** *Arise for our help.* A short, but sweet and comprehensive prayer, much to the point, clear, simple, urgent, as all prayers should be. *And redeem us for thy mercies' sake.* Here is the final plea. The favor is redemption, the plea is mercy; and this, too, in the case of faithful sufferers who had not forgotten their God. Mercy is always a safe plea, and never will any man find a better.

> "Were I a martyr at the stake.
> I would plead my Saviour's name,
> Intreat a pardon for his sake,
> And urge no other claim."[120]

Here ends this memorable Psalm, but in Heaven its power ends not, but brings down deliverance for the tried people of God.

---

120. *"Communion With Jesus." A hymn by Thomas Greene written in 1780.*

PSALM 45

PSALM 45:1–PSALM 45:17

Psalm 45:1 *My heart is inditing a good matter: I speak of the things which I have made touching the king: my tongue is the pen of a ready writer.*

EXPOSITION: Verse 1. *My heart.* There is no writing like that dictated by the heart. Heartless hymns are insults to heaven. *Is inditing a good matter.* A good heart will only be content with good thoughts. Where the fountain is good streams of good will flow forth. The learned tell us that the word may be read overflows, or as others, boils or bubbles up, denoting the warmth of the writer's love, the fullness of his heart, and the consequent richness and glow of his utterance, as though it were the ebullition[121] of his inmost soul when full of affection.

We have here no single cold expression; the writer is not one who frigidly studies the elegancies and proprieties of poetry, his stanzas are the natural outburst of his soul, comparable to the boiling jets of the geysers of Hecla[122]. As the corn offered in sacrifice was parched in the pan, so is this tribute of love hot with sincere devotion. It is a sad thing when the heart is cold with a good matter and worse when it is warm with a bad matter, but incomparably good when a warm heart and a good matter meet together. O that we may often offer to God an acceptable minchah[123], a sweet

---

121. Unrestrained emotion.
122. A geyser on Mount Hecla in Iceland.
123. Mincha is the afternoon prayer service in Judaism.

oblation fresh from the pan of hearts warmed with gratitude and admiration.

I speak of the things which I have made touching the King. This song has "the King" for its only subject, and for the King's honor alone was it composed, well might its writer call it a good matter. The psalmist did not write carelessly; he calls his poem his works, or things which he had made. We are not to offer to the Lord that which costs us nothing. Good material deserves good workmanship. We should well digest in our heart's affections and our mind's meditations any discourse or poem in which we speak of one so great and glorious as our Royal Lord. As our version reads it, the psalmist wrote experimentally things which he had made his own, and personally tasted and handled concerning the King.

My tongue is the pen of a ready writer, not so much for rapidity, for there the tongue always has the preference, but for exactness, elaboration, deliberation, and skilfulness of expression. Seldom are the excited utterances of the mouth equal in real weight and accuracy to the verba scripta[124] of a thoughtful accomplished penman; but here the writer, though filled with enthusiasm, speaks as correctly as a practiced writer; his utterances therefore are no ephemeral [short-lived] sentences, but such as fall from men who sit down calmly to write for eternity. It is not always that the best of men are in such a creative moment, and when they are they should not restrain the gush of their hallowed feelings. Such a condition of heart in a gifted mind creates that auspicious hour in which poetry pours forth her tuneful numbers to enrich the service of song in the house of the Lord.

---

124. "Spoken words fly away, written words remain."

Psalm 45:2 *Thou art fairer than the children of men: grace is poured into thy lips: therefore God hath blessed thee for ever.*

EXPOSITION: **Verse 2.** *Thou.* As though the King himself had suddenly appeared before him, the psalmist lost in admiration of his person, turns from his preface to address his Lord. A loving heart has the power to realize its object. The eyes of a true heart see more than the eyes of the head. Moreover, Jesus reveals himself when we are pouring forth our affections towards Him. It is usually the case that when we are ready Christ appears. If our heart is warm it is an indication that the sun is shining, and when we enjoy his heat we shall soon behold his light. *Thou art fairer than the children of men.* In person, but especially in mind and character, the King of saints is peerless in beauty. The Hebrew word is doubled, "Beautiful, beautiful art thou." Jesus is so emphatically lovely that words must be doubled, strained, yea, exhausted before He can be described. Among the children of men many have through grace been lovely in character, yet they have each had a flaw; but in Jesus we behold every feature of a perfect character in harmonious proportion. He is lovely everywhere, and from every point of view, but never more so than when we view him in conjugal union with His Church; then love gives a ravishing flush of glory to His loveliness.

Grace is poured into thy lips. Beauty and eloquence make a man majestic when they are united; they both dwell in perfection in the all fair, all eloquent Lord Jesus. Grace of person and grace of speech reach their highest point in Him. Grace has in the most copious manner been poured upon Christ, "for it pleased the Father that in him should all fulness dwell"[125], and now grace is in superabundance, poured forth from His lips to cheer and enrich His people. The testimony, the promises, the invitations, the consolations of our King pour forth from Him in such volumes of meaning that we cannot but contrast those cataracts of grace with the speech of Moses which did but drop as the rain, and distil as the dew. Whoever in personal communion with the Well-beloved has listened to His voice will feel that "never man spake like this man." [See John 7:46.] Well did the bride say of him, "his lips are like lilies dropping sweet smelling myrrh." [See Song of Solomon 5:13.] One word from Him dissolved the heart of Saul of Tarsus, and turned him into an apostle, another word raised up John the Divine when fainting in the Isle of Patmos. Oftentimes a sentence from His lips has turned our own midnight into morning, our winter into spring.

Therefore God has blessed thee for ever. Calvin reads it; Because God hath blessed thee for ever. Christ is blessed of God, blessed forever, and this is to us one great reason for His beauty, and the source of the gracious words which proceed out of His lips. The rare endowments of the man Christ Jesus are given Him of the Father, that by them His people may be blessed with all spiritual blessings in union with himself. But if we take our own translation, we read that the Father has blessed the Mediator as a reward for all His gracious labors; and right well does He deserve the recompense. Whom God blesses we should bless, and the more so because all His blessedness is communicated to us.

Psalm 45:3 *Gird thy sword upon thy thigh, O most mighty, with thy glory and thy majesty.*

---

125. See Colossians 1:19.

EXPOSITION: **Verse 3.** *Gird thy sword upon thy thigh.* Loving spirits jealous of the Redeemer's glory long to see Him putting forth His power to vindicate His own most holy cause. Why should the sword of the Spirit lie still, like a weapon hung up in an armory; it is sharp and strong, both for cutting and piercing: O that the divine power of Jesus were put forth to use against error. The words before us represent our great King as urged to arm himself for battle, by placing His sword where it is ready for use. Christ is the true champion of the Church, others are but underlings who must borrow strength from Him; the single arm of Immanuel is the sole hope of the faithful. Our prayer should be that of this verse. There is at this moment an apparent suspension of our Lord's former power, we must by importunate prayer call Him to the conflict, for like the Greeks without Achilles we are soon overcome by our enemies, and we are but dead men if Jesus is not in our midst. *O most mighty.* A title well deserved, and not given from empty courtesy like the serenities, excellencies and highnesses of our fellow mortals—titles, which are but sops for vain glory. Jesus is the truest of heroes. Hero worship in His case alone is commendable. He is mighty to save, mighty in love.

With thy glory and thy majesty. Let thy sword both win you renown and dominion, or as it may mean, gird on with your sword your robes which indicate your royal splendor. Love delights to see the Beloved arrayed as becomes His Excellency; she weeps as she sees Him in the garments of humiliation, she rejoices to behold Him in the vestments of His exaltation. Our precious Christ can never be made too much of. Heaven itself is but just good enough for Him. All the pomp that angels and archangels, and thrones, and dominions, and principalities, and powers can pour at His feet is too little for Him. Only His own essential glory is such as fully answers to the desire of His people, who can never extol Him enough.

Psalm 45:4 *And in thy majesty ride prosperously because of truth and meekness and righteousness; and thy right hand shall teach thee terrible things.*

EXPOSITION: **Verse 4.** *And in thy majesty ride prosperously.* The hero monarch armed and appareled is now entreated to ascend his triumphal car. Would to God that our Immanuel would come forth in the chariot of love to conquer our spiritual foes and seize by power the souls whom He has bought with blood. *Because of truth and meekness and righteousness.* These words may be rendered, ride forth upon truth and meekness and righteousness. Three noble chargers to draw the war chariot of the gospel. In the sense of our translation it is a most potent argument to urge with our Lord that the cause of the true, the humble, and the good, calls for his advocacy. Truth will be ridiculed, meekness will be oppressed, and righteousness slain, unless the God, the Man in whom these precious things are incarnated, shall arise for their vindication. Our earnest petition ought ever to be that Jesus would lay His almighty arm to the work of grace lest the good causes languish and wickedness prevails.

And thy right hand shall teach thee terrible things. Foreseeing the result of divine working, the psalmist prophesies that the uplifted arm of Messiah will reveal to the King's own eyes the terrible overthrow of His foes. Jesus needs no guide but His own right hand, no teacher but His own might; may He instruct us all in what He can perform, by achieving it speedily before our gladdened eyes.

Psalm 45:5 *Thine arrows are sharp in the heart of the king's enemies; whereby the people fall under thee.*

EXPOSITION: Verse 5. *Thine arrows.* Our King is master of all weapons: He can strike those who are near and those afar off with equal force. *Are sharp.* Nothing that Jesus does is ill done; He uses no blunted shafts, no pointless darts. *In the heart of the King's enemies.* Our Captain aims at men's hearts rather than their heads, and He hits them too; point blank are His shots, and they enter deep into the vital part of man's nature. Whether for love or vengeance, Christ never misses aim, and when His arrows stick, they cause a smart not soon forgotten, a wound which only He can heal. Jesus' arrows of conviction are sharp in the quiver of His Word, and sharp when on the bow of his ministers, but they are most known to be so when they find a way into careless hearts. They are His arrows, He made them, and He shoots them. He makes them sharp, and He makes them enter the heart. May none of us ever fall under the darts of His judgment, for none kill so surely as they. *Whereby the people fall under thee.* On either side the slain of the Lord are many when Jesus leads on the war. Nations tremble and turn to Him when He shoots abroad His truth. Under His power and presence, men are stricken down as though pricked in the heart. There is no standing against the Son of God when His bow of might is in His hands. Terrible will be that hour when His bow shall be made quite naked, and bolts of devouring fire shall be hurled upon His adversaries: then shall princes fall and nations perish.

Psalm 45:6 *Thy throne, O God, is for ever and ever: the sceptre of thy kingdom is a right sceptre.*

EXPOSITION: **Verse 6.** *Thy throne, O God, is for ever and ever.* To whom can this be spoken but our Lord? The psalmist cannot restrain his adoration. His enlightened eye sees in the royal Husband of the Church, God, and God to be adored, God reigning, God reigning everlastingly. Blessed sight! Blind are the eyes that cannot see God in Christ Jesus! We never appreciate the tender condescension of our King in becoming one flesh with His Church, and placing her at His right hand, until we have fully rejoiced in His essential glory and deity. What a mercy for us that our Savior is God, for who but a God could execute the work of salvation? What a glad thing it is that He reigns on a throne which will never pass away, for we need both sovereign grace and eternal love to secure our happiness. If Jesus could cease to reign we would cease to be blessed, and were He not God, and therefore eternal, this must be the case. No throne can endure forever, but that on which God himself sits.

The sceptre of thy kingdom is a right sceptre. He is the lawful monarch of all things that be. His rule is founded in right, its law is right, its result is right. Our King is no usurper and no oppressor. Even when He shall break His enemies with a rod of iron, He will do no man wrong; His vengeance and His grace are both in conformity with justice. Hence we trust Him without suspicion; He cannot err; no affliction is too severe, for He sends it; no judgment too harsh, for He ordains it. O blessed hands of Jesus! The reigning power is safe with you. All the just rejoice in the government of the King who reigns in righteousness.

Psalm 45:7 *Thou lovest righteousness, and hatest wickedness: therefore God, thy God, hath anointed thee with the oil of gladness above thy fellows.*

EXPOSITION: **Verse 7.** *Thou lovest righteousness,*

296

and hatest wickedness. Christ Jesus is not neutral in the great contest between right and wrong: as warmly as He loves the one He abhors the other. What qualifications for a sovereign! What grounds of confidence for a people! The whole of our Lord's life on Earth proved the truth of these words. His death to put away sin and bring in the reign of righteousness sealed the fact beyond all question. His providence, by which He rules from His mediatorial throne, when rightly understood, reveals the same; and His final assize [judicial writ] will proclaim it before all worlds. We should imitate Him both in His love and hate; they are both needful to complete a righteous character.

Therefore God, thy God, hath anointed thee with the oil of gladness above thy fellows. Jesus as Mediator owned God as His God, to whom, being found in fashion as a man, He became obedient. On account of our Lord's perfect life He is now rewarded with superior joy. Others there are to whom grace has given a sacred fellowship with Him, but by their universal consent and His own merit, He is prince among them, the gladdest of all because the cause of all their gladness. At Oriental feasts oil was poured on the heads of distinguished and very welcome guests; God himself anoints the man Christ Jesus, as He sits at the heavenly feasts, anoints Him as a reward for His work, with higher and fuller joy than any else can know; thus is the Son of man honored and rewarded for all His pains. Observe the indisputable testimony to Messiah's Deity in verse six and to His manhood in the present verse. Of whom could this be written but of Jesus of Nazareth? Our Christ is our Elohim. Jesus is God with us.

Psalm 45:8 *All thy garments smell of myrrh, and aloes, and cassia, out of the ivory palaces, whereby they have made thee glad.*

EXPOSITION: **Verse 8.** *All thy garments smell of myrrh, and aloes, and cassia.* The divine anointing causes fragrance to distil from the robes of the Mighty Hero. He is delightful to every sense, to the eyes most fair, to the ear most gracious, to the spiritual nostril most sweet. The excellences of Jesus are all most precious, comparable to the rarest spices; they are most varied, and to be likened not to myrrh alone, but to all the perfumes blended in due proportion. The Father always finds a pleasure in Him, in Him he is well pleased; and all regenerated spirits rejoice in Him, for He is made of God unto us, "wisdom, righteousness, sanctification, and redemption." [See 1 Corinthians 1:30.] Note that not only is Jesus most sweet, but even His garments are so; everything that He has to do with is perfumed by His person. All His garments are thus fragrant; not some of them, but all; we delight as much in His purple of dominion as in the white of His priesthood, His mantle as our prophet is as dear to us as His seamless coat as our friend. All His dress is fragrant with all sweetness. To attempt to spiritualize each spice here mentioned would be unprofitable, the evident sense is that all sweetness meets in Jesus, and are poured forth wherever He is present.

Out of the ivory palaces, whereby they have made thee glad. The abode of Jesus now is imperial in splendor, ivory and gold but faintly images His royal seat; there He is made glad in the presence of the Father, and in the company of His saints. Oh, to behold Him with His perfumed garments on! The very fragrance of Him from afar ravishes our spirit, what must it be to be on the other side of the pearl gate, within the palace of ivory, amid those halls of Zion, "conjubilant with song," where the throne of David is, and the abiding presence of the Prince! To think of His gladness, to know that He is full of joy, gives gladness at this moment to our souls. We poor exiles can sing in our banishment since our

King, our Well-beloved, has come to His throne.

Psalm 45:9 *Kings' daughters were among thy honourable women: upon thy right hand did stand the queen in gold of Ophir.*

EXPOSITION: **Verse 9.** *King's daughters were among thy honourable women.* Our Lord's courts lack not for courtiers, and those the fairest and noblest. Virgin souls are maids of honor to the court, the true lilies of Heaven. The lowly and pure in heart are esteemed by the Lord Jesus as His most familiar friends; their place in His palace is not among the menials but near the throne. The day will come when those who are "king's daughters" literally will count it their greatest honor to serve the Church, and, meanwhile every believing sister is spiritually a King's daughter, a member of the royal family of Heaven.

Upon thy right hand, in the place of love, honour, and power, did stand the queen in gold of Ophir:[126] the Church shares her Lord's honor and happiness, He sets her in the place of dignity, He clothes her with the best of the best. Gold is the richest of metals, and Ophir gold the purest known. Jesus bestows nothing inferior or of secondary value upon His beloved Church. In imparted and imputed righteousness the Church is divinely arrayed. Happy are those who are members of a Church so honored, so beloved; unhappy are those who persecute the beloved people, for as a husband will not endure that his wife should be insulted or maltreated, so neither will the heavenly Husband; He will speedily avenge His own elect. Mark, then, the solemn pomp of the verses we have read. The King is seen with rapture, He girds himself as a warrior, robes himself as a monarch, mounts His chariot,

---

126. The location of Ophir, also called the Port of Ophir is still unknown to this day.

darts His arrows, and conquers His foes. Then He ascends His throne with His scepter in His hand, fills the palace hall with perfume brought from His secret chambers, His retinue stand around Him, and, fairest of all, His bride is at His right hand, with daughters of subject princes as her attendants. Faith is no stranger to this sight, and every time she looks she adores, she loves, she rejoices, she expects.

Psalm 45:10 *Hearken, O daughter, and consider, and incline thine ear; forget also thine own people, and thy father's house;*

EXPOSITION: **Verse 10.** *Hearken, O daughter, and consider.* Ever is this the great duty of the Church. Faith cometh by hearing, and confirmation by consideration. No precept can be more worthy of the attention of those who are honored to be espoused to Christ than that which follows. *And incline thine ear.* Lean forward so that no syllable may be unheard. The whole faculties of the mind should be bent upon receiving holy teaching. *Forget also thine own people, and thy father's house.* To renounce the world is not easy, but it must be done by all who are affianced to the Great King, for a divided heart He cannot endure; it would be misery to the beloved one as well as dishonor to her Lord.

Evil acquaintances, and even those who are but neutral, must be forsaken, they can confer no benefits, and they must inflict injury. The house of our nativity is the house of sin—we were shaped in iniquity; the carnal mind is enmity against God, we must come forth from the house of fallen nature, for it is built in the City of Destruction. Not that natural ties are broken by grace, but ties of the sinful nature, bonds of graceless affinity. We have much to forget as well as to learn, and the unlearning is so difficult that only diligent hearing, and considering, and bending of the whole soul to it, can accomplish the work; and even these would be too feeble if divine grace did not assist. Yet why should we remember the Egypt from which we came out? Are the leeks and the garlic, and the onions anything, when the iron bondage, and the slavish tasks, and the death dealing Pharaoh of hell are remembered? We part with folly for wisdom; with bubbles for eternal joys; with deceit for truth; with misery for bliss; and with idols for the living God. O that Christians were more mindful of the divine precept here recorded; but, alas! worldliness abounds; the Church is defiled; and the glory of the Great King is veiled. Only when the whole Church leads the separated life will the full splendor and power of Christianity shine forth upon the world.

Psalm 45:11 *So shall the king greatly desire thy beauty: for he is thy Lord; and worship thou him.*

EXPOSITION: Verse 11. *So shall the king greatly desire thy beauty.* Wholehearted love is the duty and bliss of the marriage state in every case, but especially so in this lofty mystical marriage. The Church must forsake all others and cleave to Jesus only, or she will not please Him nor enjoy the full manifestation of His love. What less can He ask, what less may she dare propose than to be wholly His? Jesus sees a beauty in His Church, a beauty which He delights in most when it is not marred by worldliness. He has always been most near and precious to His saints when they have cheerfully taken up His Cross and followed Him without [outside] the camp. [See Hebrews 13:13.] His Spirit is grieved when they mingle themselves among the people and learn their ways. No great and lasting revival of religion can be granted us until the professed lovers of Jesus prove their affection by coming out from an ungodly world, being separated, and touching not the unclean thing.

For he is thy Lord; and worship thou him. He has royal rights still; His condescending grace does not lessen but rather enforce His authority. Our Savior is also our Ruler. The husband is the head of the wife; the love he bears her does not lessen but strengthen her obligation to obey. The Church must reverence Jesus, and bow before Him in prostrate adoration; His tender union with her gives her liberty, but not license; it frees her from all other burdens, but places His easy yoke upon her neck. Who would wish it to be otherwise? The service of God is Heaven in Heaven, and perfectly carried out it is Heaven upon Earth. Jesus, you are He whom your Church praises in her unceasing songs, and adores in her perpetual service. Teach us to be wholly yours. Bear with us, and work by your Spirit in us until your will is done by us on Earth as it is in Heaven.

Psalm 45:12 *And the daughter of Tyre shall be there with a gift; even the rich among the people shall intreat thy favour.*

EXPOSITION: Verse 12. *And the daughter of Tyre shall be there with a gift.* When the Church abounds in holiness, she shall know no lack of homage from the surrounding people. Her glory shall then impress and attract the heathen around, until they also unite in doing honor to her Lord. The power of missions abroad lies at home: a holy Church will be a powerful Church. Nor shall there be lack of treasure in her coffers when grace is in her heart; the free gifts of a willing people shall enable the workers for God to carry on their sacred enterprise without stint.[127] Commerce shall send in its revenue to endow, not with forced levies and imperial taxes, but with willing gifts to the Church of the Great King.

---

127. Without trying to work with a meager allotment of necessary things.

Even the rich among the people shall intreat your favour. Not by pandering to their follies, but by testifying against their sins, shall the wealthy be won to the faith of Jesus. They shall come not to favor the Church but to beg for her favor. She shall not be the hireling of the great, but as a queen shall she dispense her favors to the suppliant throng of the rich among the people. We go about to beg for Christ like beggars for alms, and many who should know better will make compromises and become reticent of unpopular truth to please the great ones of the Earth. Not so will the true bride of Christ degrade herself, when her sanctification is more deep and more visible; then will the hearts of men grow liberal, and offerings from afar, abundant and continual, shall be presented at the throne of the Peaceful Prince.

Psalm 45:13 *The king's daughter is all glorious within: her clothing is of wrought gold.*

EXPOSITION: **Verse 13.** *The king's daughter is all glorious within.* Within her secret chambers her glory is great. Though unseen of men her Lord sees her, and commends her. "It doth not yet appear what we shall be." [See 1 John 3:2.] Or the passage may be understood as meaning within herself–her beauty is not outward only or mainly; the choicest of her charms are to be found in her heart, her secret character, her inward desires. Truth and wisdom in the hidden parts are what the Lord regards; mere skin deep beauty is nothing in His eyes. The Church is of royal extraction, of imperial dignity, for she is a king's daughter; and she has been purified and renewed in nature; for she is glorious within. Note the word all. The Bridegroom was said to have all His garments perfumed, and now the bride is all glorious within—entireness and completeness are great points. There is no mixture of ill savor in Jesus, nor shall there be the alloy of unholiness in His people, His Church shall be presented without spot or wrinkle, or any such thing. *Her clothing is of wrought gold.* Best material and best workmanship. How laboriously did our Lord work out the precious material of His righteousness into a vesture for His people! No embroidery of golden threads can equal that masterpiece of holy art. Such clothing becomes one so honored by relationship to the Great King. The Lord sees to it that nothing shall be wanting to the glory and beauty of His bride.

Psalm 45:14 *She shall be brought unto the king in raiment of needlework: the virgins her companions that follow her shall be brought unto thee.*

EXPOSITION: **Verse 14.** *She shall be brought unto the king in raiment of needlework.* The day comes when the celestial marriage shall be openly celebrated, and these words describe the nuptial procession wherein the queen is brought to her royal Husband attended by her handmaidens. In the latter-day glory, and in the consummation of all things, the glory of the bride, the Lamb's wife, shall be seen by all the universe with admiration. While she was within doors, and her saints hidden ones, the Church was glorious; what will be her splendor when she shall appear in the likeness of her Lord in the day of His manifestation? The finest embroidery is but a faint image of the perfection of the Church when sanctified by the Spirit. This verse tells us of the ultimate rest of the Church—the King's own bosom; of the way she comes to it, she is brought by the power of sovereign grace; of the time when this is done—in the future, she shall be, it does not yet appear; of the state in which she shall come—clad in richest array, and attended by brightest spirits.

The virgins her companions that follow her shall be

brought unto thee. Those who love and serve the Church for her Lord's sake shall share in her bliss "in that day." In one sense they are a part of the Church, but for the sake of the imagery they are represented as maids of honor; and, though the figure may seem incongruous, they are represented as brought to the King with the same loving familiarity as the bride, because the true servants of the Church are of the Church, and partake in all her happiness. Note that those who are admitted to everlasting communion with Christ, are pure in heart—virgins, pure in company—her companions, pure in walk—that follow her. Let none hope to be brought into Heaven at last who are not purified now.

Psalm 45:15 *With gladness and rejoicing shall they be brought: they shall enter into the king's palace.*

EXPOSITION: Verse 15. *With gladness and rejoicing shall they be brought.* Joy becomes a marriage feast. What joy will that be which will be seen at the feasts of paradise when all the redeemed shall be brought home! Gladness in the saints themselves, and rejoicing from the angels shall make the halls of the New Jerusalem ring again with shouting. *They shall enter into the King's palace.* Their peaceful abodes shall be where Jesus the King reigns in state forever. They shall not be shut out but shut in. Rights of free entrance into the holiest of all shall be accorded them. Brought by grace, they shall enter into glory. If there was joy in the bringing, what in the entering? What in the abiding? The glorified are not field laborers in the plains of Heaven, but sons who dwell at home, princes of the blood, resident in the royal palace. Happy hour when we shall enjoy all this and forget the sorrows of time in the triumph of eternity.

Psalm 45:16 *Instead of thy fathers shall be thy children, whom thou mayest make princes in all the earth.*

EXPOSITION: **Verse 16.** Instead of thy fathers shall be thy children. The ancient saints who stood as fathers in the service of the Great King have all passed away; but a spiritual seed is found to fill their places. The veterans depart, but volunteers fill up the vacant places. The line of grace never becomes extinct. As long as time shall last, the true apostolical succession will be maintained. *Whom thou mayest make princes in all the earth.* Servants of Christ are kings. Where a man has preached successfully, and evangelized a tribe or nation, he gets to himself more than regal honors, and his name is like the name of the great men that are upon the Earth. Jesus is the king maker. Ambition of the noblest kind shall win her desire in the army of Christ; immortal crowns are distributed to His faithful soldiers. The whole Earth shall yet be subdued for Christ, and honored are they, who shall, through grace, have a share in the conquest—these shall reign with Christ at His coming.

Psalm 45:17 *I will make thy name to be remembered in all generations: therefore shall the people praise thee for ever and ever.*

EXPOSITION: **Verse 17.** *I will make thy name to be remembered in all generations.* Jehovah by the prophet's mouth promises to the Prince of Peace eternal fame as well as a continuous progeny. His name is His fame, His character, His person; these are dear to His people now—they can never forget them; and it shall be so as long as men exist. Names renowned in one generation have been unknown to the next era, but the laurels of Jesus shall ever be fresh, His renown

306

ever new. God will see to this; His providence and His grace shall make it so. The fame of Messiah is not left to human guardianship; the Eternal guarantees it, and His promise never fails. All down the ages the memories of Gethsemane and Calvary shall glow with an inextinguishable light; nor shall the lapse of time, the smoke of error, or the malice of hell be able to dim the glory of the Redeemer's fame.

Therefore shall the people praise thee for ever and ever. They shall confess you to be what you are, and shall render to you in perpetuity the homage due. Praise is due from every heart to Him who loved us, and redeemed us by His blood; this praise will never be fully paid, but will be ever a standing and growing debt. His daily benefits enlarge our obligations; let them increase the number of our songs. Age to age reveals more of His love, let every year swell the volume of the music of Earth and Heaven, and let thunders of song roll up in full diapason to the throne of Him that liveth, and was dead, and is alive for evermore, and has the keys of hell and of death. [See Revelation 1:18.]

> "Let him be crowned with majesty
> Who bowed his head to death,
> And be his honours sounded high
> By all things that have breath."[128]

---

128. Hymn by Isaac Watts: *"O Lord, Our Lord, How Wondrous Great is Thine Exalted Name."*

307

PSALM 46

PSALM 46:1–PSALM 46:11

Psalm 46:1 *God is our refuge and strength, a very present help in trouble.*

EXPOSITION: Verse 1. *God is our refuge and strength.*

Not our armies or our fortresses. Israel's boast is in Jehovah, the only living and true God. Others vaunt their impregnable castles, placed on inaccessible rocks, and secured with gates of iron, but God is a far better refuge from distress than all these: and when the time comes to carry the war into the enemy's territories, the Lord stands His people in better stead than all the valor of legions or the boasted strength of chariot and horse. Soldiers of the

Cross, remember this, and count you safe, and make yourselves strong in God. Forget not the personal possessive word *our*; make sure each one of your portion in God, that you may say, "He is my refuge and strength." [See Psalm 62:7.] Neither forget the fact that God is our refuge just now, in the

309

immediate present, as truly as when David penned the word. God alone is our all in all. All other refuges are refuges of lies; all other strength is weakness, for power belongs unto God: but as God is all sufficient, our defense and might are equal to all emergencies.

A very present help in trouble, or in distress He has so been found, He has been tried and proved by His people. He never withdraws himself from His afflicted. He is their help, truly, effectually, constantly; He is present or near them, close at their side and ready as their help. This is emphasized by the word *very* in our version, He is more present than friend or relative can be, yes, more closely present than even the trouble itself. To all this comfortable truth is added the consideration that His assistance comes at the needed time. He is not as the swallows that leave us in the winter; he is a friend in need and a friend indeed. When it is very dark with us, let brave spirits say, "Come, let us sing the forty-sixth Psalm."

> "A fortress firm, and steadfast rock,
> Is God in time of danger;
> A shield and sword in every shock,
> From foe well known or stranger."

Psalm 46:2 *Therefore will not we fear, though the earth be removed, and though the mountains be carried into the midst of the sea;*

EXPOSITION: **Verse 2.** *Therefore.* How fond the psalmist is of *therefores*! His poetry is no poetic rapture without reason, it is as logical as a mathematical demonstration. The next words are a necessary inference from these. *Will not we fear.* With God on our side, how irrational would fear be! Where He is all power is, and all love, why therefore should we quail[129]? *Though the earth be removed,* though the basis of all visible things should be so convulsed as to be entirely changed. *And though the mountains be carried into the midst of the sea;* though the firmest of created objects should fall to headlong ruin, and be submerged in utter destruction. The two phrases set forth the most terrible commotions within the range of imagination, and include the overthrow of dynasties, the destruction of nations, the ruin of families, the persecutions of the Church, the reign of heresy, and whatever else may at any time try the faith of believers. Let the worst come to the worst, the child of God should never give way to mistrust; since God remains faithful there can be no danger to His cause or people. When the elements shall melt with fervent heat, and the heavens and the Earth shall pass away in the last general conflagration, we shall serenely behold "the wreck of matter, and the crash of worlds,"[130] for even then our refuge shall preserve us from all evil, our strength shall prepare us for all good.

Psalm 46:3 *Though the waters thereof roar and be troubled, though the mountains shake with the swelling thereof. Selah.*

EXPOSITION: **Verse 3.** *Though the waters thereof roar and be troubled.* When all things are excited to fury, and reveal their utmost power to disturb, faith smiles serenely. She is not afraid of noise, nor even of real force, she knows that the Lord stills the raging of the sea, and holds the waves in the hollow of His hand. *Though the mountains shake with the swelling thereof.* Alps and Andes may tremble, but faith rests on a firmer basis, and is not to be moved by swelling

129. To cringe in fear.
130. From "Cato, A Tragedy" by Joseph Addison, 1713; also cited elsewhere as "the crush of worlds."

seas. Evil may ferment, wrath may boil, and pride may foam, but the brave heart of holy confidence trembles not. Great men who are like mountains may quake for fear in times of great calamity, but the man whose trust is in God needs never to be dismayed. *Selah.*

Psalm 46:4 *There is a river, the streams whereof shall make glad the city of God, the holy place of the tabernacles of the most High.*

EXPOSITION: Verse 4. *There is a river.* Divine grace like a smoothly flowing, fertilizing, full, and never failing river, yields refreshment and consolation to believers. This is the river of the water of life, of which the Church above as well as the Church below partakes evermore. It is no boisterous ocean, but a placid stream, it is not stayed in its course by earthquakes or crumbling mountains, it follows its serene course without disturbance. Happy are they who know from their own experience that there is such a river of God. *The streams whereof* in their various influences, for they are many, *shall make glad the city of God,* by assuring the citizens that Zion's Lord will unfailingly supply all their needs. The streams are not transient like Cherith[131], nor muddy like the Nile, nor furious like Kishon[132], nor treacherous like Job's deceitful brooks, neither are their waters "naught" like those of Jericho, they are clear, cool, fresh, abundant, and gladdening.

The great fear of an Eastern city in time of war was that the water supply would be cut off during a siege; if that were secured the city could hold out against attacks for an indefinite period. In this verse, Jerusalem, which represents the Church of God, is described as well supplied with water,

---

131. A small brooks that flows into the River Jordan.
132. A river that flows into the Mediterranean Sea near Haifa.

to set forth the fact that in seasons of trial all sufficient grace will be given to enable us to endure unto the end. The Church is like a well-ordered city, surrounded with mighty walls of truth and justice, garrisoned by omnipotence, fairly built and adorned by infinite wisdom. Its burgesses[133] the saints enjoy high privileges; they trade with far off lands, they live in the smile of the King; and as a great river is the very making and mainstay of a town, so is the broad river of everlasting love, and grace their joy and bliss. The Church is peculiarly the City of God, of His designing, building, election, purchasing and indwelling. It is dedicated to His praise, and glorified by His presence.

The holy place of the tabernacles of the Most High. This was the peculiar glory of Jerusalem, that the Lord within her walls had a place where He peculiarly revealed himself, and this is the choice privilege of the saints, concerning which we may cry with wonder, "Lord, how is it that thou wilt manifest thyself unto us, and not unto the world?" [See John 14:22.] To be a temple for the Holy Ghost is the delightful portion of each saint, to be the living temple for the Lord our God is also the high honor of the Church in her corporate capacity. Our God is here called by a worthy title, indicating His power, majesty, sublimity, and excellency; and it is worthy of note that under this character He dwells in the Church. We have not a great God in nature, and a little God in grace; no, the Church contains as clear and convincing a revelation of God as the works of nature, and even more amazing in the excellent glory which shines between the cherubim overshadowing that mercy seat which is the center and gathering place of the people of the living God. To have the Most High dwelling within her members is to make the Church on Earth like the Church in Heaven.

---

133. Citizens

Psalm 46:5 *God is in the midst of her; she shall not be moved: God shall help her, and that right early.*

EXPOSITION: **Verse 5.** *God is in the midst of her.* His help is therefore sure and near. Is she besieged, then He is himself besieged within her, and we may be certain that He will break forth upon His adversaries. How near is the Lord to the distresses of His saints, since He sojourns in their midst! Let us take heed that we do not grieve Him; let us have such respect to Him as Moses had when he felt the sand of Horeb's desert to be holy, and put off his shoes from off his feet when the Lord spake from the burning bush. *She shall not be moved.* How can she be moved unless her enemies move her Lord also? His presence renders all hope of capturing and demolishing the city utterly ridiculous. The Lord is in the vessel, and she cannot, therefore, be wrecked. *God shall help her.* Within her He will furnish rich supplies, and outside her walls He will lay her foes in heaps like the armies of Sennacherib, when the angel went forth and smote them.

And that right early. As soon as the first ray of light proclaims the coming day, at the turning of the morning God's right arm shall be outstretched for His people. The Lord is up early. We are slow to meet Him, but He is never tardy in helping us. Impatience complains of divine delays, but in very deed the Lord is not slack concerning His promise. Man's haste is often folly, but God's apparent delays are ever wise; and when rightly viewed, are no delays at all. Today the bands of evil may environ the Church of God, and threaten her with destruction; but before long they shall pass away like the foam on the waters, and the noise of their tumult shall be silent in the grave. The darkest hour of the night is just before the turning of the morning; and then, even then, shall the Lord appear as the great ally of His Church.

Psalm 46:6 *The heathen raged, the kingdoms were moved: he uttered his voice, the earth melted.*

EXPOSITION: **Verse 6.** *The heathen raged.* The nations were in a furious uproar, they gathered against the city of the Lord like wolves ravenous for their prey; they foamed, and roared, and swelled like a tempestuous sea. *The kingdoms were moved.* A general confusion seized upon society; the fierce invaders convulsed their own dominions by draining the population to urge on the war, and they desolated other territories by their devastating march to Jerusalem. Crowns fell from royal heads, ancient thrones rocked like trees driven of the tempest, powerful empires fell like pines uprooted by the blast: everything was in disorder, and dismay seized on all who knew not the Lord.

He uttered his voice, the earth melted. With no other instrumentality than a word the Lord ruled the storm. He gave forth a voice and stout hearts were dissolved, proud armies were annihilated, conquering powers were enfeebled. At first the confusion appeared to be worse confounded, when the element of divine power came into view; the very earth seemed turned to wax, the most solid and substantial of human things melted like the fat of rams upon the altar; but in a little while peace followed, the rage of man subsided, hearts capable of repentance relented, and the implacable were silenced. How mighty is a Word from God! How mighty the Incarnate Word. O that such a word would come from the excellent glory even now to melt all hearts in love to Jesus, and to end for ever all the persecutions, wars, and rebellions of men!

Psalm 46:7 *The Lord of hosts is with us; the God of Jacob is our refuge. Selah.*

EXPOSITION: **Verse 7.** *The Lord of hosts is with us.* This is the reason for all Zion's security, and for the overthrow of her foes. The Lord rules the angels, the stars, the elements, and all the hosts of Heaven; and the Heaven of heavens are under His sway. The armies of men though they know it not are made to subserve His will. This Generalissimo of the forces of the land, and the Lord High Admiral of the seas, is on our side—our august ally; woe unto those who fight against Him, for they shall fly like smoke before the wind when He gives the word to scatter them. *The God of Jacob is our refuge,* Immanuel is Jehovah of Hosts, and Jacob's God is our high place of defense. When this glad verse is sung to music worthy of such a jubilate, well may the singers pause and the players wait awhile to tune their instruments again; here, therefore, fitly stands that solemn, stately, peaceful note of rest, *Selah.*

Psalm 46:8 *Come, behold the works of the Lord, what desolations he hath made in the earth.*

EXPOSITION: **Verse 8.** *Come, behold the works of the Lord.* The joyful citizens of Jerusalem are invited to go forth and view the remains of their enemies that they may mark the prowess of Jehovah and the spoil which His right hand has won for His people. It would be good if we also carefully noted the providential dealings of our covenant God, and were quick to perceive His hand in the battles of His Church. Whenever we read history it should be with this verse sounding in our ears. We should read the newspaper in the same spirit, to see how the Head of the Church rules the nations for His people's good, as Joseph governed Egypt for the sake of Israel.

What desolations He hath made in the earth. The destroyers He destroys, the desolators He desolates. How forcible is the verse at this date! The ruined cities of Assyria, Babylon, Petra, Bashan, Canaan, are our instructors, and in tables of stone record the doings of the Lord. In every place where His cause and crown have been disregarded ruin has surely followed: sin has been a blight on nations, and left their palaces to lie in heaps. In the days of the writer of this Psalm, there had probably occurred some memorable interpositions of God against His Israel's foes; and as He saw their overthrow, He called on His fellow citizens to come forth and attentively consider the terrible things in righteousness which had been wrought on their behalf. Dismantled castles and ruined abbeys in our own land stand as memorials of the Lord's victories over oppression and superstition. May there soon be more of such desolations.

> "Ye gloomy piles, ye tombs of living men,
> Ye sepulchres of womanhood, or worse;
> Ye refuges of lies, soon may ye fall,
> And amid your ruins may the owl, and bat,
> And dragon find congenial resting place."

Psalm 46:9 *He maketh wars to cease unto the end of the earth; he breaketh the bow, and cutteth the spear in sunder; he burneth the chariot in the fire.*

EXPOSITION: **Verse 9.** *He maketh wars to cease unto the end of the earth.* His voice quiets the tumult of war, and calls for the silence of peace. However remote and barbarous the tribe, He awes the people into rest. He crushes the great powers till they cannot provoke strife again; He gives His people profound repose. *He breaketh the bow,* the sender of swift winged death He renders useless. *And cutteth the spear in sunder*—the lance of the mighty man He shivers.[134] *He burneth the chariot in the fire*—the proud war chariot with its death dealing scythes He commits to the flames. All sorts of weapons He piles heaps on heaps, and utterly destroys them. So it was in Judea in the days long ago, so shall it be in all lands in eras yet to come. Blessed deed of the Prince of Peace! When shall it be literally performed? Already the spiritual foes of His people are stripped of their power to destroy; but when shall the universal victory of peace be celebrated, and instruments of wholesale murder be consigned to ignominious[135] destruction? How glorious will the ultimate victory of Jesus be in the day of His appearing, when every enemy shall lick the dust!

Psalm 46:10 *Be still, and know that I am God: I will be exalted among the heathen, I will be exalted in the earth.*

EXPOSITION: Verse 10. *Be still, and know that I am God.* Hold off your hands, you enemies! Sit down and wait in patience, you believers! Acknowledge that Jehovah is God, you who feel the terrors of His wrath! Adore Him, and Him only, you who partake in the protection of His grace. Since none can worthily proclaim His nature, let "expressive silence muse His praise." The boasts of the ungodly and the timorous forebodings of the saints should certainly be hushed by a sight of what the Lord has done in past ages. *I will be exalted among the heathen.* They forget God, they worship idols, but Jehovah will yet be honored by them. Reader, the prospects of missions are bright, bright as the promises of God. Let no man's heart fail him; the solemn declarations

134. Shatters
135. Disgraceful or shameful.

of this verse must be fulfilled. *I will be exalted in the earth,* among all people, whatever may have been their wickedness or their degradation. Either by terror or love God will subdue all hearts to himself. The whole round Earth shall yet reflect the light of His majesty. All the more because of the sin, and obstinacy, and pride of man shall God be glorified when grace reigns unto eternal life in all corners of the world.

Psalm 46:11 *The Lord of hosts is with us; the God of Jacob is our refuge. Selah.*

EXPOSITION: Verse 11. *The Lord of hosts is with us; the God of Jacob is our refuge.* It was good to sing this twice over. It is a truth of which no believer wearies, it is a fact too often forgotten, and it is a precious privilege which cannot be too often considered. Reader, is the Lord on your side? Is Emmanuel, God with us, your Redeemer? Is there a covenant between you and God as between God and Jacob? If so, three times happy are you. Show your joy in holy song and in times of trouble play the man by still making music for your God. *Selah.* Here as before, lift up the heart. Rest in contemplation after praise. Still keep the soul in tune. It is easier to sing a hymn of praise than to continue in the spirit of praise, but let it be our aim to maintain the uprising devotion of our grateful hearts, and so end our song as if we intended it to be continued.

> SELAH bids the music rest.
> Pause in silence soft and blest;
> SELAH bids uplift the strain,
> Harps and voices tune again;
> SELAH ends the vocal praise,
> Still your hearts to God upraise.

PSALM 47

PSALM 47:1–PSALM 47:9

Psalm 47:1 *O clap your hands, all ye people; shout unto God with the voice of triumph.*

EXPOSITION: Verse 1. *O clap your hands.* The most natural and most enthusiastic tokens of exultation are to be used in view of the victories of the Lord, and His universal reign. Our joy in God may be demonstrative, and yet He will not censure it. *All ye people.* The joy is to extend to all nations; Israel may lead the van, but all the Gentiles are to follow in the march of triumph, for they have an equal share in that kingdom where there is neither Greek nor Jew, but Christ is all and in all. Even now if they did but know it, it is the best hope of all nations that Jehovah rules over them. If they cannot all speak the same tongue, the symbolic language of the hands they can all use. All people will be ruled by the Lord in the latter days, and all will exult in that rule; were they wise they would submit to it now, and rejoice to do so; yes, they would clap their hands in rapture at the thought. *Shout,* let your voices keep tune with your hands. *Unto God,* let Him have all the honors of the day, and let them be loud, joyous, universal, and undivided. *With the voice of triumph,* with happy sounds, consonant with such splendid victories, so great a King, so excellent a rule, and such happy subjects. Many are human languages, and yet the nations may triumph as with one voice. Faith's view of God's government is full of transport. The prospect of the universal reign of the Prince of Peace is enough to make the tongue of the dumb sing; what will the reality be? Well might the poet of the seasons bid mountains and valleys raise their joyous hymn— "For the GREAT SHEPHERD reigns, / And his unsuffering kingdom yet will come."[136]

Psalm 47:2 *For the Lord most high is terrible; he is a great King over all the earth.*

EXPOSITION: Verse 2. *For the Lord,* or JEHOVAH, the self existent and only God; *Most high,* most great in power, lofty in dominion, eminent in wisdom, elevated in glory. *Is terrible,* none can resist His power or stand before His vengeance; yet as these terrors are wielded on the behalf of His subjects, they are fit reasons for rejoicing. Omnipotence, which is terrible to crush, is almighty to protect. At a grand review of the troops of a great prince, all His loyal subjects are His foes. *He is a great King over all the earth.* Not over Judea only, but even to the utmost isles His reign extends. Our God is no local deity, no petty ruler of a tribe; in infinite majesty He rules the mightiest realm as absolute arbiter of destiny, sole monarch of all lands, King of kings, and Lord of lords. Not a hamlet or an islet is excluded from His dominion. How glorious will that era be when this is seen and known of all; when in the person of Jesus all flesh shall behold the glory of the Lord!

Psalm 47:3 *He shall subdue the people under us, and the nations under our feet.*

EXPOSITION: Verse 3. *He,* with whom is infinite power, *shall subdue the people under us.* The battle is not ours but the Lord's. He will take His own time, but He

---

136. *"Benevolent Reflections"* from *Winter* by James Thompson.

will certainly achieve victory for His Church. Truth and righteousness through grace shall climb to the ascendant. We wage no doubtful warfare. Hearts the most rebellious, and wills the most stubborn, shall submit to all conquering grace. All the Lord's people, whether Jews or Gentiles, may clap their hands at this, for God's victory will be theirs; but surely apostles, prophets, ministers, and those who suffer and labor the most, may take the largest share in the joy. Idolatry, infidelity, superstition, we shall yet tread upon, as men tread down the stones of the street. *And the nations under our feet.* The Church of God shall be the greatest of monarchies; her victory shall be signal and decisive. Christ shall take to himself His great power and reign, and all the tribes of men shall own at once His glory and the glory of His people in Him. How changed will be the position of affairs in coming ages! The people of God have been under the feet of men in long and cruel persecutions, and in daily contempt; but God will reverse the position, and the best in character shall be first in honor.

Psalm 47:4 *He shall choose our inheritance for us, the excellency of Jacob whom he loved. Selah.*

EXPOSITION: Verse 4. While as yet we see not all things put under Him, we are glad to put ourselves and our fortunes at His disposal. *He shall choose our inheritance for us.* We feel His reign to be so gracious that we even now ask to be in the fullest degree the subjects of it. We submit our will, our choice, and our desire, wholly to Him. Our heritage here and hereafter we leave to Him let Him do with us as seems good to Him. *The excellency of Jacob whom he loved.* He gave His ancient people their portion, He will give us ours, and we ask nothing better. This is the most spiritual and real manner of clapping our hands because of His sovereignty, namely, to leave all our affairs in His hands, for then our hands are empty of all care for self, and free to be used in His honor. He was the boast and glory of Israel; He is and shall be ours. He loved His people and became their greatest glory; He loves us, and He shall be our exceeding joy. As for the latter days, we ask nothing better than to stand in our appointed lot, for if we have but a portion in our Lord Jesus, it is enough for our largest desires. Our beauty, our boast, our best treasure, lies in having such a God to trust in, such a God to love us. *Selah*. Yes, pause, faithful songsters. Here is abundant room for holy meditation—

> "Muse awhile, obedient thought,
> Lo, the theme's with rapture fraught;
> See thy King, whose realm extends
> Even to earth's remotest ends.
> Gladly shall the nations own
> Him their God and Lord alone;
> Clap their hands with holy mirth,
> Hail him MONARCH OF THE EARTH.
> Come, my soul, before him bow,
> Gladdest of his subjects thou;
> Leave thy portion to his choice,
> In his sovereign will rejoice,
> This thy purest, deepest bliss,
> He is thine and thou art his."[137]

Psalm 47:5 *God is gone up with a shout, the LORD with the sound of a trumpet.*

EXPOSITION: **Verse 5.** *God is gone up with a shout.* Faith hears the people already shouting. The command of

137. Author unknown.

the first verse is here regarded as a fact. The fight is over; the conqueror ascends to His triumphant chariot, and rides up to the gates of the city which is made resplendent with the joy of His return. The words are fully applicable to the ascension of the Redeemer. We doubt not that angels and glorified spirits welcomed Him with acclamations. He came not without song; shall we imagine that He returned in silence? *The Lord with the sound of a trumpet.* Jesus is Jehovah. The joyful strain of the trumpet speaks of the splendor of His triumph. It was fitting and right to welcome one returning from the wars with martial music. Fresh from Bozrah, with His garments all red from the winepress, he ascended, leading captivity captive, and well might the clarion ring out the tidings of Immanuel's victorious return.

Psalm 47:6 *Sing praises to God, sing praises: sing praises unto our King, sing praises.*

EXPOSITION: Verse 6. *Sing praises.* What jubilation is here, when five times over the whole Earth is called upon to sing to God! He is worthy, He is Creator, and He is goodness itself. Sing praises; keep on with the glad work. Never let the music pause. He never ceases to be good, let us never cease to be grateful. Strange that we should need so much urging to attend to so heavenly an exercise.

Sing praises unto our King. Let him have all our praise; no one ought to have even a particle of it. Jesus shall have it all. Let His sovereignty be the fount of gladness. It is a sublime attribute, but full of bliss to the faithful. Let our homage be paid not in groans but songs. He asks not slaves to grace His throne; He is no despot [tyrant]; singing is fit homage for a monarch so blessed and gracious. Let all hearts that own His scepter sing and sing on forever, for there is everlasting reason for thanksgiving while we dwell under the shadow of such a throne.

Psalm 47:7 *For God is the King of all the earth: sing ye praises with understanding.*

EXPOSITION: **Verse 7.** *For God is the King of all the earth.* The Jews of our Savior's time resented this truth, but had their hearts been right they would have rejoiced in it. They would have kept their God to themselves, and not even have allowed the Gentile dogs to eat the crumbs from under His table. Alas! How selfishness turns honey into wormwood. Jehovah is not the God of the Jews only, all the nations of the Earth are, through the Messiah, yet to own Him Lord. Meanwhile His providential throne governs all events beneath the sky.

Sing ye praises with understanding. Sing a didactic [instructive] Psalm. Sound doctrine praises God. Even under the economy of types and ceremonies, it is clear that the Lord had regard to the spirituality of worship, and would be praised thoughtfully, intelligently, and with deep appreciation of the reason for song. It is to be feared from the slovenly way in which some make a noise in singing, that they fancy any sound will do. On the other hand, from the great attention paid by some to the mere music, we feel sadly sure that the sense has no effect upon them. Is it not a sin to be tickling men's ears with sounds when we profess to be adoring the Lord? What has a sensuous delight in organs, anthems, etc., to do with devotion? Do not men mistake physical effects for spiritual impulses? Do they not often offer to God strains far more calculated for human amusement than for divine acceptance? An understanding enlightened of the Holy Spirit is then and then only fully capable of offering worthy praise.

Psalm 47:8 *God reigneth over the heathen: God sitteth upon the throne of his holiness.*

EXPOSITION: **Verse 8.** Now at this moment, over the most debased idolaters, God holds a secret rule; here is work for faith. How we ought to long for the day when this truth shall be changed in its aspect and the rule now unrecognized shall be delighted in! The great truth that *God reigneth* in providence is the guarantee that in a gracious gospel sense His promises shall be fulfilled, and His Kingdom shall come. *God sitteth upon the throne of his holiness.* Unmoved He occupies an undisputed throne, whose decrees, acts, and commands are holiness itself. What other throne is like this? Never was it stained with injustice, or defiled with sin. Neither is He who sits upon it dismayed, or in a dilemma. He sits in serenity, for He knows His own power, and sees that His purposes will not miscarry. Here is reason enough for holy song.

Psalm 47:9 *The princes of the people are gathered together, even the people of the God of Abraham: for the shields of the earth belong unto God: he is greatly exalted.*

EXPOSITION: **Verse 9.** *The princes of the people are gathered together.* The prophetic eye of the psalmist sees the willing subjects of the great King assembled to celebrate His glory. Not only the poor and the men of low estate are there, but nobles bow their willing necks to His sway. "All kings shall bow down before him." [See Psalm 72:11.] No people shall be unrepresented; their great men shall be good men, their royal ones regenerate ones. How august will be the parliament where the Lord Jesus shall open the court, and princes shall rise up to do Him honor.

Even the people of the God of Abraham. That same God, who was known only here and there to a patriarch like the father of the faithful, shall be adored by a seed as

327

many as the stars of Heaven. The covenant promise shall be fulfilled, "In thee and in thy seed shall all the nations of the earth be blessed." [See Genesis 28:14.] Shiloh shall come, and "to him shall the gathering of the people be." [See Genesis 49:10.] Babel's dispersion shall be obliterated by the gathering arm of the Great Shepherd King. *For the shields of the earth belong unto God.* The insignia of pomp, the emblems of rank, the weapons of war, all must pay loyal homage to the King of all.

Those who are right honorable must honor Jesus, and majesties must claim Him to be far more majestic. Those who are Earth's protectors, the shields of the commonwealth, derive their might from Him, and are His. All principalities and powers must be subject unto Jehovah and His Christ, for *He is greatly exalted.* In nature, in power, in character, in glory, there is none to compare with Him. Oh, glorious vision of a coming era! Make haste, you wheels of time! Meanwhile, you saints, "Be ye steadfast, unmovable, always abounding in the work of the Lord, forasmuch as ye know that your labour is not in vain in the Lord." [See 1 Corinthians 15:58.]

PSALM 48

PSALM 48:1–PSALM 48:14

Psalm 48:1 *Great is the Lord, and greatly to be praised in the city of our God, in the mountain of his holiness.*

EXPOSITION: Verse 1. *Great is the Lord.* How great Jehovah is essentially none can conceive; but we can all see that He is great in the deliverance of His people, great in their esteem who are delivered, and great in the hearts of those enemies whom He scatters by their own fears. Instead of the mad cry of Ephesus, "Great is Diana," we bear the reasonable, demonstrable, self evident testimony, "Great is Jehovah." There is none great in the Church but the Lord. Jesus is "the great Shepherd," He is "a Savior, and a great one," our great God and Savior, our great High Priest. His Father has divided Him a portion with the great, and His name shall be great unto the ends of the Earth.

And greatly to be praised. According to His nature should His worship be; it cannot be too constant, too laudatory, too earnest, too reverential, and too sublime. *In the city of our God.* He is great there, and should be greatly praised there. If all the world renounced Jehovah's worship, the chosen people in His favored city would continue to adore Him, for in their midst and on their behalf His glorious power has been so manifestly revealed. In the Church the Lord is to be extolled though all the nations rage against Him. Jerusalem was the peculiar abode of the God of Israel, the seat of the theocratic government, and the center of prescribed worship, and even thus is the Church the place of divine manifestation.

In the mountain of his holiness. Where His holy temple, His holy priests, and His holy sacrifices might continually be seen. Zion was a mount, and as it was the most renowned part of the city, it is mentioned as a synonym for the city itself. The Church of God is a mount for elevation and for conspicuousness, and it should be adorned with holiness, her sons being partakers of the holiness of God. Only by holy men can the Lord be fittingly praised, and they should be incessantly occupied with His worship.

Psalm 48:2 *Beautiful for situation, the joy of the whole earth, is mount Zion, on the sides of the north, the city of the great King.*

EXPOSITION: **Verse 2.** *Beautiful for situation.* Jerusalem was so naturally, she was styled the Queen of the East; the Church is so spiritually, being placed near God's heart, within the mountain of His power, upon the hills of His faithfulness, in the center of providential operations. The elevation of the Church is her beauty. The more she is above the world the fairer she is. *The joy of the whole earth is Mount Zion.* Jerusalem was the world's star; whatever light lingered on Earth was borrowed from the oracles preserved by Israel. An ardent Israelite would esteem the holy city as the eye of the nations, the most precious pearl of all lands. Certainly the Church of God, though despised of men, is the true joy and hope of the world.

On the sides of the north, the city of the great King. Either meaning that Jerusalem was in the northern extremity of Judah, or it may denote that part of the city that lay to the north of Mount Zion. It was the glory of Jerusalem to be God's city, the place of His regal dwelling, and it is the joy of the Church that God is in her midst. The great God is the great King of the Church, and for her sake He rules all the nations. The people among whom the Lord deigns to dwell are privileged above all others; the lines have fallen unto them in pleasant places, and they have a goodly heritage. We who dwell in Great Britain in the sides of the north, have this for our chief glory, that the Lord is known in our land, and the abode of His love is among us.

Psalm 48:3 *God is known in her palaces for a refuge.*

EXPOSITION: Verse 3. *God is known in her palaces for a refuge.* We worship no unknown God. We know Him as our refuge in distress, we delight in Him as such, and run to Him in every time of need. We know nothing else as our refuge. Though we are made kings, and our houses are palaces, yet we have no confidence in ourselves, but trust in the Lord Protector, whose well known power is our bulwark.

Psalm 48:4 *For, lo, the kings were assembled, they passed by together.*

EXPOSITION: Verse 4. *The kings were assembled, they passed by together.* They came and they went. No sooner together than scattered. They came one way and fled twenty ways. Boastful the gathering hosts with their royal leaders, despairing the fugitive bands with their astonished captains. They came like foam on the angry sea, like foam they melted away. This was so remarkable that the psalmist puts in a note of exclamation, Lo! What! have they so suddenly fled! Even thus shall the haters of the Church vanish from the field. Papists, Ritualists, Arians, Skeptics, they shall each have their day, and shall pass on to the limbo of forgetfulness.

Psalm 48:5 *They saw it, and so they marvelled; they were troubled, and hasted away.*

EXPOSITION: **Verse 5.** *They saw it, and so they marvelled.* They came, they saw, but they did not conquer. There was no veni, vidi, vici[138] for them. No sooner did they perceive that the Lord was in the Holy City, than they took to their heels. Before the Lord came to blows with them, they were faint hearted, and beat a retreat. *They were troubled and hasted away.* The troublers were troubled. Their haste in coming was nothing to their hurry in going. Panic seized them, horses were not fleet enough; they would have borrowed the wings of the wind. They fled dishonorably like children in a fright. Glory be to God, it shall be even thus with the foes of His church; when the Lord comes to our help, our enemies shall be as nothing. Could they foresee their dishonorable defeat, they would not advance to the attack.

Psalm 48:6 *Fear took hold upon them there, and pain, as of a woman in travail.*

EXPOSITION: **Verse 6.** *Fear took hold upon them there.* They were in Giant Despair's grip. Where they hoped to triumph, there they quivered with dismay. They did not take the city, but fear took hold on them. *And pain, as of a woman in travail.* They were as much overcome as a woman whose fright causes premature delivery; or, as full of pain as a poor mother in her pangs—a strong expression, commonly employed by Orientals to set forth the extremity of anguish. When the Lord arises for the help of His church, the proudest of His foes shall be as trembling women, and their dismay shall be but the beginning of eternal defeat.

---

138. I came, I saw, I conquered.

Psalm 48:7 *Thou breakest the ships of Tarshish with an east wind.*

EXPOSITION: **Verse 7.** *Thou breakest the ships of Tarshish with an east wind.* As easily as vessels are driven to shipwreck, do you overturn the most powerful adversaries; or it may mean the strength of some nations lies in their ships, whose wooden walls are soon broken; but our strength is in our God, and therefore, it fails not. Or there may be another meaning, though you are our defense, yet you take vengeance on our inventions, and while you preserve us, yet our ships, our comforts, our earthly ambitions, are taken from us that we may look alone to you alone. God is seen at sea, but He is equally present on land. Speculative heresies, pretending to bring us wealth from afar, are constantly assailing the Church, but the breath of the Lord soon drives them to destruction. The Church too often relies on the wisdom of men, and these human helps are soon shipwrecked; yet the Church itself is safe beneath the care of her God and King.

Psalm 48:8 *As we have heard, so have we seen in the city of the Lord of hosts, in the city of our God: God will establish it for ever. Selah.*

EXPOSITION: **Verse 8.** *As we have heard, so have we seen in the city of the Lord of hosts, in the city of our God.* Our father's stories are reproduced before our very eyes. We heard the promise, and we have seen the fulfillment. The records of Zion, wonderful as they are, are proved to be truthful, because present facts are in perfect harmony therewith. Note how the Lord is first spoken of as Lord of hosts, a name of power and sovereignty, and then as our God, a name of covenant relation and condescension. No wonder that since the Lord bears both titles, we find Him dealing with us after the precedents of His loving-kindness, and the faithfulness of His promises. *God will establish it for ever.* The true church can never be disestablished. That which kings establish can last for time only, that which God establishes endures to all eternity. *Selah.* Here is a fit place to pause, viewing the past with admiration, and the future with confidence.

Psalm 48:9 *We have thought of thy lovingkindness, O God, in the midst of thy temple.*

EXPOSITION: **Verse 9.** *We have thought.* Holy men are thoughtful men; they do not suffer God's wonders to pass before their eyes and melt into forgetfulness, but they meditate deeply upon them. *Of thy lovingkindness, O God.* What a delightful subject! Devout minds never tire of so divine a theme. It is good to think of past loving-kindness in times of trial, and equally profitable to remember it in seasons of prosperity. Grateful memories sweeten sorrows and sober joys. *In the midst of thy temple.* Fit place for so devout a meditation. Where God is most seen He is best loved. The assembled saints constitute a living temple, and our deepest musings when so gathered together should have regard to the loving-kindness of the Lord, exhibited in the varied experiences of each of the living stones. Memories of mercy should be associated with continuance of praise. Hard by the table of show bread commemorating His bounty, should stand the altar of incense denoting our praise.

Psalm 48:10 *According to thy name, O God, so is thy praise unto the ends of the earth: thy right hand is full of righteousness.*

EXPOSITION: **Verse 10.** *According to thy name, O God, so is thy praise unto the ends of the earth.* Great fame is due to His great name. The glory of Jehovah's exploits overleaps the boundaries of Earth; angels behold with wonder, and from every star delighted intelligences proclaim His fame beyond the ends of the Earth. What if men are silent, yet the woods, and seas, and mountains, with all their countless tribes, and all the unseen spirits that walk them, are full of the divine praise? As in a shell we listen to the murmurs of the sea, so in the convolutions of creation we hear the praises of God. *Thy right hand is full of righteousness.* Your scepter and your sword, your government and your vengeance, are altogether just. Your hand is never empty, but full of energy, of bounty, and of equity. Neither saint nor sinner shall find the Lord to be an empty handed God; He will in both cases deal out righteousness to the full: to the one, through Jesus, He will be just to forgive, to the other just to condemn.

Psalm 48:11 *Let mount Zion rejoice, let the daughters of Judah be glad, because of thy judgments.*

EXPOSITION: **Verse 11.** *Let mount Zion rejoice.* As the first of the cities of Judah, and the main object of the enemies' attack, let her lead the song. *Let the daughters of Judah be glad,* let the smaller towns join the chorus, for they join in the common victory. Let the women, who fare worst in the havoc of war, be among the gladdest of the glad, now that the spoilers have fled. All the Church, and each individual member, should rejoice in the Lord, and magnify His name. *Because of thy judgments.* The righteous acts of the Lord are legitimate subjects for joyful praise. However it may appear on Earth, yet in Heaven the eternal ruin of the wicked will be the theme of adoring song. *"Alleluia; salvation, and glory, and honour, and power, unto the Lord* *our God. For true and righteous are his judgments; for he hath judged the great whore which did corrupt the earth with her fornication, and hath avenged the blood of his servants at her hand. And again they said, Alleluia, and her smoke rose up for ever and ever."* [See Revelation 19:1-3.] Justice which to our poor optics now seems severe, will then be perceived to be perfectly consistent with God's name of love, and to be one of the brightest jewels of His crown.

Psalm 48:12 *Walk about Zion, and go round about her: tell the towers thereof.*

EXPOSITION: **Verse 12.** *Walk about Zion;* often beat her bounds, even as Israel marched around Jericho. With leisurely and careful inspection survey her. *And go round about her.* Encircle her again and again with loving perambulations .[139] We cannot too frequently or too deeply consider the origin, privileges, history, security, and glory of the Church. Some subjects deserve but a passing thought; this is worthy of the most patient consideration. *Tell the towers thereof.* See if any of them have crumbled, or have been demolished. Is the Church of God what she was in doctrine, in strength and in beauty? Her foes counted her towers in envy first, and then in terror, let us count them with sacred exultation. The city of Lucerne, encircled by its ancient walls, adorned with a succession of towers, is a visible illustration of this figure; and as we have gone around it, and paused at each picturesque tower, we have realized the loving lingering inspection which the metaphor implies.

Psalm 48:13 *Mark ye well her bulwarks, consider her palaces; that ye may tell it to the generation following.*

---

139. Walks

PSALM 48

EXPOSITION: Verse 13. *Mark ye well her bulwarks.* Consider most attentively how strong her ramparts are, how safely her inhabitants are entrenched behind successive lines of defense. The security of the people of God is not a doctrine to be kept in the background, it may be safely taught, and frequently pondered; only to base hearts will that glorious truth prove harmful. The sons of perdition make a stumbling stone even of the Lord Jesus himself, it is little wonder that they pervert the truth of God concerning the final perseverance of the saints. We are not to turn away from inspecting Zion's ramparts, because idlers skulk behind them. *Consider her palaces.* Examine with care the fair dwellings of the city. Let the royal promises which afford quiet resting places for believers be attentively inspected. See how sound the defenses are, and how fair are the pleasures of "that ancient city," of which you are citizens.

A man should be best acquainted with his own home; and the Church is our dear and blest abode. I pray to God that Christians were more considerate of the condition of the Church; so far from telling the towers, some of them scarcely know what or where they are; they are too busy counting their money, and considering their ledgers. Freehold and copyhold, and leasehold, men measure to an inch, but Heaven hold and grace hold are too often treated as less important and neglected in sheer heedlessness. *That ye may tell it to the generation following* is an excellent reason for studious observation. We have received and we must transmit. We must be students that we may be teachers. The debt we owe to the past we must endeavor to repay by handing down the truth to the future.

Psalm 48:14 *For this God is our God for ever and ever: he will be our guide even unto death.*

337

EXPOSITION: Verse 14. *For this God is our God for ever and ever.* A good reason for preserving a record of all that He has wrought. Israel will not change her God so as to wish to forget, nor will the Lord change so as to make the past mere history. He will be the covenant God of His people world without end. There is no other God, we wish for no other, we would have no other even if there were. There are some who are so ready to comfort the wicked, that for the sake of ending their punishment they weaken the force of language, and make forever and ever mean but a time; nevertheless, despite their interpretations we exult in the hope of an eternity of bliss, and to us "everlasting," and "for ever and ever" mean what they say.

He will be our guide even unto death. Throughout life, and to our dying couch, He will graciously conduct us, and even after death He will lead us to the living fountains of waters. We look to Him for resurrection and eternal life. This consolation is clearly derivable from what has gone before; hitherto our foes have been scattered, and our bulwarks have defied attack, for God has been in our midst, therefore all possible assaults in the future shall be equally futile.

> "The church has all her foes defied
> And laughed to scorn their rage;
> Even thus for aye she shall abide
> Secure from age to age."

Farewell, fear. Come hither, gratitude and faith, and sing right joyously.[140]

---

140. Author unknown.

PSALM 49

PSALM 49:1–PSALM 49:20

Psalm 49:1 *Hear this, all ye people; give ear, all ye inhabitants of the world:*

EXPOSITION: **Verse 1-4.** In these four verses the poet prophet calls universal humanity to listen to his didactic hymn. **Verse 1.** *Hear this, all ye people.* All men are concerned in the subject, it is of them, and therefore to them that the psalmist would speak. It is not a topic which men delight to consider, and therefore he who would instruct them must press them to give ear. Where, as in this case, the theme claims to be wisdom and understanding, attention is very properly demanded; and when the style combines the conciseness of the proverb with the sweetness of poetry, interest is readily excited.

Give ear, all ye inhabitants of the world. "He that hath ears to hear let him hear." [See Matthew 11:15.] Men dwelling in all climes are equally concerned in the subject, for the laws of providence are the same in all lands. It is wise for each one to feel I am a man, and therefore everything which concerns mortals has a personal interest to me. We must all appear before the Judgment Seat, and therefore we all should give earnest heed to holy admonition which may help us to prepare for that dread event. He who refuses to receive instruction by the ear, will not be able to escape receiving destruction by it when the Judge shall say, "Depart, ye cursed." [See Matthew 25:41.]

Psalm 49:2 *Both low and high, rich and poor, together.*

EXPOSITION: **Verse 2.** *Both low and high, rich and poor, together.* Sons of great men, and children of mean men, men of large estate, and you who pine in poverty, you are all bidden to hear the inspired minstrel as he touches his harp to a mournful but instructive lay. The low will be encouraged, the high will be warned, the rich will be sobered, the poor consoled, there will be a useful lesson for each if they are willing to learn it. Our preaching ought to have a voice for all classes, and all should have an ear for it. To suit our word to the rich alone is wicked sycophancy,[141] and to aim only at pleasing the poor is to act the part of a demagogue.[142] Truth may be so spoken as to command the ear of all, and wise men seek to learn that acceptable style. Rich and poor must soon meet together in the grave, they may well be content to meet together now. In the congregation of the dead all differences of rank will be obliterated, they ought not now to be obstructions to united instructions.

Psalm 49:3 *My mouth shall speak of wisdom; and the meditation of my heart shall be of understanding.*

EXPOSITION: **Verse 3.** *My mouth shall speak of wisdom.* Inspired and therefore lifted beyond himself, the prophet is not praising his own attainments, but extolling the divine Spirit which spoke in him. He knew that the Spirit of truth and wisdom spoke through him. He who is not sure that his matter is good has no right to ask a hearing. *And the meditation of my heart shall be of understanding.* The same Spirit who made the ancient seers eloquent, also made them thoughtful. The help of the Holy Ghost was never

141. Fawning
142. Politician

meant to supersede the use of our own mental powers. The Holy Spirit does not make us speak as Balaam's ass, which merely uttered sounds, but never meditated; He first leads us to consider and reflect, and then He gives us the tongue of fire to speak with power.

Psalm 49:4 *I will incline mine ear to a parable: I will open my dark saying upon the harp.*

EXPOSITION: Verse 4. *I will incline mine ear to a parable.* He who would have others hear, begins by hearing himself. As the minstrel leans his ear to his harp, so must the preacher give his whole soul to his ministry. The truth came to the psalmist as a parable, and he endeavored to understand the meaning of it for popular use; he would not leave the truth in obscurity, but he listened to its voice until he so well understood it as to be able to interpret and translate it into the common language of the multitude.

Still of necessity it would remain a problem, and a dark saying to the unenlightened many, but this would not be the songster's fault, for, saith he, *I will open my dark saying upon the harp.* The writer was no mystic, delighting in deep and cloudy things, yet he was not afraid of the most profound topics; he tried to open the treasures of darkness, and to uplift pearls from the deep. To win attention he cast his proverbial philosophy into the form of song, and tuned his harp to the solemn tone of his subject. Let us gather round the minstrel of the King of kings, and hear the Psalm which first was led by the chief musician, as the chorus of the sons of Korah lifted up their voices in the temple.

Psalm 49:5 *Wherefore should I fear in the days of evil, when the iniquity of my heels shall compass me about?*

EXPOSITION: **Verse 5.** *Wherefore should I fear in the days of evil, when the iniquity of my heels shall compass me about?* The man of God looks calmly forward to dark times when those evils which have dogged his heels shall gain a temporary advantage over him. Iniquitous [sinful] men, here called in the abstract iniquity, lie in wait for the righteous, as serpents that aim at the heels of travelers: the iniquity of our heels is that evil which aims to trip us up or impede us. It was an old prophecy that the serpent should wound the heel of the woman's seed, and the enemy of our souls is diligent to fulfill that premonition. In some dreary part of our road it may be that evil will wax stronger and bolder, and gaining upon us will openly assail us; those who followed at our heels like a pack of wolves, may perhaps overtake us, and compass us about. What then? Shall we yield to cowardice? Shall we be a prey to their teeth? God forbid. Nay, we will not even fear, for what are these foes? What indeed, but mortal men who shall perish and pass away? There can be no real ground of alarm to the faithful. Their enemies are too insignificant to be worthy of one thrill of fear. Does not the Lord say to us, "I, even I, am he that comforteth thee; who art thou, that thou shouldest be afraid of a man that shall die, and of the son of man which shall be made as grass?" [See Isaiah 51:12.] Scholars have given other renderings of this verse, but we prefer to keep to the authorized version when we can, and in this case we find in it precisely the same meaning which those would give to it who translate my heels, by the words "my supplanters."

Psalm 49:6 *They that trust in their wealth, and boast themselves in the multitude of their riches;*

EXPOSITION: **Verse 6.** What if the good man's foes are among the great ones of the Earth! Yet he need not fear them. *They that trust in their wealth.* Poor fools, to be content with such a rotten confidence. When we set our rock in contrast with theirs, it would be folly to be afraid of them. Even though they are loud in their brags, we can afford to smile. What if they glory *and boast themselves in the multitude of their riches?* Yet while we glory in our God we are not dismayed by their proud threatenings. Great strength, position, and estate, make wicked men very lofty in their own esteem, and tyrannical towards others; but the heir of Heaven is not overawed by their dignity, nor cowed by their haughtiness. He sees the small value of riches, and the helplessness of their owners in the hour of death, and therefore he is not so concerned as to be afraid of such a short lived thing as a moth, or a bubble.

Psalm 49:7 *None of them can by any means redeem his brother, nor give to God a ransom for him:*

EXPOSITION: Verse 7. *None of them can by any means redeem his brother.* With all their riches, the whole of them put together could not rescue a comrade from the chill grasp of death. They boast of what they will do with us, let them see to themselves. Let them weigh their gold in the scales of death, and see how much they can buy therewith from the worm and the grave. The poor are their equals in this respect; let them love their friend ever so dearly, *nor give to God a ransom for him.* A king's ransom would be of no avail, a Monte Rosa[143] of rubies, an America of silver, a world of gold, a sun of diamonds, would all be utterly condemned. O you boasters, think not to terrify us with your worthless wealth, go and intimidate death before you

---

143. Monte Rosa is the highest mountain in Switzerland.

threaten men in whom is immortality and life.

Psalm 49:8 *(For the redemption of their soul is precious, and it ceaseth for ever:)*

EXPOSITION: Verse 8. For the redemption of their soul is precious, and it ceaseth for ever. Too great is the price, the purchase is hopeless. For ever must the attempt to redeem a soul with money remain a failure. Death comes and wealth cannot bribe him; hell follows and no golden key can unlock its dungeon. Vain, then, are your threatenings, you possessors of the yellow clay; your childish toys are despised by men who estimate the value of possessions by the shekel of the sanctuary.

Psalm 49:9 *That he should still live for ever, and not see corruption.*

EXPOSITION: Verse 9. No price could secure for any man *that he should still live for ever, and not see corruption.* Mad are men now after gold, what would they be if it could buy the elixir of immortality? Gold is lavished out of the bag to cheat the worm of the poor body by embalming it, or enshrining it in a coffin of lead, but it is a miserable business, a very burlesque and comedy. As for the soul, it is too subtle a thing to be detained when it hears the divine command to soar through tracks unknown. Never, therefore, will we fear those base nibblers at our heels, whose boasted treasure proves to be so powerless to save.

Psalm 49:10 *For he seeth that wise men die, likewise the fool and the brutish person perish, and leave their wealth to others.*

EXPOSITION: Verse 10. *For he seeth that wise men die.*
Everyone sees this. The proud persecuting rich man cannot
help seeing it. He cannot shut his eyes to the fact that wiser
men than he are dying, and that he also, with all his craft,
must die. *Likewise the fool and the brutish person perish.*
Folly has no immunity from death. Off goes the jester's cap,
as well as the student's gown. Jollity cannot laugh off the
dying hour; death who visits the university, does not spare
the tavern. Thoughtlessness and brutishness meet their end
as surely as much care and wasting study. In fact, while the
truly wise, so far as this world is concerned, die, the fool has
a worse lot, for he perishes, is blotted out of remembrance,
bewailed by none, remembered no more.

And leave their wealth to others. Not a farthing can
they carry with them. Whether heirs male of their own
body, lawfully begotten, inherit their estates, or they remain
unclaimed, it matters not, their hoardings are no longer theirs;
friends may quarrel over their property, or strangers divide
it as spoil, they cannot interfere. You boasters, hold your
own, before you dream of despoiling the sons of the living
God. Keep shoes to your own feet in death's dark pilgrimage,
before you seek to bite our heels.

Psalm 49:11 *Their inward thought is, that their
houses shall continue for ever, and their dwelling
places to all generations; they call their lands after
their own names.*

EXPOSITION: Verse 11. *Their inward thought is, their
houses shall continue for ever, and their dwelling places to
all generations.* He is very foolish who is more a fool in
his inmost thought than he dare to be in his speech. Such
rotten fruit, rotten at the core, are worldlings. Down deep
in their hearts, though they dare not say so, they fancy that

earthly goods are real and enduring. Foolish dreamers! The frequent dilapidation of their castles and manor houses should teach them better, but still they cherish the delusion. They cannot tell the mirage from the true streams of water; they fancy rainbows to be stable, and clouds to be the everlasting hills. *They call their lands after their own names.* Common enough is this practice. His grounds are made to bear the groundling's name, he might as well write it on the water. Men have even called countries by their own names, but what are they the better for the idle compliment, even if men perpetuate their nomenclature?

Psalm 49:12 *Nevertheless man being in honour abideth not: he is like the beasts that perish.*

EXPOSITION: **Verse 12.** *Nevertheless man being in honour abideth not.* He is but a lodger for the hour, and does not stay a night: even when he dwells in marble halls his notice to quit is written out. Eminence is evermore in imminence of peril. The hero of the hour lasts but for an hour. Scepters fall from the paralyzed hands which once grasped them, and coronets slip away from skulls when the life is departed.

He is like the beasts that perish. He is not like the sheep which are preserved of the Great Shepherd, but like the hunted beast which is doomed to die. He lives a brutish life and dies a brutish death. Wallowing in riches, surfeited with pleasure, he is fatted for the slaughter, and dies like the ox in the shambles. Alas! that so noble a creature should use his life so unworthily, and end it so disgracefully. So far as this world is concerned, wherein does the death of many men differ from the death of a dog? They go down "To the vile dust from whence they sprung, / Unwept, unhonoured, and unsung."[144]

What room is there, then, for fear to the godly when such natural brute beasts assail them? Should they not in patience possess their souls?

Psalm 49:13 *This their way is their folly: yet their posterity approve their sayings. Selah.*

EXPOSITION: Verse 13. Their vain confidences are not casual aberrations from the path of wisdom, but their way, their usual and regular course; their whole life is regulated by such principles. *This their way is their folly.* They are fools ingrained. From first to last brutishness is their characteristic, groveling stupidity the leading trait of their conduct. *Yet their posterity approve their sayings.* Those who follow them in descent follow them in folly, quote their worldly maxims, and accept their mad career as the most prudent mode of life. Why do they not see by their father's failure their father's folly? No, the race transmits its weakness. Grace is not hereditary, but sordid worldliness goes from generation to generation. The race of fools never dies out. No need of missionaries to teach men to be earthworms, they crawl naturally to the dust. *Selah.* Well may the minstrel pause, and bid us muse upon the deep seated madness of the sons of Adam. Take occasion, reader, to reflect upon your own.

Psalm 49:14 *Like sheep they are laid in the grave; death shall feed on them; and the upright shall have dominion over them in the morning; and their beauty shall consume in the grave from their dwelling.*

EXPOSITION: Verse 14. *Like sheep they are laid in the grave.* As dumb driven cattle, they are hurried to their

---

144. "The Lay of the Last Minstrel" by Sir Walter Scott.

doom, and are penned in within the gates of destruction. As sheep that go whither they are driven, and follow their leader without thought, so these men who have chosen to make this world their all, are urged on by their passions, until they find themselves at their journey's end, that end the depths of Hades. Or if we keep to our own translation, we have the idea of their dying peaceably, and being buried in quiet, only that they may wake up to be ashamed at the last great day. *Death shall feed on them.* Death like a grim shepherd leads them on, and conducts them to the place of their eternal pasturage, where all is barrenness and misery. The righteous are led by the Good Shepherd, but the ungodly have death for their shepherd, and he drives them onward to hell. As the power of death rules them in this world, for they have not passed from death unto life, so the terrors of death shall devour them in the world to come. As grim giants, in old stories, are said to feed on men whom they entice to their caves, so death, the monster, feeds on the flesh and blood of the mighty.

And the upright shall have dominion over them in the morning. The poor saints were once the tail, but at the day break they shall be the head. Sinners rule till night fall; their honors wither in the evening, and in the morning they find their position utterly reversed. The sweetest reflection to the upright is that "the morning" here intended begins an endless, changeless, day. What a vexation of spirit to the proud worldling, when the Judge of all the Earth holds His morning session, to see the man whom he despised, exalted high in Heaven, while he himself is cast away!

And their beauty shall consume in the grave from their dwelling. Whatever of glory the ungodly had shall disappear in the tomb. Form and comeliness shall vanish from them, the worm shall make sad havoc of all their beauty. Even their last dwelling place, the grave, shall not be able to protect the relics committed to it; their bodies shall dissolve, no trace shall remain of all their strong limbs and lofty heads, no vestige of remaining beauty shall be discoverable. The beauty of the righteous is not yet revealed, it waits its manifestations; but all the beauty the wicked will ever have is in full bloom in this life; it will wither, fade, decay, rot, and utterly pass away. Who, then, would envy or fear the proud sinner?

Psalm 49:15 *But God will redeem my soul from the power of the grave: for he shall receive me. Selah.*

EXPOSITION: **Verse 15.** *But God will redeem my soul from the power of the grave.* Forth from that temporary resting place we shall come in due time, quickened by divine energy. Like our risen Head we cannot be held by the bands of the grave; redemption has emancipated us from the slavery of death. No redemption could man find in riches, but God has found it in the blood of His dear Son. Our Elder Brother has given to God a ransom, and we are the redeemed of the Lord: because of this redemption by price we shall assuredly be redeemed by power out of the hand of the last enemy.

For he shall receive me. He shall take me out of the tomb, take me up to Heaven. If it is not said of me as of Enoch, "He was not, for God took him," yet shall I reach the same glorious state. [See Genesis 5:24.] My spirit God will receive, and my body shall sleep in Jesus until, being raised in His image, it shall also be received into glory. How infinitely superior is such a hope to anything which our oppressors can boast! Here is something which will bear meditation, and therefore again let us pause, at the bidding of the musician, who inserts a *Selah.*

Psalm 49:16 *Be not thou afraid when one is made rich, when the glory of his house is increased;*

EXPOSITION: Verse 16. In these last verses the psalmist becomes a preacher, and gives admonitory lessons which he has himself gathered from experience. *Be not thou afraid when one is made rich.* Let it not give you any concern to see the godless prosper. Raise no questions as to divine justice; suffer no foreboding to cloud your mind. Temporal prosperity is too small a matter to be worth fretting about; let the dogs have their bones, and the swine their draff.[145] *When the glory of his house is increased.* Though the sinner and his family are in great esteem, and stand exceedingly high, never mind; all things will be righted in due time. Only those whose judgment is worthless will esteem men the more because their lands are broader; those who are highly estimated for such unreasonable reasons will find their level before long, when truth and righteousness come to the forefront.

Psalm 49:17 *For when he dieth he shall carry nothing away: his glory shall not descend after him.*

EXPOSITION: Verse 17. *For when he dieth he shall carry nothing away.* He has but a leasehold of his acres, and death ends his tenure. Through the river of death man must pass naked. Not a rag of all his raiment, not a coin of all his treasure, not a joy of all his honor, can the dying worldling carry with him. Why then fret ourselves about so fleeting a prosperity?

His glory shall not descend after him. As he goes down, down, down forever, none of his honors or possessions will follow him. Patents of nobility are invalid in the sepulcher. His worship, his honor, his lordship, and his grace, will alike find their titles ridiculous in the tomb. Hell knows no aristocracy. Your dainty and delicate sinners shall find

---

145. Refuse

350

that eternal burnings have no respect for their affectations and refinements.

Psalm 49:18 *Though while he lived he blessed his soul: and men will praise thee, when thou doest well to thyself.*

EXPOSITION: Verse 18. *Though while he lived he blessed his soul.* He pronounced himself happy. He had his good things in this life. His chief end and aim were to bless himself. He was charmed with the adulation of flatterers. *And men will praise thee, when thou doest well to thyself.* The generality of men worship success, however it may be gained. The color of the winning horse is no matter; it is the winner, and that is enough. "Take care of Number One," is the world's proverbial philosophy, and he who gives good heed to it is "a clever fellow," "a fine man of business," "a shrewd common sense tradesman," "a man with his head put on the right way." Get money, and you will be "respectable," "a substantial man," and your house will be "an eminent firm in the city," or "one of the best county families." To do good wins fame in Heaven, but to do good to yourself is the prudent thing among men of the world. Yet not a whisper of worldly congratulation can follow the departing millionaire; they say he died worth a mint of money, but what charm has that fact to the dull cold ear of death? The banker rots as fast as the shoeblack, and the peer becomes as putrid as the pauper. Alas! poor wealth, thou art but the rainbow coloring of the bubble, the tint which yellows the morning mist, but adds not substance to it.

Psalm 49:19 *He shall go to the generation of his fathers; they shall never see light.*

EXPOSITION: **Verse 19.** *He shall go to the generation of his fathers.* Where the former generations lie, the present shall also slumber. The sires beckon to their sons to come to the same land of forgetfulness. Mortal fathers beget not immortal children. As our ancestors have departed, so also must we. *They shall never see light.* To this upper region the dead worldling shall never return again to possess his estates, and enjoy his dignities. Among the dead he must lie in the thick darkness, where no joy or hope can come to him. Of all his treasures there remains not enough to furnish him one poor candle; the blaze of his glory is out for ever, and not a spark remains to cheer him. How then can we look with fear or envy upon a wretch doomed to such unhappiness?

Psalm 49:20 *Man that is in honour, and understandeth not, is like the beasts that perish.*

EXPOSITION: **Verse 20.** The song ends with the refrain, *Man that is in honour, and understandeth not, is like the beasts that perish.* Understanding differences men from animals, but if they will not follow the highest wisdom, and like beasts find their all in this life, then their end shall be as mean and dishonorable as that of beasts slain in the chase, or killed in the shambles. From the loftiest elevation of worldly honor to the uttermost depths of death is but a step. Saddest of all is the reflection, that though men are like beasts in all the degradation of perishing, yet not in the rest which animal perishing secures, for, alas! it is written, "These shall go away into everlasting punishment." [See Matthew 25:46.] So ends the minstrel's lay. Comforting as the theme is to the righteous, it is full of warning to the worldly. Hear it, O you rich and poor. Give ear to it, you nations of the Earth.

PSALM 50

PSALM 50:1–PSALM 50:23

Psalm 50:1 *The mighty God, even the Lord, hath spoken, and called the earth from the rising of the sun unto the going down thereof.*

EXPOSITION: **Verse 1.** *The mighty God, even the Lord.* El, Elohim, Jehovah, three glorious names for the God of Israel. To render the address the more impressive, these august titles are mentioned, just as in royal decrees the names and dignities of monarchs are placed in the forefront. Here the true God is described as Almighty, as the only and perfect object of adoration and as the self- existent One. *Hath spoken, and called the earth from the rising of the sun until the going down thereof.* The dominion of Jehovah extends over the whole Earth, and therefore to all mankind is His decree directed. The east and the west are bidden to hear the God who makes His sun to rise on every quarter of the globe. Shall the summons of the great King be despised? Will we dare provoke Him to anger by slighting His call?

Psalm 50:2 *Out of Zion, the perfection of beauty, God hath shined.*

EXPOSITION: **Verse 2.** *Out of Zion, the perfection of beauty, God hath shined.* The Lord is represented not only as speaking to the Earth, but as coming forth to reveal the glory of His presence to an assembled universe. God of old dwelt in Zion among His chosen people, but here the beams of His splendor are described as shining forth upon all nations. The sun was spoken of in the first verse, but here is a far brighter sun. The majesty of God is most conspicuous among His own elect, but is not confined to them; the Church is not a dark lantern, but a candlestick. God shines not only in Zion, but out of her. She is made perfect in beauty by His indwelling, and that beauty is seen by all observers when the Lord shines forth from her. Observe how with trumpet voice and flaming ensign the infinite Jehovah summons the heavens and the Earth to hearken to His Word.

Psalm 50:3 *Our God shall come, and shall not keep silence: a fire shall devour before him, and it shall be very tempestuous round about him.*

EXPOSITION: **Verse 3.** *Our God shall come.* The psalmist speaks of himself and his brethren as standing in immediate anticipation of the appearing of the Lord upon the scene. "He comes," they say, "our covenant God is coming;" they can hear His voice from afar, and perceive the splendor of His attending train. Even thus should we await the long promised appearing of the Lord from Heaven. *And shall not keep silence.* He comes to speak, to plead with His people, to accuse and judge the ungodly. He has been silent long in patience, but soon He will speak with power. What a moment of awe when the Omnipotent is expected to reveal himself! What will be the reverent joy and solemn expectation when the poetic scene of this Psalm becomes in the last great day an actual reality!

A fire shall devour before him, and it shall be very tempestuous round about him. Flame and hurricane are frequently described as the attendants of the divine appearance. "Our God is a consuming fire." [See Hebrews 12:29.] "At the brightness that was before him his thick clouds passed, hailstones and coals of fire." [See Psalm 18:12.] "He rode upon a cherub, and did fly; yea, he did fly upon the wings of the wind." [See Psalm 18:10.] "The Lord Jesus shall be revealed from heaven with his mighty angels, in flaming fire taking vengeance on them that know not God." [See 2 Thessalonians 1:7-8.] Fire is the emblem of justice in action, and the tempest is a token of His overwhelming power. Who will not listen in solemn silence when such is the tribunal from which the Judge pleads with Heaven and Earth?

Psalm 50:4 *He shall call to the heavens from above, and to the earth, that he may judge his people.*

EXPOSITION: **Verse 4.** *He shall call to the heavens from above, and to the earth.* Angels and men, the upper and the lower worlds, are called to witness the solemn scene. The whole creation shall stand in court to testify to the solemnity and the truth of the divine pleading. Both Earth beneath and Heaven above shall unite in condemning sin; the guilty shall have no appeal, though all are summoned that they may appeal if they dare. Both angels and men have seen the guilt of mankind and the goodness of the Lord, they shall therefore confess the justice of the divine utterance, and say "Amen" to the sentence of the supreme Judge. Alas, you despisers! What will you do and to whom will you fly? *That he may judge his people.* Judgment begins at the house of God. The trial of the visible people of God will be a most awful ceremonial. He will thoroughly purge His floor. He will discern between His nominal and His real people, and that in open court, the whole universe looking on. My soul, when this actually takes place, how will it fare with you? Can you endure the day of His coming?

355

Psalm 50:5 *Gather my saints together unto me; those that have made a covenant with me by sacrifice.*

EXPOSITION: **Verse 5.** *Gather my saints together unto me.* Go, you swift winged messengers, and separate the precious from the vile. Gather out the wheat of the heavenly garner. Let the long scattered, but elect people, known by my separating grace to be my sanctified ones, be now assembled in one place. All are not saints who seem to be so—a severance must be made; therefore let all who profess to be saints be gathered before my throne of judgment, and let them hear the word which will search and try the whole, that the false may be convicted and the true revealed.

Those that have made a covenant with me by sacrifice; this is the grand test, and yet some have dared to imitate it. The covenant was ratified by the slaying of victims, the cutting and dividing of offerings; this the righteous have done by accepting with true faith the great propitiatory sacrifice, and this the pretenders have done in merely outward form. Let them be gathered before the throne for trial and testing, and as many as have really ratified the covenant by faith in the Lord Jesus shall be attested before all worlds as the objects of distinguishing grace, while formalists shall learn that outward sacrifices are all in vain. Oh, solemn assize [judicial writ], how my soul bow in awe at the prospect thereof!

Psalm 50:6 *And the heavens shall declare his righteousness: for God is judge himself. Selah.*

EXPOSITION: **Verse 6.** *And the heavens shall declare his righteousness.* Celestial intelligences and the spirits of just men made perfect, shall magnify the infallible judgment of the divine tribunal. Now they doubtless wonder at the hypocrisy of men; then they shall equally marvel at the exactness of the severance between the true and the false. *For God is judge himself.* This is the reason for the correctness of the judgment. Priests of old, and churches of later times, were readily deceived, but not so the all discerning Lord. No deputy judge sits on the great white throne; the injured Lord of all himself weighs the evidence and allots the vengeance or reward. The scene in the Psalm is a grand poetical conception, but it is also an inspired prophecy of that day which shall burn as an oven, when the Lord shall discern between him that fears and him that fears Him not. *Selah.* Here we may well pause in reverent prostration, in deep searching of heart, in humble prayer, and in awe struck expectation.

EXPOSITION:

Verses 7–15. The address which follows is directed to the professed people of God. It is clearly, in the first place, meant for Israel; but is equally applicable to the visible Church of God in every age. It declares the futility of external worship when spiritual faith is absent, and the mere outward ceremonial is rested in.

Psalm 50:7 *Hear, O my people, and I will speak; O Israel, and I will testify against thee: I am God, even thy God.*

EXPOSITION: Verse 7. *Hear, O my people, and I will speak.* Because Jehovah speaks and they are avowedly His own people, they are bound to give earnest heed. "Let me speak," saith the great I AM. The heavens and Earth are but listeners, the Lord is about both to testify and to judge. *O Israel, and I will testify against thee.* Their covenant name is mentioned to give point to the address; it was a double evil that the chosen nation should become so carnal, so unspiritual, so false, so heartless to their God.

God himself, whose eyes sleep not, who is not misled by rumor, but sees for himself, enters on the scene as witness against His favored nation. Alas! for us when God, even our fathers' God, testifies to the hypocrisy of the visible Church.

I am God, even thy God. He had taken them to be his peculiar people above all other nations, and they had in the most solemn manner avowed that He was their God. Hence the special reason for calling them to account. The law began with, "I am the Lord thy God, which brought thee up out of the land of Egypt," [See Exodus 20:2.], and now the session of their judgment opens with the same reminder of their singular position, privilege, and responsibility. It is not only that Jehovah is God, but your God, O Israel; this is that which makes you so amenable to His searching reproofs.

Psalm 50:8 *I will not reprove thee for thy sacrifices or thy burnt offerings, to have been continually before me.*

EXPOSITION: Verse 8. *I will not reprove thee for thy sacrifices or thy burnt offerings, to have been continually before me.* Though they had not failed in maintaining His outward worship, or even if they had, He was not about to call them to account for this: a more weighty matter was now under consideration. They thought the daily sacrifices and the abounding burnt offerings to be everything: He counted them nothing if the inner sacrifice of heart devotion had been neglected. What was greatest with them was least with God. It is even so today. Sacraments (so called) and sacred rites are the main concern with unconverted but religious men, but with the Most High the spiritual worship which they forget is the sole matter. Let the external be maintained by all means, according to the divine command, but if the secret and spiritual are not in them, they are a vain oblation, a dead ritual, and even an abomination before the Lord.

Psalm 50:9 *I will take no bullock out of thy house, nor he goats out of thy folds.*

EXPOSITION: Verse 9. *I will take no bullock out of thy house.* Foolishly they dreamed that bullocks with horns and hoofs could please the Lord, when indeed He sought for hearts and souls. Impiously they fancied that Jehovah needed these supplies, and that if they fed His altar with their fat beasts, He would be content. What He intended for their instruction, they made their confidence. They remembered not that "to obey is better than sacrifice, and to hearken than the fat of rams." [See 1 Samuel 15:22.]

Nor he goats out of thy folds. He mentions these lesser victims as if to rouse their common sense to see that the great Creator could find no satisfaction in mere animal offerings. If He needed these, He would not appeal to their scanty stalls and folds; in fact, He here refuses to take so much as one, if they brought them under the false and dishonoring view, that they were in themselves pleasing to Him. This shows that the sacrifices of the law were symbolical of higher and spiritual things, and were not pleasing to God except under their typical aspect. The believing worshipper looking beyond the outward was accepted, the unspiritual who had no respect to their meaning was wasting his substance, and blaspheming the God of Heaven.

Psalm 50:10 *For every beast of the forest is mine, and the cattle upon a thousand hills.*

EXPOSITION: Verse 10. *For every beast of the forest is mine.* How could they imagine that the Most High God, possessor of Heaven and Earth, had need of beasts, when all the countless hordes that find shelter in a thousand forests and wildernesses belong to Him? *And the cattle upon a thousand hills.* Not alone the wild beasts, but also the tamer creatures are all His own. Even if God cared for these things, He could supply himself. Their cattle were not, after all, their own, but were still the great Creator's property, why then should He be beholden to them. From Dan to Beersheba, from Nebaioth to Lebanon, there fed not a beast which was not marked with the name of the great Shepherd; why, then, should He crave oblations of Israel? What a slight is put here even upon sacrifices of divine appointment when wrongly viewed as in themselves pleasing to God! And all this to be so expressly stated under the law! How much clearer this is under the gospel, when it is so much more plainly revealed, that "God is a Spirit, and they that worship him must worship him in spirit and in truth"? [See John 4:24.] You Ritualists[146], you Sacramentarians[147], you modern Pharisees, what do you say to this?

Psalm 50:11 *I know all the fowls of the mountains: and the wild beasts of the field are mine.*

EXPOSITION: Verse 11. *I know all the fowls of the mountains.* All the winged creatures are under my inspection and near my hand; what then can be the value of your pairs of turtledoves, and your two young pigeons? The great Lord not only feeds all His creatures, but is well acquainted with each one; how wondrous is this knowledge!

---

146. Those who emphasize rituals and liturgical ceremony, a great debate in the Anglican Church during the 19th century.
147. Sacramentarians: During the Protestant Reformation these Christians denied Roman Catholic Transubstantiation and Lutheran Sacramental Union.

And the wild beasts of the fields are mine. The whole population moving over the plain belongs to me; why then should I seek your beef and rams? In me all things live and move; how mad are you to suppose that I desire your living things! A spiritual God demands other life than that which is seen in animals; He looks for spiritual sacrifice; for the love, the trust, the praise, the life of your hearts.

Psalm 50:12 *If I were hungry, I would not tell thee: for the world is mine, and the fulness thereof.*

EXPOSITION: **Verse 12.** *If I were hungry, I would not tell thee.* Strange conception, a hungry God! Yet if such an absurd ideal could be truth, and if the Lord hungered for meat, He would not ask it of men. He could provide for himself out of His own possessions; He would not turn suppliant to His own creatures. Even under the grossest ideal of God, faith in outward ceremonies is ridiculous. Do men think that the Lord needs banners, music, incense, and fine linen? If He did, the stars would emblazon His standard, the winds and the waves become His orchestra, ten thousand times ten thousand flowers would breathe forth perfume, the snow should be His alb,[148] the rainbow His girdle, the clouds of light His mantle. "O fools and slow of heart," ye worship ye know not what! [See Luke 24:25.] *For the world is mine, and the fulness thereof.* What can He need who is owner of all things and able to create as He wills? Thus overwhelmingly does the Lord pour forth His arguments upon formalists.

Psalm 50:13 *Will I eat the flesh of bulls, or drink the blood of goats?*

148. Vestment

EXPOSITION: Verse 13. Will I eat the flesh of bulls, or drink the blood of goats? Are you so infatuated as to think this? Is the great I AM subject to corporeal wants, and are they to be thus grossly satisfied? Heathens thought thus of their idols, but do you dare think thus of the God who made the heavens and the Earth? Can you have fallen so low as to think thus of me, O Israel? What vivid reasoning is here! How the fire flashes dart into the idiot faces of those who trust in outward forms! You dupes of Rome, can you read this and be unmoved? The expostulation is indignant; the questions utterly confound; the conclusion is inevitable; heart worship can only be acceptable with the true God. It is inconceivable that outward things can gratify Him, except so far as through them our faith and love express themselves.

Psalm 50:14 *Offer unto God thanksgiving; and pay thy vows unto the most High:*

EXPOSITION: Verse 14. *Offer unto God thanksgiving.* No longer look at your sacrifices as in themselves gifts pleasing to me, but present them as the tributes of your gratitude; it is then that I will accept them, but not while your poor souls have no love and no thankfulness to offer me. The sacrifices, as considered in themselves, are contemned [disdained], but the internal emotions of love consequent upon a remembrance of divine goodness, are commended as the substance, meaning, and soul of sacrifice. Even when the legal ceremonials were not abolished, this was true, and when they came to an end, this truth was more than ever made manifest. Not for want of bullocks on the altar was Israel blamed, but for want of thankful adoration before the Lord. She excelled in the visible, but in the inward grace, which is the one thing needful, she sadly failed. Too many in these days are in the same condemnation.

And pay thy vows unto the most High. Let the sacrifice be really presented to the God who sees the heart, pay to Him the love you promised, the service you covenanted to render, the loyalty of heart you have vowed to maintain. O for grace to do this! O that we may be graciously enabled to love God, and live up to our profession! To be, indeed, the servants of the Lord, the lovers of Jesus, this is our main concern. What avails our baptism, to what end our gatherings at the Lord's table, to what purpose our solemn assemblies, if we have not the fear of the Lord, and vital godliness reigning within our bosoms?

Psalm 50:15 *And call upon me in the day of trouble: I will deliver thee, and thou shalt glorify me.*

EXPOSITION: Verse 15. *And call upon me in the day of trouble.* Oh blessed verse! Is this then true sacrifice? Is it an offering to ask an alms of Heaven? It is even so. The King himself so regards it. For herein is faith manifested, herein is love proved, for in the hour of peril we fly to those we love. It seems a small thing to pray to God when we are distressed, yet is it a more acceptable worship than the mere heartless presentation of bullocks and he goats. This is a voice from the throne, and how full of mercy it is! It is very tempestuous round about Jehovah, and yet what soft drops of mercy's rain drop from the bosom of the storm! Who would not offer such sacrifices? Troubled one, haste to present it now! Who shall say that Old Testament saints did not know the gospel? Its very spirit and essence breathes like frankincense all around this holy Psalm.

I will deliver thee. The reality of your sacrifice of prayer shall be seen in its answer. Whether the smoke of burning bulls is sweet to me or not, certainly your humble prayer shall be, and I will prove it so by my gracious reply to your supplication. This promise is very large, and may refer both to temporal and eternal deliverances; faith can turn it every way, like the sword of the cherubim.

And thou shalt glorify me. Your prayer will honor me, and your grateful perception of my answering mercy will also glorify me. The goats and bullocks would prove a failure, but the true sacrifice never could. The calves of the stall might be a vain oblation, but not the calves of sincere lips. Thus we see what is true ritual. Here we read inspired rubrics.[149] Spiritual worship is the great, the essential matter; all else without it is rather provoking than pleasing to God. As helps to the soul, outward offerings were precious, but when men went not beyond them, even their hallowed things were profaned in the view of Heaven.

--- **EXPOSITION:** ---

Verses 16–21. Here the Lord turns to the manifestly wicked among His people; and such there were even in the highest places of His sanctuary. If moral formalists had been rebuked, how much more these immoral pretenders to fellowship with Heaven? If the lack of heart spoiled the worship of the more decent and virtuous, how much more would violations of the law, committed with a high hand, corrupt the sacrifices of the wicked?

Psalm 50:16 *But unto the wicked God saith, What hast thou to do to declare my statutes, or that thou shouldest take my covenant in thy mouth?*

EXPOSITION: **Verse 16.** *But unto the wicked God saith.* To the breakers of the second table He now addresses himself; He had previously spoken to the neglectors of the first. *What hast thou to do to declare my statutes?* You

---

149. An authoritative rule of conduct or procedure.

violate openly my moral law, and yet are great sticklers for my ceremonial commands! What have you to do with them? What interest can you have in them? Do you dare to teach my law to others, and profane it yourselves? What impudence, what blasphemy is this! Even if you claim to be sons of Levi, what of that? Your wickedness disqualifies you, disinherits you, puts you out of the succession. It should silence you, and would if my people were as spiritual as I would have them, for they would refuse to hear you, and to pay you the portion of temporal things which is due to my true servants. You count up your holy days, you contend for rituals, you fight for externals, and yet the weightier matters of the law you despise! Ye blind guides, ye strain out gnats and swallow camels; your hypocrisy is written on your foreheads and manifest to all. [See Matthew 23:24.]

Or that thou shouldest take my covenant in thy mouth. You talk of being in covenant with me, and yet trample my holiness beneath your feet as swine trample upon pearls; do you think I can allow this? Your mouths are full of lying and slander, and yet you mouth my words as if they were fit morsels for such as you! How horrible and evil it is, that to this day we see men explaining doctrines who despise precepts! They make grace a coverlet for sin, and even judge themselves to be sound in the faith, while they are rotten in life. We need the grace of the doctrines as much as the doctrines of grace, and without it an Cross of Christ.

Psalm 50:17 *Seeing thou hatest instruction, and casteth my words behind thee.*

EXPOSITION: Verse 17. *Seeing thou hatest instruction.* Profane professors are often too wise to learn, too besotted with conceit to be taught of God. What a monstrosity that men should declare those statutes which with their hearts they do not know, and which in their lives they openly disavow! Woe unto the men who hate the instruction which they take upon themselves to give. *And castest my words behind thee.* Despising them, throwing them away as worthless, putting them out of sight as obnoxious. Many boasters of the law did this practically; and in these last days there are pickers and choosers of God's words who cannot endure the practical part of Scripture; they are disgusted at duty, they abhor responsibility, they disembowel texts of their plain meanings, they wrest[150] the Scriptures to their own destruction. It is an ill sign when a man dares not look a Scripture in the face, and an evidence of brazen impudence when he tries to make it mean something less condemnatory of his sins, and endeavors to prove it to be less sweeping in its demands. How powerful is the argument that such men have no right to take the covenant of God into their mouths, seeing that its spirit does not regulate their lives!

Psalm 50:18 *When thou sawest a thief, then thou consentedst with him, and hast been partaker with adulterers.*

EXPOSITION: Verse 18. *When thou sawest a thief, then thou consentedst with him.* Moral honesty cannot be absent where true grace is present. Those who excuse others in trickery are guilty themselves; those who use others to do unjust actions for them are doubly so. If a man is ever so religious, if his own actions do not rebuke dishonesty, he is an accomplice with thieves. If we can acquiesce in anything which is not upright, we are not upright ourselves, and our religion is a lie.

---

150. Twist

And hast been partaker with adulterers. One by one the moral precepts are thus broken by the sinners in Zion. Under the cloak of piety, those who live an unclean life conceal themselves. We may do this by smiling at unchaste jests, listening to indelicate expressions, and conniving [encouraging or allowing licentious behavior] at licentious behavior in our presence; and if we thus act, how dare we preach, or lead public prayer, or wear the Christian name? See how the Lord lays righteousness to the plummet. How plainly all this declares that without holiness no man shall see the Lord! No amount of ceremonial or theological accuracy can cover dishonesty and fornication: these filthy things must be either purged from us by the blood of Jesus, or they will kindle a fire in God's anger which will burn even to the lowest hell.

Psalm 50:19 *Thou givest thy mouth to evil, and thy tongue frameth deceit.*

EXPOSITION: **Verse 19.** *Thou givest thy mouth to evil.* Sins against the ninth commandment are here mentioned. The man who surrenders himself to the habit of slander is a vile hypocrite if he associates himself with the people of God. A man's health is readily judged by his tongue. A foul mouth, a foul heart. Some slander almost as often as they breathe, and yet are great upholders of the Church, and great sticklers for holiness. To what depths will not they go in evil, who delight in spreading it with their tongues.

And thy tongue frameth deceit. This is a more deliberate sort of slander, where the man dexterously elaborates false witness, and concocts methods of defamation. There is an ingenuity of calumny [slander] in some men, and, alas! even in some who are thought to be followers of the Lord Jesus. They manufacture falsehoods, weave them in their loom, hammer them on their anvil, and then retail their wares in

367

every company. Are these accepted with God? Though they bring their wealth to the altar, and speak eloquently of truth and of salvation, have they any favor with God? We should blaspheme the holy God if we were to think so. They are corrupt in His sight, a stench in His nostrils. He will cast all liars into hell. Let them preach, and pray, and sacrifice as they will; until they become truthful, the God of truth loathes them utterly.

Psalm 50:20 *Thou sittest and speakest against thy brother; thou slanderest thine own mother's son.*

EXPOSITION: **Verse 20.** *Thou sittest and speakest against thy brother.* He sits down to it, makes it his meat, studies it, resolves upon it, becomes a master of defamation, occupies the chair of calumny [slander]. His nearest friend is not safe, his dearest relative escapes not. *Thou slanderest thine own mother's son.* He ought to love him best, but he has an ill word for him. The son of one's own mother was to the Oriental a very tender relation; but the wretched slanderer knows no claims of kindred. He stabs his brother in the dark, and aims a blow at him who came forth of the same womb; yet he wraps himself in the robe of hypocrisy, and dreams that he is a favorite of Heaven, an accepted worshipper of the Lord. Are such monsters to be met with nowadays? Alas! they pollute our churches still, and are roots of bitterness, spots on our solemn feasts, wandering stars for whom is reserved the blackness of darkness forever. Perhaps some such may read these lines, but they will probably read them in vain; their eyes are too dim to see their own condition, their hearts are waxen gross [hard and flagrantly bad], their ears are dull of hearing; they are given up to a strong delusion to believe a lie, that they may be damned.

Psalm 50:21 *These things hast thou done, and I kept silence; thou thoughtest that I was altogether such an one as thyself: but I will reprove thee, and set them in order before thine eyes.*

EXPOSITION: Verse 21. *These things hast thou done, and I kept silence.* No swift judgment overthrew the sinner— longsuffering reigned; no thunder was heard in threatening, and no bolt of fire was hurled in execution. *Thou thoughtest that I was altogether such an one as thyself.* The inference drawn from the Lord's patience was infamous; the respited[151] culprit thought his judge to be one of the same order as himself. He offered sacrifice, and deemed it accepted; he continued in sin, and remained unpunished, and therefore he rudely said, "Why need believe these crazy prophets? God cares not how we live so long as we pay our tithes. Little does he consider how we get the plunder, so long as we bring a bullock to His altar." What will not men imagine of the Lord? At one time they likened the glory of Israel to a calf, and another unto their brutish selves.

But I will reprove thee. At last I will break silence and let them know my mind. *And set them in order before thine eyes.* I will marshall your sins in battle array. I will make you see them, I will put them down item by item, classified and arranged. You shall know that if silent awhile, I was never blind or deaf. I will make you perceive what you have tried to deny. I will leave the seat of mercy for the throne of judgment, and there I will let you see how great the difference is between you and me.

Psalm 50:22 *Now consider this, ye that forget God, lest I tear you in pieces, and there be none to deliver.*

151. Reprieved

EXPOSITION: **Verse 22.** *Now* or oh! It is a word of entreaty, for the Lord is loathe even to let the most ungodly run on to destruction. *Consider this; ye that forget God,* take these truths to heart, you who trust in ceremonies and you who live in vice, for both of you sin in that ye forget God. Think how unaccepted you are, and turn unto the Lord. See how you have mocked the eternal, and repent of your iniquities. *Lest I tear you in pieces,* as the lion rends his prey, *and there be none to deliver,* no Savior, no refuge, no hope. You reject the Mediator: beware, for you will sorely need one in the day of wrath, and none will be near to plead for you. How terrible, how complete, how painful, how humiliating, will be the destruction of the wicked! God uses no soft words, or velvet metaphors, nor may His servants do so when they speak of the wrath to come. O reader, consider this.

Psalm 50:23 *Whoso offereth praise glorifieth me: and to him that ordereth his conversation aright will I shew the salvation of God.*

EXPOSITION: **Verse 23.** *Whoso offereth praise glorifieth me.* Praise is the best sacrifice; true, hearty, gracious thanksgiving from a renewed mind. Not the lowing of bullocks bound to the altar, but the songs of redeemed men are the music which the ear of Jehovah delights in. Sacrifice your loving gratitude, and God is honored thereby.

And to him that ordereth his conversation aright will I shew the salvation of God. Holy living is a choice evidence of salvation. He who submits his whole way to divine guidance, and is careful to honor God in his life, brings an offering which the Lord accepts through His dear Son; and such a one shall be more and more instructed, and made experimentally to know the Lord's salvation. He needs salvation, for the best ordering of the life cannot save us, but that salvation He shall have. Not to ceremonies, not to unpurified lips, is the blessing promised, but to grateful hearts and holy lives. O Lord, give us to stand in the judgment with those who have worshipped you aright and have seen your salvation.

STUDY GUIDE

1.) In Psalm 27:1, the psalmist is praising and thanking God for three of the His mighty promises and blessings He is to us. List those three promises.

_____

_____

_____

_____

2.) Psalm 29:2 tells us to: *Give unto the Lord the glory due unto his name; worship the Lord in the beauty of holiness.* What does to worship Him in the beauty of holiness mean to you?

_____

_____

_____

_____

3.) In Psalm 31:3, the psalmist is praising God because He is our rock and fortress in times of trouble. As you read Spurgeon's exposition on that psalm what requirement does this place upon us?

_____

_____

_____

_____

4.) In Psalm 31:16, the psalmist asks God to make His face shine upon him. How does Spurgeon say that affects the soul?

_____

_____

_____

_____

_____

5.) In his exposition of Psalm 32:2, Spurgeon mentions three words that describe sin and three words that describe pardon. List them below.

_____

_____

_____

_____

_____

6.) In Psalm 34:1, we are taught all through Scripture to praise the Lord at all times. Fill in the blanks: David said: "I will bl_____ the LORD at all times: his pr_____ shall continually be in my mouth."

7.) In Psalm 37:11, this promise is repeated by Christ Jesus in Matthew 5:5. Fill in the blank: "But the m_____ shall inherit the earth; and shall delight themselves in the abundance of peace."

8.) Psalm 40:5a says, "Many, O LORD my God, are thy wonderful works which thou hast done, and thy thoughts which are to us-ward." In his exposition, how does Spurgeon describe God's thoughts toward us in his exposition?

_____

_____

_____

_____

_____

9.) In Psalm 41:13, may the last verse of this psalm serve as the heartfelt prayer of the universal Church in all ages. Fill in the last three words of this Psalm: "Blessed be the LORD God of Israel from everlasting, and to everlasting. ____, ____ ____."

10.) Psalm 44:8 says, "In God we boast all the day long, and praise thy name for ever. Selah." What does the term "Selah" mean?

_____

_____

11.) In his exposition of Psalm 50:23, how does Spurgeon describe praise to God?

_____

_____

_____

Pure Gold Classics
Timeless Truth in a Distinctive, Best-Selling Collection

An Expanding Collection of the Best-Loved Christian Classics of All Time.
AVAILABLE AT FINE BOOKSTORES.
FOR MORE INFORMATION, VISIT WWW.BRIDGELOGOS.COM

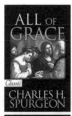
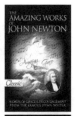

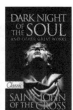

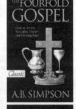

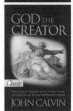

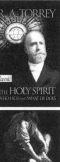
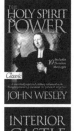

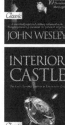

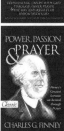
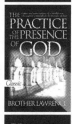

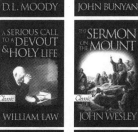
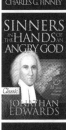

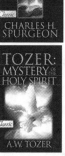
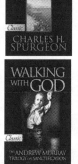
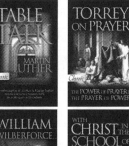
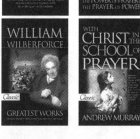